LEGISLATURES IN PLURAL SOCIETIES

PUBLICATIONS OF THE CONSORTIUM
FOR COMPARATIVE LEGISLATIVE STUDIES

Malcolm E. Jewell
General Editor

G. R. Boynton and Chong Lim Kim, Editors, *Legislative Systems in Developing Countries*

Abdo I. Baaklini, *Legislative and Political Development: Lebanon, 1842–1972*

Allan Kornberg and William Mishler, *Influence in Parliament: Canada*

Peter Vanneman, *The Supreme Soviet: Politics and the Legislative Process in the Soviet Political System*

Albert F. Eldridge, Editor, *Legislatures in Plural Societies: The Search for Cohesion in National Development*

Forthcoming titles to be announced

LEGISLATURES IN PLURAL SOCIETIES: THE SEARCH FOR COHESION IN NATIONAL DEVELOPMENT

Edited by
ALBERT F. ELDRIDGE

Duke University Press, Durham, North Carolina 1977

© 1977, Duke University Press
L.C.C. card no. 76-28916
I.S.B.N. 0-8223-0373-6
Printed in the United States of America

PREFACE

This volume reflects the efforts of a group of scholars who share a common concern in the problems of ethnic communalism and the processes of modernization. Basically two standards were adopted in inviting participation: (1) Was the individual currently engaged in or planning research dealing with the topic? (2) Had the individual's previous work demonstrated an interest and competence in related topics, e.g., problems of societal fragmentation, comparative legislative analysis, or national integration and development? As we expected, there was a large pool of scholars who met the second criteria, and a much smaller number who actually were engaged in or planning research dealing with legislatures and integration. Ten of the fifteen people originally invited tentatively accepted; of this group, two withdrew in the early stages of the volume's preparation, and two more withdrew later, when it was decided that their research was moving into areas outside of our immediate interest. The remaining contributors, three of whom are nationals of their referent countries, completed their projects in less than two years. Their findings are presented here for the first time.

In the preparation and execution of their research, the contributors were requested to focus their analyses and discussion in terms of the theme, "The Integrative Functions of Legislatures." We asked the individuals preparing papers to pay particular attention to questions dealing with the functions commonly associated with legislatures. No attempt was made to impose a single conceptual or theoretical framework on the various projects; rather, a more casual form of mutual guidance evolved through our correspondence. As the various projects progressed we found that these informal guidelines insured as much topical integrity as we could expect. All seven of the resulting papers can be said to focus explicitly on the integrative functions of legislatures; six of the papers are data based, and one is essentially a "think-piece." Since there is a lack of scholarly agreement on definitions for some of the central concepts such as "national integration" or "legitimation," we saw no need to impose conceptual unity where none existed. Surprisingly, the definitional variations were minimal.

Research method per se has become a subject of growing concern in recent years. One of the more frequent criticisms of the case-study method which is used throughout this volume has been that it generates a great deal of specific information concerning the unique features of an event or institution but not much general information.

Yet there is no reason why case-study data cannot suggest general propositions and contribute directly to the development of theory. The research reported in this volume has had some immediate payoffs, both substantive and theoretical.

The six essays in this volume frame a single issue that has multiple dimensions. Where there is probably insufficient definitional or theoretical unity, there is unity in conceptual focus, research method, and the attempt to place the study of the integrative functions of legislatures within the broad context of the sociocultural, institutional, and developmental systems of which the issue is a part. We believe that these studies have made a marked contribution to research in an important but still relatively neglected area of inquiry.

There are a number of individuals whose assistance and support I wish to acknowledge. Without the funds granted to the Comparative Legislative Studies Program of Duke University from the Agency for International Development this volume would not have been possible. While the contributors are grateful for the agency's support, we naturally absolve it of any responsibility for the viewpoints and interpretations made in this work.

I am especially indebted to Allan Kornberg and Malcolm E. Jewell for their assistance. Both made substantial contributions to the preparation of this book. As with any manuscript, the final product benefits from the labor of many valued associates. I wish particularly to thank Anne Morris and Alice Falcone for their editorial assistance. Doris Ralston and Louise Walker typed various portions of the chapters and made additional editorial comments. Finally, I would like to thank Mary Eldridge for her active support during the preparation of the manuscript.

Albert F. Eldridge

CONTRIBUTORS

Abdo I. Baaklini is Associate Director for International Programs, State University of New York at Albany. He received his doctorate in political science from the State University of New York at Albany in 1972. A citizen of Lebanon, he has had extensive field experience in the Middle East. He is author of *Legislative and Political Development: Lebanon, 1842–1972* (1976).

Ian Budge is Reader in Government at the University of Essex, Colchester, England. He is author of *Agreement and the Stability of Democracy* (1970), *Political Stratification and Democracy* (1972), and *Belfast: Approach to Crisis* (1973) and is coauthor of *Scottish Political Behaviour* (1966). He has also contributed many articles to *Political Studies,* the *British Journal of Political Science,* and the *Midwest Journal of Political Science.*

Lenard J. Cohen is a doctoral candidate in the Department of Political Science at Columbia University and a lecturer in the Department of Political Science at Queens College of the City University of New York. During 1968 and 1969 he conducted field research in Yugoslavia. He is coeditor of *Communist Systems in Comparative Perspective* (1974) and a contributor to the edited volume, *Opinion-Making Elites in Yugoslavia* (1973).

Albert F. Eldridge is Associate Professor of Political Science at Duke University. He received his Ph.D. in political science from the University of Kentucky. He has written numerous articles for scholarly journals and collections.

Samuel M. Hines is a doctoral candidate in the Department of Political Science at Duke University and an instructor in the Department of Political Science at the College of Charleston.

Malcolm E. Jewell is Professor of Political Science at the University of Kentucky. He received his doctorate in political science from Pennsylvania State University. His professional activities include chairmanship of the American Political Science Association's Committee of Departmental Chairmen (1971–72) and editor of the *Midwest Journal of Political Science* (1966–70). He is author of *The State Legislature* (1962) and *Legislative Representation in the Contemporary Society* (1967), and is coauthor of *The Legislative Process in the United States* (1966) and *Kentucky Politics* (1968).

Allan Kornberg is Professor of Political Science at Duke University. He received his doctorate in political science from the University of Michigan. Currently he is engaged in a cross-national study of political socialization and recruitment funded by the National Science Foundation and the Canada Council. He is author of *Canadian Legislative Behavior: A Study of the 25th Parliament* (1967), editor and coauthor of *Legislatures in Developmental Perspective* (1970), and coauthor of *Influence in Parliament: Canada* (1976). He also has contributed articles to a number of professional journals, including the *American Political Science Review,* the *Midwest Journal of Politics,* and the *Journal of Politics.*

Cornelius O'Leary is a Reader in the Department of Political Science at Queen's University of Belfast. He holds a doctorate from Oxford University. Currently his research interests are in British and Irish politics, especially party systems and electoral behavior. His publications include *The Irish Republic and Its Experiments with Proportional Representation* (1961) and *Belfast: Approach to Crisis* (1973, with Ian Budge). He has contributed articles to such professional journals as the *Political Quarterly* and the *Midwest Journal of Politics.*

Lawrence L. Shrader is Professor of Government at Mills College. He received his Ph.D. from the University of California at Berkeley, where he was a research assistant with the *Indian Press Digest*. He was a Fulbright Fellow in India from 1961 to 1962, and a Fellow of the Institute for International Studies, University of California, Berkeley, 1969, studying political leadership in India. In collaboration with Ram Joshi he has published a study of Zilla Parishad elections in one district of Maharashtra in the *Asian Survey*, contributed a study of politics in Rajasthan to Myron Weiner, ed., *State Politics in India*, and coauthored with Richard Sisson *Legislative Recruitment and Political Integration: Patterns of Political Linkage in an Indian State*. He is currently engaged in research on comparative state legislatures in India.

Richard Sisson received his doctorate in political science from the University of California, Berkeley, in 1967. From 1963 to 1965 he held a Foreign Area Training Fellowship and conducted field research in Rajasthan, India. He was in military service from 1965 to 1968 and served as a member of the faculty of the Department of Social Sciences, United States Military Academy, West Point. From 1968 to 1970 he was Assistant Professor of Political Science at the University of California at Los Angeles where he currently holds the rank of Professor. He was a contributor to *Caste in Indian Politics* (1970), coeditor of "Elections and Party Politics in India" (*Asian Survey*, November 1970), and is author of *Political Institutionalization in a Developing Society: The Congress System in Rajasthan* (1971).

Marvin G. Weinbaum is Associate Professor of Political Science at the University of Illinois. He received his doctorate in political science from Columbia University. Currently he is undertaking field research in Afghanistan. He is author of *Metro Decision Processes* (1969), coauthor of *Presidential Elections: A Simulation Report* (1969), and a contributor to the *Midwest Journal of Political Science* and the *National Civil Review*.

LEGISLATURES IN PLURAL SOCIETIES

INTRODUCTION:
ON LEGISLATURES IN PLURAL SOCIETIES

ALBERT F. ELDRIDGE

The House of Representatives in Belgium passed a bill that granted parity to parochial and public schools. The legislation effectively reduced the salience of church-state divisions, particularly in the area of educational policy.

In Ceylon single-member district boundaries are drawn in such a way as to facilitate the representation of ethnic, religious, and caste minorities. This districting technique protects the interests of minority groups by producing relatively homogeneous districts and giving minority groups a proportionate share of the districts dominated by them.

In Northern Ireland (until the mid-1960s) all Unionist MPs were members of the Orange Order. The order is militantly anti-Catholic, and its annual processions celebrating the Protestant Ascendancy have been the source of repeated instances of civil violence. The Unionist party has dominated the Stourmont Parliament for the past 50 years.

The Belgian parliament enacted a series of language reform bills. These and later reforms contributed to a radicalization of the electoral process within the Flemish and French communities, one result of which was a dramatic gain in parliamentary elections by extremist linguistic parties. Within a span of three years, two coalition governments would fall as a result of the "language issue"—an issue that the parliament had articulated but had failed to resolve.

These experiences are broadly similar. In each case the legislative system must function in a social environment that is acutely divided. In each country ethnic, religious, racial, and other comparable interests are institutionalized. The political salience of these minority groups is visible in the functioning of the legislature where minorities often hold the key to either stability and unity or instability and factionalism. In the last analysis, for each of these political systems the ultimate justification for accepting, maintaining, and strengthening the legislature is its ability to contribute, along with other institutions, to reconciling diverse communal interests with broader national concerns.

These examples and others that could be cited suggest that legislative systems may either promote or hinder national integration. It is important to determine under what conditions, and in what ways legislatures perform integrative or disintegrative functions in multiethnic societies. The purpose of this volume is to explore the basic elements of the integration issue, to define the questions that need to be answered concerning the roles of legislatures, to analyze the actual functions of legislatures in various nations, and to offer suggestions for future research based on these initial findings.

THE INTEGRATION ISSUE

Because the issue with which we are dealing is complex, a brief discussion of its several dimensions is in order. In every nation the problem of national integration exists, but for some nations the task is complicated by the presence of multiple divisions in the social order. Where these divisions reinforce each other, the resulting groups often seek expression of their particularistic values through institutional structures such as political parties, fraternal groups, and even paramilitary forces. These associational forms often have the capacity to channel social mobilization, and, like their national counterparts, these institutions will achieve various levels of development. Neither the national nor the communal institution is its own master (Enloe, 1973). The presence of parallel and often competing institutions within a multiethnic state is likely to generate problems, particularly for the national government. For various reasons communal institutions pose an explicit and formidable challenge to the authority and legitimacy of the central government. The nature of this challenge varies. In Lebanon, for instance, it takes the form of intense competition for political support among numerous communal parties. Among the results are a multiplicity of constituencies, the fragmentation of political allegiances, and the inability to create a system of effective party government (Rabushka and Shepsle, 1972). In Nigeria, where the central government was unable to resolve long-standing communal-class grievances between the Ibos and the Hausa-Fulani, the consequence was ethnic violence resulting in seccession and civil war (von der Mehden, 1973). The appropriateness of any regime's strategy for dealing with various ethnic groups must be measured by the success of its institutions and processes in fostering national integration.

Depending upon their definitions of national integration, governments may follow several strategies. One immediate course has been to seek minimal political cohesion and security by granting decisional, institutional, or even territorial concessions to ethnic groups in return for their loyalty to the central government. Examples of this strategy can be found in Lebanon, with its meticulous apportionment of government positions among Christians and Muslims, and in Malaysia, where the dominant national Alliance party has a Chinese branch (Enloe, 1973: 85). Another strategy is to minimize, but not obliterate, ethnic identities and loyalties by fostering the development of a broader national identity. This may be accomplished by inducements such as jobs, education, or status, or by institutions that cut across ethnic allegiances. Ultimately the success of any of these strategies will depend upon the level of security that the government can provide contending groups, and the level of responsiveness that these groups can demonstrate to the commonality and legitimacy of all interests (Grossholtz, 1970: 94).

As if the integration issue were not complex enough, there is a developmental dimension to the problem as well. Multiethnic states are often undergoing modernization. The literature dealing with the concept of modernization and its equivalents (development, growth) is voluminous. No attempt will be made to discuss it here. Borrowing Kornberg's description of the term, we may define it simply as "the enhanced capacity of a social system to accommodate itself to simultaneous rapid change within its sectors and events in the total outside environment" (Kornberg, 1973: 475). While there is some dispute over optimum strategies for achieving this "enhanced capacity," most scholars and nation builders agree that functional modernity demands administrative centralization and nationalization of policy priorities (Huntington, 1968). Without such centralization, governments cannot maximize the use of their nation's limited resources and cannot assure the coordination of necessary "national" activities.

Development and integration processes are related. In the Canadian and Indian case studies in this volume the authors discuss various aspects of this relationship. Allan Kornberg and Samuel M. Hines point out, for instance, that the purpose of Canadian integration is to insure "balance" and as a result maintain "order" within the nation. They contend that without this order a nation would find it difficult to modernize itself, since its ability to accommodate rapid change would be hampered. Yet, as Richard Sisson and Lawrence L. Shrader point out in the case study of Rajasthan, the quest for development may generate "discrepancies" between the conditions of integration and the requisites for development. Enloe (1973: 84–85) has pointed out that many nations find that integration-oriented policies may create political subdivisions (e.g., as the result of federalism) that are not capable of effectively making or administering public policy. Thus the unification of a multiethnic society may often be achieved, at least initially, at the expense of development. Some governments, of course, may stress the development priority, or even periodically shift priorities. Canada and Yugoslavia are cases in point. The Canadian example further illustrates that integration crises do not always come at a nation's birth; they frequently come during a later stage when the government attempts to redefine jurisdictional and institutional boundaries in light of changing developmental priorities. Consequently, federal structures of government which initially may promote integration may also become a future obstacle to development and precipitate a delayed integration-development crisis. It is essential that we recognize that the integration issue is complex. The existing theories of national integration are ambiguous; empirical findings are often contradictory, and the delineations of the exact dimensions of the problem are disputed. Furthermore, in spite of our emphasis in this volume on societal, institutional, and developmental dimensions of the issue, we realize that there may be other factors of equal or greater import for analysis. With these words of caution, I shall turn to an examination of the primary research question: What, if any, is the integrative function of legislatures?

THE INTEGRATIVE FUNCTIONS OF LEGISLATURES

It has been suggested in a number of previous studies (e.g., Binder, 1964) that political institutions are, or can be, vehicles for national integration and development. When political institutions have been the focus of analysis in integration research, legislatures have received low priority compared with such agencies as parties, bureaucracies, and the military. There are a number of reasons for this lack of scholarly interest including, for example, the belief that legislatures in developing states are obstacles to developmental change (Kornberg and Musolf, 1970), that legislatures are "declining" vis-a-vis other institutions, or that they have no real influence in the political system (Balutis, 1974). These and other reasons that can be cited (Kornberg, 1973) may account for the previous disregard of legislative research in developing countries. Consequently, the role of legislatures in national integration is unclear, in part, because so few attempts have been made to determine what that role may be.

With the emergence of comparative legislative research, a growing number of scholars are beginning to examine the relevance of legislative functions for national integration. None of the authors of the studies reported in this volume assumes that there is anything inherent in the legislative process that would insure integration. Rather, each author attempts to assess systematically what functions legislatures actually carry out in multiethnic countries, and whether these functions are related to national integration. There are a few hints in the existing literature on where and how analysis might progress. Malcolm E. Jewell's chapter reviews and synthesizes this literature, then raises a number of important questions and offers guidelines for analysis.

Using Jewell's chapter as a guide, it may be useful to identify the several functions that have been ascribed to legislative systems and then briefly examine their possible effects on national integration. The contributing authors to this volume have analyzed the integrative impact of legislatures basically in terms of three general legislative functions: (1) representation, (2) policy making, and (3) legitimation. The representation function refers to the provisions and processes of formal access to legislative assemblies for representatives of diverse groups. As Jewell, Abdo I. Baaklini, Ian Budge and Cornelius O'Leary, and Sisson and Shrader point out in their respective chapters, analysis of the representational function requires not only concurrent examination of electoral systems, party nominating strategies, and slating procedures but also an analysis of a series of legislative-environmental relationships. In addition to these foci of analysis, one may also include under the representation category an analysis of the legislator's behavior. Marvin G. Weinbaum's chapter, for instance, focuses on the legislative role behavior of the Afghan *wakil* while Sisson and Shrader analyze the relationship between the Indian MLA and various groups. The term "policy making" refers to both decisional processes and tangible policy outputs. There are any number of different legislative policies that could be analyzed, as Lenard J. Cohen and Kornberg and Hines illustrate in their respective studies of Yugoslavia and Canada. The policies they include in their analyses are measures that provide for security against external aggression, that stimulate economic growth, that insure administrative stability, and that heighten national awareness. The last function, legitimation, refers to building support for an institution and compliance with its judgments. The term "support" refers to a predisposition to obey voluntarily a regime's regulations, and accept the relative primacy and appropriateness of its goals (Sisson, 1972). The legitimating process endows governmental decisions with moral oughtness and, as others have contended, even where legislatures perform a questionable decisional function, some link to the generation of public support can be demonstrated (Balutis, 1974; Boynton, Patterson, and Hedlund, 1968). By discharging either of the other two functions, or by simply existing over time, legislatures may generate specific and diffuse support. Jewell's analysis of various representational systems, Kornberg's and Hines's analysis of Canadian parliamentary policies, and Baaklini's discussion of Lebanon's long-standing National Pact illustrate each of the respective methods for generating legitimacy.

THE RESEARCH QUESTIONS

The problem of the scholar, then, is to determine how the experience of representational, decisional, and legitimating functions may affect national integration. From this general question each of the contributing authors derived a number of specific research propositions to direct his analysis. Jewell, for example, contends that in order for the legislature to serve as an arena in which representatives of diverse groups can meet and discuss divergent interests, there must be electoral access to the system. Furthermore, he contends that representation provides minorities with symbolic and tangible benefits that may reduce communalism and strengthen support for the central regime. In order to analyze the problem of minority representation, he poses a series of questions to direct his research, including the following: Do systems of separate electorates affect minority representation? Why have proportional representation systems not been utilized in acutely divided states? Do leaders of minority groups try to organize separate parties? What are the role perceptions of minority legislators? Do they have loyalties to party or to legislative subgroups?

Some nations confront integration problems that have less to do with creating channels for effective multiethnic participation than with the inability of the central government to fulfill its decision-making duties. Where legislative outputs are the main issue, scholars will focus on policy-related questions. These may include such concerns as how districting legislation, for instance, affects minority representation, or in which areas of legislation minority legislators have been most effective for their constituents. Kornberg's and Hines's analysis of Canada's historical experience is based on the contention that legislation can facilitate national integration if it insures balanced economic growth. They then ask what types of legislation did the first Canadian MPs emphasize, whether they contributed to economic development and whether, consequently, this facilitated integration? Both the questions dealing with representation and those focusing on legislation tell us something about a legislature's ability to generate support, and as a result build legitimacy.

The "general" findings of the research reported in this volume will be dealt with in the concluding chapter. Some of the specific results that emerged from the six essays are presented here.

In Chapter 1, in addition to providing an overview and synthesis of legislative research, Malcolm E. Jewell examines the impact that party systems have on the representational function of legislatures. His survey examines experiments with various electoral systems in multiethnic societies. These include separate electorates in Pakistan and India, the reserved-seats system in Lebanon, and single-member districting with plurality elections in Malaysia. The results of his analysis suggest that the influence of any electoral system on minority representation is mitigated by the party system. Since parties control nominations and influence both voters and legislators through party identity and loyalty, future studies might examine directly the relationship between the party system and national integration.

In Chapter 2 Richard Sisson and Lawrence L. Shrader explore the character of elite-mass relations and their salience for political integration in the Indian state of Rajasthan. Their analysis is confined largely to structural elements of integration and of legislative-environmental relationships. These relationships include associational and representational linkages between legislators and their constituencies, as well as formal assembly and party associations. Using both structural and attitudinal data in their analysis, the authors conclude that the legislators are markedly distinct from the mass society with regard to education, mobility, and occupation. There are, however, important indications of social integration in public life which include close ties between the legislator and his constituency and linkages within and between political parties.

In the second of the case studies (Chapter 3) Marvin G. Weinbaum generates and analyzes data to demonstrate that the individual Afghan legislator, not the parliament, contributes to integration. Influenced by a wholly personal and particularistic role concept, the legislator engages in ombudsmanlike behavior that links the outlying regions and tribes to the national bureaucracies and agencies. Weinbaum's findings give additional support to those who have urged greater attention to role variables in integration research.

The study of another group of legislators, by Allan Kornberg and Samuel M. Hines in Chapter 6, demonstrates that MPs in the first three Canadian Parliaments (1865–77) were more concerned with national security and economic development than potentially divisive sociocultural issues. The legislators' "neglect" of particularistic demands and pursuit of national economic objectives facilitated the political and economic development of Canada. However, the failure to recognize and reconcile sociocultural cleavages may account, in part, for Canada's current integration problems. More generally, these findings suggest that immediate and tangible economic rewards often generate sufficient regime legitimacy so that central political institutions can control sociocultural divisions.

In Chapter 7 Abdo Baaklini contends that the fragile basis for consociational agreement among Lebanese elites precludes legislative action on any sensitive sociopolitical issues. Denied any legislative power, the function of the legislature is to provide an institutional setting for manipulating and submerging the overt conflict generated by sectarianism. In a similar vein, Ian Budge and Cornelius O'Leary, in Chapter 5, analyze sectarian divisions in Northern Ireland. But, in tracing the effect of sectarianism on Parliament's development, the authors describe a legislature where there are restrictions in accessibility, representation, and accountability. As in Lebanon, sectarianism permeates all levels of the legislative system; yet in Northern Ireland this has the effect of transforming Parliament into an appendage of the sectarian majority, and thus Parliament's very existence becomes an obstacle to national integration.

An important dimension of Lenard Cohen's analysis of the Yugoslavian legislature in Chapter 4 is his evaluation of the relative utility of attempting to employ parliamentary institutions in managing societal divisions. Cohen's findings suggest that when the Yugoslav Federal Assembly has provided a minimum of integrative services, it has done so at a cost either to its effectiveness as a decision-making body, or to its development vis-à-vis other contending political institutions such as the party and executive agencies.

The comparative study of legislatures in plural societies may offer some answers to the questions about the relationships among pluralism, social cleavage, economic exploitation, and political domination. The countries that are examined in these six essays are even now undergoing rapid and sweeping social, economic, and political change. For example, since Baaklini completed his chapter on Lebanon, that country was plunged into violent civil war as a result of its sectarian divisions and foreign intervention. As research continues, it might be possible in the future to specify more precisely some of the legislative conditions that govern the possibility of either peaceful change or divisive conflict.

REFERENCES

BALUTIS, A. P. (1974) "The role of national legislatures in civilian control of the military in developing nations." Mimeographed paper. Buffalo: State Univ. of New York.

BINDER, L. (1964) "National integration and political development." American Political Science Review 58 (Sept.): 622–31.

BOYNTON, G. R., S. C. PATTERSON, and R. D. HEDLUND (1968) "The structure of public support for legislative institutions." Midwest Journal of Political Science 14 (May): 163–80.

ENLOE, C. H. (1973) Ethnic Conflict and Political Development. Boston: Little, Brown.

GROSSHOLTZ, J. (1970) "Integrative factors in the Malaysian and Philippine legislatures." Comparative Politics 3 (Oct.): 93–113.

HUNTINGTON, S. P. (1968) Political Order in Changing Societies. New Haven, Conn.: Yale Univ. Press.

KORNBERG, A., Ed. (1973) Legislatures in a Comparative Perspective. Beverly Hills, Calif.: Sage Publications.

KORNBERG, A., and L. D. MUSOLF, eds. (1970) Legislatures in Developmental Perspective. Durham, N.C.: Duke University Press.

RABUSHKA, A., and K. A. SHEPSLE (1972) Politics in Plural Societies: A Theory of Democratic Instability. Columbus, Ohio: Merrill.

SISSON, R. (1972) Legislative Recruitment and Political Integration: Patterns of Political Linkage in an Indian State. Berkeley: Univ. of California Press.

VON DER MEHDEN, F. R. (1973) Comparative Political Violence. Englewood Cliffs, N.J.: Prentice-Hall.

Chapter 1

LEGISLATIVE REPRESENTATION AND NATIONAL INTEGRATION

MALCOLM E. JEWELL

The problem of national integration is common to every political system in the world, but it is particularly acute in nations that are deeply divided along racial, linguistic, religious, caste, or other comparable lines. Where such divisions are deep enough, there may be constant danger of civil war and secession. Even where these dangers are unlikely, such divisive forces may create deadlocks in policy making, instability in government, or a fractionalization of political parties and interest groups.

One of the most important topics being studied by students of legislative systems is the legislature's ability to promote integration in a political system. It is important to determine under what conditions a legislature facilitates integration and under what conditions it becomes a vehicle for disintegration. Among the characteristics of the legislative system that may affect this is the process of representation and its effect on minorities. The representation of minorities needs to be studied in all of its aspects, including the apportionment and elections processes, the party system, and the roles and behavior of legislators elected by minority constituencies.

The purpose of this chapter is to explore this problem, defining the questions that need to be answered in cross-national research, summarizing what is already known about the problem as a result of research in a number of countries, and offering suggestions for future research. Although there have been a number of studies in single countries and a few cross-national surveys of specific aspects of the problem, no effort has been made to synthesize the research.

I must first define what I mean by national integration, borrowing Grossholtz's description of the term (1970: 94):

> Integration is here treated as a process and, specifically, as a process leading to political cohesion and sentiments of loyalty toward central political institutions. Integration is not merely unification; it is more than simply bringing diverse groups or political units under central control. Integration implies some level of effective commitment to the commonality of all groups or political levels, but it does not require the obliteration of primary identifications of race, religion, family, or culture. The process of national integration involves the penetration of the primary, occupational, or geographic groups by a broader national identification. . . . The acceptability of the central political institutions and associations depends on the level of security that contending groups feel is provided them and their interests, and on the recognition on the part of the contenders that the interests of other groups are legitimate. Integration is defined as the acceptance on the part of primary, bureaucratic, and associational groups of the fact that other group interests are legitimate and must also be satisfied.

I must also define what I mean by minorities. A workable definition is provided by LaPonce (1960: 6): "A minority is a group of people who, because of a common racial, linguistic, religious, or national heritage which singles them out from the politically dominant cultural group, fear that they may either be prevented from integrating themselves into the national community of their choice or be obliged to do so at the expense of their identity." The definition excludes economic and social classes primarily because an individual's membership in such groupings is less permanent. At the same time, it must be recognized that minority racial, linguistic, and other groups often are concentrated in the lowest economic and social classes. (In a country such as India, I would define lower castes as minorities because the caste system has a rigidity that distinguishes it from economic and social classes). It should be emphasized that LaPonce's definition, being subjective as well as objective, recognizes that "a minority is a group that thinks of itself as a minority" (1960: 4).

THE INTEGRATIVE FUNCTION OF LEGISLATURES

It is commonly argued that the legislature is, or can be, a vehicle for national integration. Many writers have emphasized the legitimizing function of the legislature, and we generally assume that its representative function also serves the purposes of integration. In a political system where minorities are a major source of disintegration, the legislature provides an arena in which representatives of these minorities may meet with representatives of the dominant group or groups and try to compromise their differences. Representation in the legislature may provide minorities with both symbolic and tangible benefits and may serve to strengthen their support of the political regime.

It is possible, however, that a legislature may fail to perform an integrative function or may even contribute to disintegration, for any of several reasons. The election system may fail to provide adequate representation for minorities because of the mechanics of districting, the tactics followed by parties, or other reasons. Those legislators who are elected by minority constituencies may not be effective in satisfying the demands of their constituents because they fail to recognize this as their proper role, because they perform this role ineptly, or because they simply do not have enough political power in the legislature. Another possibility is that the election of minority representatives and their vigorous activities on behalf of constituents may have the effect of exacerbating conflict and intensifying both the demands of the minority groups and the determination of the dominant groups to resist these demands.

There is no reason to suppose that there is something inherent in the legislative process that guarantees either integration or disintegration in a deeply divided society. Rather, it is assumed that the impact of the legislature depends on how that legislative system operates: the mechanics of elections, the party system, the roles and behavior of legislators. My goal is to try to determine under what conditions and in what ways legislatures perform an integrative function. Does it make any difference whether single-member districts or proportional representation is used? Can political parties contribute to or overcome conflicts between groups through their slating policies? Exactly what does a legislator do to represent a minority constituency, and what are the consequences of change? If the districting system is changed, or a new party coalition is established, or minority legislators begin to vote as a bloc, does this further integration, deter it, or have no effect either way?

A few words of caution are in order. It is important to start out without any preconceptions about the answers to be found, without any bias in favor of legislatures as vehicles of integration. It is essential to recognize that the problem is complex and that no single feature of a legislative system, such as proportional representation, is likely to be the key to integration in a divided society. Moreover, despite my concentration on the legislative system, it should be recognized that there may be other factors—socioeconomic, geographical, or historical perhaps—that determine the impact of the legislature on integration. It is possible that legislatures can serve an integrative function only in societies where the divisions have not reached a certain depth. If a society is on the brink of civil war, it may be too late for any changes in the legislature to prevent such a conflict. In other words, we must be aware of possible limits on the legislature's potential for integration.

I will begin by summarizing briefly some of the efforts to achieve integration through a federal structure. Then I will examine in some detail the effects of five different methods for selecting legislators: separate electorates, reserved seats, single-member district plurality systems, multimember district plurality systems, and methods of proportional representation. The effects of any of these systems on minority representation depend very largely on the strategies employed by party and group leaders regarding the nomination of legislative candidates. Moreover, the effectiveness of representation depends on the roles and behavior of the elected members, and I will review the sparse literature on this topic. Finally, I will consider the problem of measuring the effects that legislative outputs actually have on minority interests. These latter topics are fully as important as the electoral methods, but they can be discussed more briefly because very little has been written about them.

FEDERAL STRUCTURES OF GOVERNMENT

Federalism is one structural device that may be used in an effort to integrate a nation while preserving the rights of minorities.[1] There may, of course, be other reasons for the establishment of a federal system; in the United States it was an essential method for uniting colonies that had previously been independent. Whether federalism is proposed as a method of handling minority problems depends in large part on the geographical distribution of those minorities. If an important minority is geographically concentrated, and particularly if this minority constitutes a majority in one or more provinces, it is likely to demand decentralization of decision making by means of a federal system. At the same time, if the concentration of cultural minorities does coincide with provincial boundaries, the rivalries between provinces are likely to be more intense, and the problems of creating a workable federal system may be magnified.

It must be emphasized that geographic concentration of minorities is not a sufficient condition for federalism to serve minority interests. In the United States, the blacks, although concentrated in southern states until recent years, did not benefit from federalism because they did not have political control of any states. In fact, the state governments in which blacks consituted the largest minority were generally the ones that adopted the most repressive legislation. The protection of black rights in the twentieth century came first from the national government, and it can be argued that blacks would have benefited more from a unitary system of government in the United States. We must look for federalism to be used as a device for integration and minority protection in those countries where ethnic, linguistic, tribal, or other groups have a dominant political position in particular political subunits.

There are two distinct ways in which federalism might be expected to serve minority interests. First, it provides for a division of power between the national and subnational unit to determine policies with respect to those issues that come within its jurisdiction. These are likely to include issues of particular importance to the minority, such as education, religion, language, and cultural autonomy. In some federal systems minorities may also benefit from an apportionment system in one house of a bicameral legislature that overrepresents those subnational units controlled by these minorities. In other words, federalism may give minorities in control of subnational units a disproportionate voice in national policy making as well as exclusive control over local policy making. It may not be possible for every federal system to provide both kinds of benefits. In Canada, for example, where the French-speaking population has a majority only in the province of Quebec, federalism provides this minority with authority over provincial matters, but does not give it an enlarged voice in national policy making.

Second, a federal system, by creating multiple units of government, may create a variety of majorities and minorities and may complicate the relationships among them. LaPonce (1960: 68, 82) points out that one consequence of federalism, if national minorities control some areas, is "to reduce, in certain parts of the state, the nationally dominant group to the status of a local minority." He argues that "by becoming local majorities, minorities derive the advantage from federalism of being given hostages." Milnor (1969: 140) is less optimistic about the consequences of federalism for subminorities in a region, particularly as a substitute for an electoral system benefiting minorities:

> In fact, since the federal device is supposed to be more effective than some form of electoral protection for minorities—such as proportional representation—the type of electoral system used in state elections will probably be a system which assumes social homogeneity within the state and whose major concern will not be representation but the preservation of a united state front against groups from other regions. . . . the existence of dissident subgroups within the large cultural regions suggests the possibility of a very large degree of underrepresentation for these minorities. And the perhaps less than gentle treatment accorded these state minorities may feed fires in other regions that potentially can have disastrous effects upon the whole nation.

Further, Milnor (1969: 141) argues that these subminorities may find it very difficult to win redress for their grievances at the national level, both because they lack representation in the national government (in the absence of proportional representation) and because the national government has delegated authority over most of the issues concerning these groups to the regional governments.

The recent history of federal systems, particularly in Africa, casts doubt on the effectiveness of federalism as a device for integration and the protection of minorities. The experience of Nigeria illustrates very well Milnor's arguments. The country was divided into three regions or states (northern, western, and eastern) under a federal plan adopted in 1950, a decade before independence. Each of the regions was dominated by a different tribe, but each contained a diversity of tribal groups, and as a consequence there was continuing agitation for the establishment of a larger number of states. In 1957–58 a British commission was established "to enquire into the fears of minorities and the means of allaying them." The commission rejected proposals for the establishment of additional states, which might perpetuate disintegrative forces. It recognized that the rights of various minorities were most seriously jeopardized by the regional governments, and it sought to use the central government as a vehicle for protecting these rights, as the British government had done in the past. But after independence was granted in 1960 the central government proved unable or unwilling to satisfy the demands of various minorities for protection. A major reason for the failure of the federal system in Nigeria was the fact that each of the major political parties that developed in the 1960s drew its strength primarily from a single tribal group. The parties tended to exacerbate rather than to overcome tribal and regional differences. Because the national government was controlled by a party dominated by a single major tribe, it was not an effective vehicle for protecting minorities against repressive state legislation. The collapse of the federal system came in 1967 when the state of Biafra seceded, and the civil war broke out (Milnor, 1969: 140–41; Schwartz, 1965).

Federalism also failed in Kenya. The original constitution in that country established a number of regional governments and gave them considerable authority to handle such questions as local law and order, tribal questions, and land rights. The constitution also established a bicameral legislature, with a Senate that was supposed to protect regional and tribal rights. The single-member districts in the Senate were drawn up on the basis of tribally homogeneous constituencies with the apportionment favoring the smaller and less advanced tribes (unlike the House districting). But the dominant KANU party, led by Kenyatta, the father of Kenyan independence, was concerned that this federal structure would be a source of disintegration. Once the KANU party had established firm political control over the nation following independence, it succeeded in passing constitutional amendments, first to reduce the powers of the regional governments and later to abolish the Senate, which had been designed to protect regional and minority tribal rights (Stultz, 1970).

If federalism failed in Kenya because the pressure for national integration was too great, the Federation of Rhodesia and Nyasaland failed because the forces of disintegration, primarily racial forces, were too great. This federal system was an abortive effort by the British in 1953 to create a multiracial nation. The northern states, however, were under black control, and in 1964 they succeeded in breaking away from the federation and establishing two independent states (Malawi and Zambia). The remaining member of the federation, Rhodesia, was a state in which the white minority maintained political control by disenfranchising the black majority and resisted pressures from the British government to adopt reforms that would increase black participation in the political process.[2]

The federal system has been used in Malaysia, but it has not been the major device for integrating a nation that is split into several ethnic groups, primarily Malay and Chinese. Although the ethnic balance differs substantially among the states, most states have substantial minority blocs, and consequently minority rights cannot be preserved simply by delegating authority to the states. The strongest force for integration in Malaysia has been the Alliance party, an alliance of Malay and Chinese political groups (discussed in more detail later in this chapter). In 1963 Malaya (which included 11 states) was expanded to include Singapore and two other states, and was renamed Malaysia. Singapore was predominantly Chinese, and the ethnic conflicts with the Malay majority in Malaysia as well as other political conflicts led two years later to the secession of Singapore. The federal system had failed to offer Singapore sufficient autonomy or influence in the national political system to satisfy it, and the influence of the Alliance party as an integrative force did not extend to Singapore, where other parties predominated (Means, 1970).

Perhaps the best example of a federal system being used to deal with the problems of integration and minority interests is in India, where one of the sources of division is linguistic diversity. Although the national government during the early years of independence resisted pressures for linguistic autonomy, it has gradually accepted the reorganization of state boundaries and an increase in the number of states to make possible greater linguistic homogeneity in the states. The changes have come about in part because the national government has been unable to guarantee effectively the rights of linguistic minorities in the states. In some cases the changes have been precipitated by large-scale rioting by minority groups. It is obviously not possible to expand the number of states sufficiently to eliminate the problem of linguistic minorities and for that reason federalism appears to be an imperfect solution to the linguistic problem, but it has worked better than any other device in India.

There is not enough evidence to evaluate the effectiveness of federalism as a method for achieving integration in a divided society. In some countries, such as Kenya and Nigeria, it did not get a fair trial. In most countries it has not been studied fully enough to make evaluation possible. The most serious limitation of federalism is that the boundaries of states rarely coincide with the boundaries between significant minority groups and the federal structure provides no answers to the problems of minorities within states. Whether federalism contributes significantly to integration in a plural society depends on a number of other factors, including the nature of powers given to the states, provisions for state representation in the national government, measures to protect minorities within states, the nature of the party system, and the electoral system used for the choice of legislators at both the state and national level.

METHODS OF ELECTING LEGISLATORS

The extent to which any group within the electorate is represented in the legislature depends to a large extent on the electoral system that is used for choosing legislatures. The scholarly literature on electoral systems has demonstrated how party strength in the electorate is translated into party seats in the legislature under each system, but it has provided less information about the representation of minority groups in the legislature. Electoral systems do have an effect on the legislative power of any group in a country, whether it is members of a party, an ethnic group, a tribe, or region. Exactly what the effect may be often depends on the geographic concentration or dispersion of the group, as well as on its ability to organize in order to take advantage of the electoral system.

It may be useful to identify the various electoral systems before describing the effects of each. The system of *separate electorates* used in a few countries most directly affects the representation of groups. Under this system, the members of a group (religious, nationality, racial) vote for a number of legislators who are responsible only to that group. In other words, the constituencies or districts are organized not along geographic lines but strictly along ethnic, racial, or other group lines. This guarantees a group that there will be a number of legislators responsible only to it, but it does not necessarily guarantee that group a number of legislators proportionate to its population, because this system can be used with an apportionment formula that discriminates either in favor of or against a minority group. A variation on this system is the use of *reserved seats* (see Baaklini, chap. 7 in this volume). There is a common election roll, but a certain number of seats are reserved for legislators belonging to a particular group. In order to win election to a reserved seat a candidate may have to win votes from persons outside as well as those inside the group.

The system of districting used in legislative elections also affects the representation of groups. The *single-member district plurality* system common to the United States, Britain, Canada, and former British colonies gives disproportionately greater numbers of seats to majorities (partisan or group). A minority can win seats only to the extent that it constitutes a majority (or at least a plurality) in some districts. The extent to which this system diminishes the legislative representation of a minority group depends on whether that minority is dispersed throughout the state or has pockets of strength. It also may depend on whether the district lines are drawn in such a way as to maximize or minimize the minority group's voting strength. A less familiar system, often used in local and state legislative elections in the United States, is the *multimember district plurality* system, which discriminates even more against minority parties and groups, with the degree of discrimination depending on the size of the multimember districts. There are many systems of *proportional representation,* all designed to represent parties or other groups proportionately in the legislature. How much a minority group benefits from the use of such a system depends on the exact electoral method used and also on the ability of the group to organize in such a way (perhaps through a party) as to take advantage of the system.

SEPARATE ELECTORATES

Separate electorates for the selection of legislators were used in the early twentieth century in a number of European countries that contained religious or nationality minorities, including Austria, Cyprus, Greece, and Poland (LaPonce, 1960: 113). The use of separate electorates has been most common, however, in the British colonies; in some of these the transition to independence has been marked by debates over perpetuation or abolition of separate electorates. There were several reasons why the British originally established separate electorates in India, Ceylon, a number of African colonies, and other possessions. These countries often included ethnic or religious groups so diverse in background and interests that the British believed the interests of each could be protected only by legislators responsive to separate electorates. Some of these groups, like the Muslims in India, demanded separate electorates. Moreover, in the African colonies, where the franchise was extended only gradually to black citizens, the early legislative councils consisted primarily of elected Europeans, with representatives of black Africans at first appointed in small numbers. The system of separate electorates also made it easy to overrepresent specific groups. The minority Muslims in India during the preindependence period demanded and got a share of seats under the separate electorate plan that was larger than their share of the population. In most of the African colonies prior to independence the separate electorate plan gave the white voters a vastly greater share of seats in legislative councils than their proportion of the population.

The system of separate electorates was often criticized for two reasons. In those countries where the system was used to diminish the numerical representation of some electorates compared to others, the groups that were discriminated against frequently objected (Mackenzie, 1954). There is nothing inherent in separate electoral rolls that guarantees such discrimination; the "one-man, one-vote" principle could be applied to all persons, whatever electorate they belonged to. A more fundamental criticism was that separate electorates undermined national integration because each legislator was elected by and responsive to only a single group. This point was made by the Commission of Inquiry in Ceylon that recommended in 1931 the elimination of separate electorates, in a statement that is often quoted: "In surveying the position in Ceylon, we have come unhesitatingly to the conclusion that communal representation is, as it were, a canker on the body politic, eating deeper and deeper into the vital energies of the people, breeding self-interest, suspicion and animosity, poisoning the new growth of political consciousness and effectively preventing the development of a national or corporate spirit" (LaPonce, 1960: 114).

In Rhodesia a white minority that constitutes barely 5% of the population has maintained political control over the black majority by means of separate election rolls for whites and for blacks as well as stringent limits on black enfranchisement through income and property qualifications. In South Africa the separate election roll has been one tool in a policy of even more absolute control by a white minority. In both countries, however, the separate election rolls are relatively minor features of a white supremacy policy that depends primarily on stringently restricting the exercise of black political power.

Separate electorates were tried more extensively and debated more thoroughly during the years prior to independence in India than in any other country. In 1909 Muslim leaders won a demand for separate Muslim electorates and representatives in national and provincial legislative councils, and in 1919 the principle was extended to other minorities such as Sikhs, Europeans, Anglo-Indians, and Indian Christians; it was reaffirmed in the 1935 Government of India Act, which reserved roughly half of the seats in the national legislative council for these minorities. The policy was opposed by the predominantly Hindu Congress party and maintained reluctantly by the British government. The consequences of this policy have not been the subject of detailed research, but scholars have concluded that the establishment of a separate electorate for the large Muslim minority contributed to the partition of India and the creation of Pakistan. One scholar (Smith, 1963: 87) concludes: "The system of separate representation undoubtedly stimulated the further growth of communalism. It encouraged the very defect it sought to remedy. The system encouraged the most vociferous and aggressive Muslim politicians; there was no need for the moderation which is inevitably developed when a candidate has to appeal to all groups." When the constituent assembly drew up a constitution for India after partition, there was consensus that separate elections—which were blamed for contributing to partition—should be abolished. Serious consideration was given to the possibility of reserved seats for the Muslims remaining in India, but this proposal was abandoned, and the electoral system that was adopted gave no advantage or protection to the Muslim minority (Smith, 1963: 407–09).

In the years following partition the question of separate electorates was frequently debated in Pakistan. Although the Muslims were a majority in the new Pakistani state, they generally argued in favor of separate electorates, while the minority Hindus supported the principle of joint electorates. This may not have been as illogical as it appears. The Hindus were concerned that separate electorates would relegate them and their political parties to a permanent minority influence. The dominant political organization in Pakistan, the Muslim League, did not want to accept Hindus into its ranks or appeal for Hindu votes as a system of joint electorates might require. Another aspect of the conflict was the tension between West and East Pakistan. Most of the Hindus were located in East Pakistan, and the political leaders of West Pakistan calculated that separate electorates would divide the political strength of East Pakistan. Muslim leaders doubted the loyalty of Hindus to Pakistan and feared that they would use their political power to undermine the fragile unity of the country (Callard, 1957: 240–57). In 1961 a constitution commission warned that the demand of Hindus for joint electorates "was due to a desire to influence the elections against the ideology of Pakistan" and "until we can be reasonably certain that they have reconciled themselves to the continuance of Pakistan, it does not appear safe to have joint electorates" (Smith, 1966: 27). Muslim leaders in the East were much more sympathetic to the principle of joint electorates. At various times the electoral laws of Pakistan provided for (1) separate electorates throughout the country, (2) separate electorates only in the West, and (3) joint electorates everywhere. The consequences of various electoral systems in Pakistan have not been studied carefully, largely because the legislature did not operate long enough under any system to make comparisons possible.

The controversy over separate or joint electorates in Pakistan is significant because it illustrates how the support for and effects of institutional devices may be affected by political forces. In most countries separate electorates have been criticized by those persons and groups who were seeking national integration. The Muslim leadership of Pakistan (and particularly West Pakistan), however, hoped to use separate electorates as a device for dividing and isolating those political groups whom they perceived as a threat to national unity. The Muslim leadership in the West was less interested in integrating Hindus into the Pakistan nation than in preventing them from cooperating with Muslim politicians in the East.

One British colony that rejected separate election rolls despite a wide ethnic diversity was the Federation of Malaya (later Malaysia). A committee appointed in 1953 (four years prior to independence) to study the method of choosing members for the Federal Legislative Council unanimously rejected separate communal election rolls because such a system "would not be in keeping with the agreed object of promoting national unity amongst the people of Malaya and might arrest the process of assimilation and cooperation which is so essential if the country is to have a single united people" (Ratnam, 1965: 176). The committee was controlled by members of political groups that were either dominated by Malays (the majority ethnic group) or were committed to an electoral strategy of alliance among the major ethnic groups. (The effects of party strategy on the electoral system in Malaysia are discussed later in this chapter.)

The experiment of the Fiji Islands with separate voting rolls is less well known than that of India or Pakistan, but it illustrates how such a policy has evolved through time. In the mid-fifties the population was 50% Indian, 42% Fijian, and less than 5% European, with a scattering of other nationalities. A legislative council gradually evolved in the early twentieth century in response to the demands of Europeans. Indians as well as Europeans were added to the membership, with an increasing proportion being elected rather than appointed and with separate electoral rolls. The Indians, who greatly outnumbered the Europeans, pressed unsuccessfully for a common election roll. By 1937 the three ethnic groups gained parity of representation, with all the Fijian members being appointed until

1963. Meller and Anthony (1968: chap. 7), analyzing the 1963 election, concluded that the separate election system was dysfunctional because the candidates had parochial viewpoints and constituencies and ignored the major issues facing the country, most of which were unrelated to communal differences. Fiji achieved full independence in 1970 under a complicated formula that represented a compromise between the demands of the Indians for a joint electorate and the preferences of other groups for separate electorates. The system provided that some legislators would be chosen by separate electorates and some by a combined national electorate, with seats reserved for specified numbers of legislators from each group. The system provided parity between Indian and Fijian legislators and a smaller number of European and other legislators (Great Britain Parliamentary Papers, 1970).

RESERVED SEATS

Separate electorates and reserved seats are both systems that should guarantee the election of legislators who are members of minority groups. The difference is that under a reserved-seat system the minority legislators may have to depend for election in part on the votes of persons outside the minority group. In theory this should make the minority legislator less parochial in his outlook and more willing to compromise in the legislature. This electoral system may serve the purposes of national integration better than a policy of separate electorates. From the viewpoint of the minority group, however, this form of representation may not be fully satisfactory because, in some cases, only those legislative candidates from the group can win who can get the approval of electors outside the group.

The actual operation of a reserved-seat system depends on how district lines are drawn. In a single-member district system, if a minority group has a majority in a particular district, it probably does not need a reserved seat in that district in order to get one of its own members elected. If it lacks a majority in a reserved-seat district, however, it can only elect a member who is acceptable to the other group(s) in the district, while the other group(s) are forced to accept a representative from a minority group. In a multimember district with one or more reserved seats, the operation of a reserved-seat policy may be more complicated, particularly if voters are able to cast as many votes as there are seats. In analyzing the consequences of this policy, it is important to distinguish between the practice of reserving some seats for a particular minority group (as in India) and that of reserving all seats for specific minorities (as in Lebanon; see Baaklini, chap. 7 in this volume).

The policy of reserved seats has been used in India for what are called the scheduled castes and scheduled tribes. The first are lower-caste Hindus, the group once referred to as "untouchables"; the latter are relatively small, isolated, generally backward groups scattered throughout India. Together they represent roughly one-seventh of the population of India. The scheduled castes were given reserved seats in national and provincial legislative bodies in 1935. The British government, in response to pressure from the leaders of lower-caste groups, first announced that they would be given separate electorates. Gandhi strongly opposed this plan as one that would further divide the Hindus politically and started a "fast unto death" in protest. He won his point, and the policy of reserved seats was established instead (Dushkin, 1967: 629–31; Smith, 1963: 303).

After Indian independence the new constitution provided for reserved seats in the House of the People (Lok Sabha) and in the state legislative assemblies for both the scheduled castes and scheduled tribes. The number of reserved seats in the Lok Sabha in various sessions has ranged from 97 to 114 of a total membership that has ranged from 490 to 521. The proportion of reserved seats in legislative assemblies has been about the same, roughly 21% (Desai, 1969: 93). The framers of the constitution believed that the policy of reserved seats should be a temporary one until the scheduled castes and tribes gained enough political strength to win legislative elections without a guarantee of seats. Consequently, the constitution provided that the reserved-seat policy would last for only ten years. But the policy was extended for ten years more by an amendment in 1959 and again in 1969, so that it will remain in effect at least until 1980 (Desai, 1969).

Members of the scheduled castes are not concentrated in a few areas or localities in India but are dispersed throughout many parts of the country. Some of the population identified as belonging to scheduled tribes is concentrated, but much of it is scattered. This means that the members of these minority groups generally constitute only a minority in the districts which have reserved seats for them. Indian legislators have generally been elected from single-member districts, but in the 1952 and 1957 elections all of the reserved seats for scheduled castes, and about half of those for tribes, were found in two-member districts. (The single-member reserved seats for tribes were in districts where tribal membership was more concentrated) (Morris-Jones, 1957: 95). In these two-member districts one of the two seats was reserved for a member of a scheduled caste or tribe and the other was a general seat. Voters were entitled to cast two votes, one of which had to go to a scheduled caste (or tribe) candidate; the other vote could go to either another scheduled caste candidate or some other candidate (Dushkin, 1967: 634). The scheduled caste candidate with the largest number of votes was elected, and it was possible for two scheduled caste candidates to be elected in one district if they ran first and second in the voting. In the 1957 elections to the Lok Sabha, scheduled caste (or tribe) candidates won both seats in about 5% of the two-member districts. The winner of the reserved seat ran unopposed in 6% of the districts, ran ahead of all candidates in 27% of the districts, ran second in 54%, and ran third in 8%. It was common for the strongest parties in a district to run a slate of two candidates, one for the reserved seat and one for the regular one, and straight-ticket voting appeared to be common. In 78% of the two-member districts in 1957, the two winning candidates belonged to the same party.[3]

In the 1962 and subsequent elections single-member districts have been used for all of the legislative seats in both the Lok Sabha and the state legislatures. None of these constituencies for the Lok Sabha in the 1962 and 1967 elections had a population more than one-fourth of which belonged to the scheduled castes, and in many districts the proportion was below 10%. In only a few of the urban districts in legislative assemblies did the scheduled caste voters approach a majority of the population (Dushkin, 1967: 634). Consequently the success of candidates for reserved seats has depended very heavily on the votes of members from other castes and on the party affiliation of candidates.

The reserved-seat policy has not encouraged, and may have discouraged, the election of scheduled caste and tribe candidates to general seats. The number elected from general seats in the Lok Sabha fell from nine to three after two-member constituencies were abandoned in 1962. The number elected to general seats in state legislative assemblies reached a high of 48 (out of about 2,500 nonreserved seats) in the 1963–66 period and then dropped to 26 in the late 1960s (Desai, 1969: 91).

In Lebanon reserved seats are used, not to insure some representation for a particular minority, but to allocate all of the legislative seats to members of particular religious groups. The political system in Lebanon has been built precariously on a delicate balance between Christian and Muslim sects. This balance extends to legislative representation. Even since the 1926 Constitution was adopted, a system of joint electorates and reserved seats has been used for the election of legislators. Since 1943 the size of the Chamber of Deputies has varied from 55 to 99 members, but the ratio of Christian to Muslim members has always been six to five, and each seat in the Chamber has been assigned specifically to one of the eight different Christian and Muslim sects (Hudson, 1968: 212–19).

The theory of joint electorates is that candidates for reserved seats must depend in part on votes from outside their group to get elected. How this system works in practice depends in large part on the size and composition of districts (see Baaklini, chap. 7 in this volume). The larger the district and the more heterogeneous its composition, the greater the reliance a candidate must place on getting votes from members of other sects. Political parties are weak in Lebanon, but the practice of slating is widely used in legislative elections. These slates are drawn up by local political leaders and include candidates for each of the seats in the district. The joint electorate system forces political leaders and candidates of various seats in a district to work together in an effort to win elections. In the 1940s, when each of the five provinces constituted a district, the dominant political figures of each province controlled the slate making. The reduction in the number of districts in the 1950s was designed to weaken the power of these provincial leaders and strengthen the influence of national leaders, particularly the president (Hudson, 1968: 213–19).

The reserved-seat policies in India and Lebanon, though very different in some respects, have had similar consequences. Candidates for reserved seats have had to win votes from outside their own caste or sect, and in order to do so have usually run on a party ticket or a slate. Whether those elected to reserved seats in the two countries have been more responsive to the caste or sect they represent or to the leadership of a party or slate is a question that needs further exploration.

SINGLE-MEMBER DISTRICTS WITH PLURALITY ELECTIONS

Single-member districts with plurality elections are commonly used in the United States, Britain, the Commonwealth countries, and other former British colonies. In most of their colonies the British established legislative councils with single-member districts, and when independence was achieved the constitutions of the new nations perpetuated the single-member district system. This explains why a number of the countries with serious problems of minority integration—such as India, Malaysia, the Fiji Islands, and several African countries—have stuck to single-member districts. Although the British were seriously concerned about the protection of minorities, they were so committed to the British principle of single-member districts that they did not seriously explore the potential of proportional representation systems for assuring legislative seats for minorities. Instead they relied to some extent on separate electorates or reserved seats.

The effects of a single-member district system on minorities depend to a very large extent on the geographic distribution of those minorities. In order to elect legislators, the minorities must have enough political control in some districts to win a plurality vote for their candidates. The French-speaking voters of Canada are sure of electing a substantial number of legislators because they control most of the districts in the province of Quebec. Members of the scheduled castes in India, however, are so thinly dispersed that they do not have a majority in any Lok Sabha district. If minorities are geographically concentrated, it is possible that the single-member district system will give them a share of seats proportionate to—or even larger than—their share of the population.

If a minority is concentrated enough so that it is plausible to expect that it can control some districts, its exact share of districts depends on how district boundaries are drawn. It is possible to draw the boundary lines so as to either maximize or minimize the number of seats controlled by the minority group. Any single-member district system wastes votes. The group or party that gets the greatest advantage from any districting plan is the one that wastes the fewest votes; the district boundaries should permit it to win some seats by small margins and lose others by large margins. Another tactic that gives an advantage to a group is to create smaller districts (in terms of population) in the areas where that group is strong.

In discussing districting techniques, I am assuming that the goal of any group is to control (win a plurality in) as many districts as possible. This is normally the case, just as it is the goal of a party. It is possible, however, that a minority group would prefer a districting pattern that gave it control over somewhat fewer districts while giving it a strong minority in a larger number of districts and therefore some influence over a larger number of legislators.

Ceylon is often cited as an example of a country where single-member districts have been drawn deliberately in such a way as to protect the interests of minority groups, and the evidence supports this assertion. The Delimitation Commission in Ceylon can and does draw single-member district boundaries in such a way as to facilitate the representation of ethnic, religious, or caste minorites. It is also authorized to create multimember districts to make possible the representation of scattered minorities, and it has done so in a few cases to assure representation of a Muslim minority. The minority group benefiting primarily from single-member district boundaries is the Ceylon Tamils. (Another minority, the Indian Tamils, is largely without citizenship.) In recent elections the Tamils have held about 12% of the seats in the House of Representatives and the Muslims 7%, both very close to their percentages of the total citizen population. The concentration of population and the districting policy have together resulted in relatively homogeneous districts. In nearly half at least 90% of the population belongs to one ethnic group, and in almost three-quarters the dominant group constitutes at least three-quarters of the population. An analysis of the 1970 elections shows that of the 19 Tamils elected 10 came from districts with at least 90% Tamil population, and all but 2 came from districts with a Tamil majority (Kearny, 1973).

It is probably relatively easy for a large majority (as in Ceylon) to allocate a proportionate share of districts to small minority groups. In Malaysia the problems of equitable districting are more serious because the balance among ethnic groups is much closer. The Malays constitute about half of the population and the Chinese a little more than one-third, with most of the remainder being Indian. Because in the 1950s the requirements for citizenship favored the Malays, they had a much higher percentage of citizens and therefore of eligible voters than of population, but the Malay electoral advantage has been smaller in recent years.

In 1954, three years before independence, the Constituency Delineation Commission announced its criteria for establishing 52 single-member districts: "We have, in delineating constituencies, wholly ignored racial considerations; but we have taken into account community of interest where it exists" (quoted in Ratnam, 1965: 183–84). But in the years that followed, the racial composition of districts was a source of continuing controversy in Malaya. The first districts, used in the 1955 election, included 50 with a Malay majority, only 2 with a Chinese majority, and none in which Indians had more than 15% of the vote. The Chinese electorate was only 11% of the total at that time (because of the restrictions on citizenship), and its share of seats was even less. By 1959, when the next election was held, a much larger number of Chinese had qualified for citizenship, and they now constituted 36% of the electorate. The number of legislative districts was doubled simply by dividing the existing districts, and the result was to give the Chinese the largest share of the vote in a number of districts that approximated their proportion of the electorate. (See Table 1.1.) Following the 1959 election an election commission proposed a new set of 100 legislative districts, but it was rejected by the government, which feared that the dominant party, and particularly its Malayan wing, would lose seats as a result of it. A constitutional amendment was adopted in 1962 that restored the districts used in 1959 as the basis for the 1964 elections, even though there were serious differences in size of districts that discriminated against urban areas. The Indian population has not been large enough or concentrated enough to win a plurality in any district, but the Chinese have not been handicapped by the districting system since their share of the electorate increased to about one-third (Ratnam, 1965: 185; Vasil, 1965: 37; Ratnam and Milne, 1967: 63–66).

The racial balance of elected members has depended not only on the composition of districts but on the shifting fortunes and tactics of coalition politics (Table 1.1). The dominant political force, the Alliance party, was established before the 1955 election as a coalition among Malay, Chinese, and Indian parties. In the 1955 election the Alliance endorsed a disproportionately large number of Chinese candidates, and 15 of them were elected. As the Chinese share of the electorate has increased, the bargaining among the partners in the Alliance party has become more intense, and the Malay wing of the party has succeeded in keeping the proportion of Chinese and Indian Alliance candidates below their percentages of the electorate. In both the 1959 and 1964 elections there were a few districts in which the winning candidate's racial background was different from the largest racial group in the district, an outcome that resulted from the slating practices and competitive position of the parties in the district (Ratnam, 1965: 185–99, 202; Ratnam and Milne, 1967: 84–87).

In the years before partition and independence in India representa-

TABLE 1.1
RACIAL CHARACTERISTICS OF ELECTORATES, DISTRICTS, AND ELECTED MEMBERS IN MALAYAN ELECTIONS, 1955, 1959, 1964
(IN PERCENTAGES)

Year	Malays			Chinese			Indians and Others		
	In Total Electorate	Districts with Malay Plurality	Malay Members Elected	In Total Electorate	Districts with Chinese Plurality	Chinese Members Elected	In Total Electorate	Districts with Indian Plurality	Indian Members Elected
1955	84	96	67	11	4	29	5	0	4
1959	56	61	64	36	39	27	8	0	9
1964	54	60	66	38	40	31	8	0	3

Sources: Ratnam (1965: 186, 199, 202, 207); Ratnam and Milne (1967: 368); Vasil (1965: 61).

tion was guaranteed to lower-caste Hindus through reserved seats and to Muslims through separate electorates. After independence the scheduled castes kept their reserved seats, but nothing was done to assure representation under the single-member district system for the Muslims who stayed in India after the partition, representing about one-tenth of the population. The Muslim population is widely dispersed in India. Except for the disputed state of Kashmir, none of the Indian states has a population that is more than one-fourth Muslim. There are very few Lok Sabha districts in which the Muslims constitute a majority or even the largest religious group. The Indian states are divided into more than 300 administrative districts. Data on the religious composition of these districts show that two-thirds of them have less than 10% Muslim population, and 89% have less than 20% Muslims, while only 4% have at least 40% Muslims (Baxter, 1969). Because voting districts for the Lok Sabha are somewhat smaller, the proportion with a concentration of Muslim voters may be slightly higher. In general we can conclude that the single-member district system in India has wasted Muslim votes by scattering most of them in districts where Muslims are badly outnumbered by Hindus and other groups.

The number of Muslim legislators in the Lok Sabha has been very modest indeed. In 1952 Muslims contested 50 seats out of 489 and won 22. In 1957 they contested 55 seats out of 494 and won 24. The proportion of Muslims elected in the state legislative assemblies has been about the same, 170 in 1952 and 159 in 1957 out of roughly 3,300 and 3,200 seats in those years (Gupta, 1962: 371–74). Since nearly all those elected to the Lok Sabha, and most of those elected to state assemblies, have been chosen in districts with only a minority of Muslims, the success of Muslim candidates has depended largely on their ability to win nomination on the ticket of a party that was strong in the district. During the 1950s most successful Muslim candidates in national and state legislative races were elected on the Congress party ticket. In 1952 the Congress party slated 27 Muslims, 20 of whom were elected, and in 1957 it slated 29 and elected 19 of them (Gupta, 1962: 372). Muslims have sometimes been nominated because Muslims voters were perceived by a party as holding the balance of power in a district; the Congress party has also put pressure on its district branches to nominate some Muslims in order to maintain the party's nonsectarian image. Given the geographic dispersion of Muslims in India, the single-member district system has not only reduced the number of Muslim legislators but has assured that most of those who won election were dependent on the help of a non-Muslim party and the votes of non-Muslim constituents.

There is no state any more torn by disintegration today than Northern Ireland (see Budge and O'Leary, chap. 5 in this volume). Since the partition of Ireland in 1922 the government of Northern Ireland has been completely dominated by the Protestant majority, and the Catholic minority (one-third of the population) has been subjected to various forms of political and economic discrimination. An obvious question, in the context of this chapter, is whether the electoral system has contributed to the disintegration of Northern Ireland. The first election for the Northern Irish parliament in 1921 was conducted under a system of proportional representation and produced a 40–12 majority for the Protestant-dominated Unionist party. Northern Ireland adopted a single-member district plurality system for local government in 1922 and for elections to the parliament (the Stormont) in 1928.

This change in the electoral system did not bring about any significant change in the party balance within the Stormont. The Unionist party continued to win about 37 to 40 seats and the opposition parties kept on getting 12 to 15 seats. Catholic voters were concentrated enough so that they could win about as many seats in districts as they had won under proportional representation. There was, however, a sharp increase in the number of uncontested seats, to a level of 40–50% of all the seats. More importantly, the single-member district system contributed to the polarization of politics in Northern Ireland. It eliminated smaller parties, including those that sought to develop class-based rather than sectarian support. It reinforced the sectarian base of the major parties. The Unionist party ran Protestant candidates in Protestant districts and won; the Nationalist and other opposition parties carried Catholic districts with Catholic candidates. In a system of proportional representation each party might have slated both Protestant and Catholic candidates in an effort to broaden the base of its support (Budge and O'Leary, chap. 5 in this volume; Lakeman, 1970: 238–40).

The electoral system is just one of many policies followed by the Unionist government in order to maintain total Protestant domination over the political life of Northern Ireland. The particular significance of the electoral system is that it reinforced the polarization of politics along religious lines and created a strong barrier to political forces that sought to change the sectarian base of Irish politics.

MULTIMEMBER DISTRICTS WITH PLURALITY ELECTIONS

In the British model plurality elections are normally associated with single-member districts, but in some American state and local legislative bodies plurality elections are used in multimember districts. Voters cast as many votes as there are seats to be filled, and the votes are counted on a plurality basis. Such a system gives a greater advantage to the majority and discriminates more against the minority than is the case with single-member districts. The differences can be easily illustrated in the case of partisan elections. If most voters vote a straight party ticket, the majority party is likely to win all of the seats in a five-member district, for example, although a minority party might expect to be able to carry one or two seats if the larger district were divided into single-member districts. Multimember districts are likely to weaken the political power of any minority group (ethnic, religious, economic) that is large enough and concentrated enough so that it could expect to control one or more districts if a single-member district plan were followed. The larger the number of members chosen in such a district, of course, the greater the effect of discrimination against minorities.

A number of American state legislatures have made some use of multimember districts. In 1970 more than one-fourth of all state senators and about half of all state representatives were chosen in multimember districts. Many of these districts contain only two or three members and in some cases have been used to get greater population equality while maintaining county or city boundaries. Large metropolitan counties have been used, however, as multimember districts for electing state legislators in some American states, particularly in the South. As reapportionment in the 1960s increased the number of metropolitan seats, some of these metropolitan districts came to elect as many as 10 or 12, or in one case 17, legislators. In the late 1960s and early 1970s a number of states abolished these large multimember districts. A study (Jewell, 1969: 15–18) of several metropolitan counties that had used or were using large multimember districts showed that the practice not only severely handicapped the minority party but also made it very difficult to elect black legislators even in counties where there was a large black minority. When several of these states changed to single-member districts, there was a dramatic increase in the number of black legislators. Examples can be found in metropolitan counties in Ohio,

Tennessee, and Georgia during the 1960s. Because black voters tend to be concentrated geographically in metropolitan counties, the single-member district system—unlike a county-wide district—offered them some chance of electing a number of legislators roughly proportional to their population.

The use of multimember districts in state legislatures has been challenged in the courts, with mixed results. In 1965, in a Georgia case, the Supreme Court suggested that the use of multimember districts might be discriminatory if it could be shown that such a system "would operate to minimize or cancel out the voting strength of racial or political elements of the voting population" (Fortson v. Dorsey, 379 U.S. 433 at 439). In 1969, however, the Supreme Court refused to invalidate the county-wide district used for legislative elections in Marion County (Indianapolis), Indiana, even though the black voters, who comprised about one-sixth of the population, had rarely been able to elect black legislators. The Court appeared to reject the idea that any minority group is entitled to elect its own members through single-member districts, and it also failed to find that the Indiana policy was deliberately intended to discriminate against black voters (Whitcomb v. Chavis, 403 U.S. 124). Several cases have arisen under the Voting Rights Act of 1965 in which lower courts have invalidated multimember district systems for state or local legislatures when these appeared to be designed specifically to discriminate against black voters. In a couple of these cases the Supreme Court has indicated approval of the use of single-member districts where multimember districts appear to have a discriminatory purpose (Derfner, 1972).

Many American city governments elect all members of their legislative bodies at large, without any districting. The at-large election policy was adopted earlier in this century as part of the reform movement that included nonpartisan elections and the use of professional city managers. It was designed to overcome what were perceived as the ills of "ward politics." The consequence may be to elect a city council consisting entirely of persons from one socioeconomic level, one race, or one area of the city. The system minimizes the political power of ethnic, racial, or other minorities in a city. This policy is also being challenged in the courts, particularly in southern states where the Voting Rights Act of 1965 is applicable. Recent decisions suggest that cities may not annex outlying areas, thereby reducing the black proportion of the city's population, unless a single-member district system is used.

There is considerable evidence that multimember plurality systems in state and local legislative bodies of the United States have substantially reduced the number of legislators who could be elected directly by black voters and other minority groups. Those who were elected usually were ones who were slated by a party or another political organization. There is also evidence that the electoral systems are changing under both political and judicial pressures.

PROPORTIONAL REPRESENTATION SYSTEMS

In theory, proportional representation systems should protect the interests of minorities because they are designed to represent each group or party in a political system in proportion to its numerical strength, and a group does not have to have majority status in any geographic area or district to elect members to the legislature. In practice, it is more difficult to assess the consequences of PR systems because they have seldom been used in those countries that have had the most serious problems of integrating minority groups.

A number of different electoral systems are covered by the term "proportional representation," and the effects of a system on minorities depend on the exact details of its operation. For example, if a country is divided into a number of districts or regions and uses a list system of PR in each district, the size and boundaries of the district will affect a minority group's chances of electing members. If a nation is divided into districts electing five members each by PR, a minority with only 10% of the population in most districts will gain little advantage from PR. I have emphasized that minority groups that are geographically dispersed rather than concentrated are most handicapped by a single-member district system. Such groups would benefit most from a PR system that is nationwide or uses a relatively small number of large districts.

The effects of a PR system in practice, like the effects of single-member districts, depend very largely on the operation of the party system. When PR is combined with a party-list system, the leaders of a minority may organize a political party in order to mobilize the voters of that minority group behind a single slate of candidates. Alternatively (or in addition), the leadership of one or more parties may decide to include some candidates from the minority group on their slate in an effort to win the support of the minority-group voters for the entire slate. In a PR system the leaders of a minority have a choice of running their own slate or participating in a larger party slate, and the minority voters may have a choice between supporting a minority or a coalition slate. These options are usually not available in a single-member district system because the minority group is forced to adopt coalition tactics in any district where it lacks the votes to elect its own member. It is debatable whether PR systems are more likely than single-member districting to have an integrative effect. On the one hand, the major parties have a greater incentive to add minority-group candidates to their slate, and if some of these are elected the party should be responsive to, but not dominated by, the interests of that group. On the other hand, PR makes it possible for a minority group, even though not geographically concentrated, to elect legislators responsible solely to that group and thus perhaps likely to make uncompromising demands in the legislature.

Critics of the single-member district system used in Northern Ireland often argue that the proportional representation system used in Ireland (Eire) has been much more successful. The system is a single-transferable vote plan with districts of five or fewer members. It has usually produced majority governments, rather than coalitions, but has generally produced small majorities and some representation of small parties and independents. Proposals to adopt a single-member plurality system were twice defeated by the voters, by a narrow margin in 1959 and by a large margin in 1968. Although PR is often credited with promoting integration and minimizing sectarian conflict in Ireland, it should be recognized that religious conflict is much less serious there than in Northern Ireland because the Protestant minority is only about 5% of the population (Lakeman, 1970: 242–50).

Belgium is divided into two major ethnic-linguistic groups, the Flemings in the northern part of the state and the French-speaking Walloons in the south. The adoption of a proportional representation system (with party lists) in that country in 1899 has been described as a major step toward integration of that seriously divided country. When it was adopted, the Catholic party was a Flemish party, and the Liberals and Socialists won nearly all their votes from the Walloons. The PR system made it possible for the three major parties to extend their bases of support so that all of them have substantial strength in both parts of the country. But the PR system has not eliminated parties that draw their support entirely from one section, and these parties have been gaining legislative strength in recent years (Lakeman, 1970: 184–87; LaPonce, 1960: 146–47).

In other countries, where ethnic divisions are less serious, proportional representation systems facilitate the efforts of party leaders to construct balanced tickets in an attempt to win votes from a variety of groups in a society. The consequence is to produce legislative parties that represent more than a single ethnic, religious, or other interest. One example is Germany, where party leaders, particularly in the Christian Democratic party, try to maintain the proper balance among Protestant and Catholic candidates and among other interests (Loewenberg, 1967: 63–84). Another example is Israel, which uses a nationwide district system of PR and where elaborate negotiations take place between parties and a variety of groups in the construction of party slates (Czudnowski, 1970).

POLITICAL STRATEGY, SLATING, AND VOTING PATTERNS

The point has repeatedly been made in this chapter that the effects of particular electoral systems on minority representation depend to a large extent on the strategy of party and group leaders concerning the nomination of legislative candidates. It should be equally obvious that the representation of minority groups depends on the voting behavior of both minority and majority members of the electorate. The operation of the party system has a pervasive effect on minority representation because parties control nominations, many voters cast their ballots on the basis of party loyalty, and the political parties in many legislatures act in a cohesive fashion and exercise some degree of control over those legislators who represent minority groups.

In order to understand the politics of minority representation, there are a number of questions we need to ask, though we may not find the answers to all of them in the literature:

1. Do the leaders of minority groups try to organize separate parties or factions?
2. Do they, instead, try to establish coalitions with other groups or parties, through which they can gain broader support for their candidates in return for supporting some candidates who are outside the minority group?
3. Do the established political parties seek to build such coalitions with minority groups and are they willing to include minority candidates on their nominating slates?
4. What is the behavior of the voters? Do minority voters vote consistently for minority candidates? Are minority voters

more likely to be influenced by other loyalties, such as class or party, in their voting? Do voters, both members of minorities and others, follow the slating recommendations of coalition parties?

There is evidence available from some countries to answer these questions. Much of the evidence is descriptive in nature, pertaining to the tactics of political leaders and parties. Some aggregate voting data have been analyzed in the literature, and these data are available in many cases for further analysis. There seems to be very little survey data available, however, to answer more precise questions about how and why voters make their decisions.

In some districts where there are seats reserved for particular minority groups, the leaders of those groups have an obvious advantage in negotiating with party leaders, but the nature of that advantage depends on the size of the group within the districts as well as its cohesiveness. I have pointed out that the members of scheduled castes and tribes in India generally comprise only a minority of the population in districts with reserved seats. The winning candidate is likely to be the one who can get the nomination of the strongest party in the area. Party leaders, in turn, may look for a candidate who has support, particularly within his own caste or tribal group. The Congress party has been particularly successful in winning reserved seats; in the 1967 election it won 54% of all seats in the Lok Sabha, but two-thirds of the reserved seats.

There are a growing number of case studies dealing with elections in particular Indian districts, but not enough research has been done to provide any comprehensive picture of the negotiations that occur over nominations for reserved seats, the nature of campaigning for such seats, or the factors that influence the voting of persons who are members, or nonmembers, of the scheduled castes and tribes in these districts. There is little evidence to show whether members of scheduled castes and tribes are any less influenced by party loyalties than other voters or whether they engage in bloc voting either for reserved seats or in other districts. In the introduction to a book of case studies on the 1962 election, Weiner and Kothari summarized the impact of ethnic loyalties on voting. Their comments are applicable to all types of voters and districts in Indian elections (1965: 8):

Almost all the reports suggest that many factors cut into ethnic loyalties. In none of the elections described here does one find that a candidate won merely because he had the support of members of his own community. In some constituencies the political cohesion of ethnic groups was high, but in others factional and leadership conflicts within the community made it possible for candidates of many parties to win some support. Virtually all reports . . . note that voters, as individuals or as members of groups, simultaneously have attachments to parties, kin groups, factions, castes and individual leaders, and that rather than be burdened by traditional attachments, the individual has many loyalties to choose from. Under these circumstances it is very difficult for parties or community leaders to simply "herd" their voters to the polls. Indeed, the bargaining, bribery, intimidation and the promise must continue until the eve of the elections.

There is some survey evidence concerning this broader question of the importance of caste in Indian electoral politics. It comes from a 1967 national survey of voting behavior based on a stratified random sample (Ahmed, 1970). The survey shows that two-thirds of the voters had perceptions about how their caste voted, and almost half perceived other castes to be engaged in bloc voting. Almost half believed that a particular party best served the interests of their caste. On the other hand, only one-fourth believed that it was important for a legislator to work for the interests of his caste, and only one-fifth considered it important to vote the way the leaders of their caste voted. Urban voters were somewhat less likely than rural voters to consider caste as salient to voting. Members of the scheduled castes and tribes were somewhat more likely than those in more heterogeneous castes to perceive caste as being important. It is also noteworthy that Muslims, who were asked comparable questions about their religious group, were more likely than any of the Hindu castes to be familiar with the endorsements of their leaders, to believe that one party would serve their group interests, and to say that it was important to vote with their group.

There is considerably less research available on Lebanon, our other example of an electoral system with reserved seats. The practice of slating has been common in Lebanon for many years, and, in the absence of strong parties, this slating is often managed by local political leaders, landlords, and other influential figures. But little is known about how these negotiations are carried out or the frequency with which nonslated candidates run. We also lack published analyses of either aggregate voting data or survey data that would shed much light on voting patterns and answer such basic questions as whether there is bloc voting among members of a sect and whether such members usually vote for all of the seats in the district or only for those reserved for their sect.

The tactics used by the Muslim leadership in India in trying to become politically effective have been examined in some detail by several writers (Wright, 1969; 1966a, 1966b; Quraishi, 1968). In the first three national elections (1952, 1957, 1962) the Muslim leadership, and apparently most Muslim voters, supported the Congress party. The policy was a logical one for several reasons: the Congress party was the dominant one, it was pursuing a secular policy that served the interests of Muslims, and the major opposition parties included those committed to Hindu communalism. In turn, the Congress party was willing to slate Muslim candidates in a few districts. In more recent years, however, many Muslim leaders have concluded that the Congress party was taking Muslim voters for granted. They have pursued a policy of trying to bargain with opposition parties as well as with the Congress party in an effort to gain support for some of the Muslim goals that have not been achieved by the Congress government.

In the 1967 election an organization known as the Majlis was established in an effort to unify Muslim political activity. It drew up a manifesto of policy proposals particularly pertinent to Muslim interests (including a demand for adoption of proportional representation). The Majlis proceeded to bargain with parties and candidates and to endorse candidates who supported its goals. Only a small proportion of its endorsed candidates were Muslims, and most of the candidates were not members of the Congress party. The new policy had mixed results. Half of the incumbents in the Lok Sabha whom it endorsed were defeated, but the number of newly elected members whom it endorsed more than made up for the losses. The number of Muslims in the Lok Sabha was increased, most of them for the first time being members of parties other than the Congress party. In the assemblies of states where the Majlis was active there was a slight reduction in the total number of Muslim members and a decrease in the proportion belonging to the Congress Party (Wright, 1969; Quraishi, 1968).

In the two southernmost states, Kerala and Madras, Muslim leaders have followed another tactic, the establishment of a separate political party—the Muslim League. (The Majlis did not operate in these states). At the same time the Muslim League in these states has bargained with members of other parties to encourage the slating of more Muslim candidates, and from time to time it has formed coalitions with other parties (Wright, 1969). It should be kept in mind that the tactics of Muslim leaders in various states are likely to vary because power in the state assemblies, as well as seats in the Lok Sabha, are at stake, and the balance of power among the parties differs from state to state.

I should note briefly some of the studies in other countries dealing with the political tactics and voting patterns of minority groups. Ratnam and Milne have studied the Malayan elections of 1955, 1959, and 1964 in great detail (Ratnam, 1965; Ratnam and Milne, 1967). They have discussed the factors that led to the formation of the Alliance party by Malay, Chinese, and Indian organizations and the frequent intraparty dissension that has arisen among these three groups. The Alliance party has been opposed by several communal parties appealing entirely or primarily to one racial group and also by several parties that, like the Alliance, have multiracial bases of support. Although there are not any survey data available on Malayan elections, Ratnam and Milne have analyzed the aggregate data very carefully, with particular attention to the racial aspects of voting. One significant finding concerning the 1964 election was that "the Alliance did best in seats where the racial composition was 'mixed,' where it was neither overwhelmingly Malay nor non-Malay . . . it may be suggested that in seats which are predominantly Malay or predominantly non-Malay, to vote for an appropriate communal party may simply be a way of expressing that one belongs to that community. A Malay is more likely to vote 'Malay-communal' when he is surrounded by many other Malays; a Chinese is most likely to vote 'Chinese-communal' when surrounded by many other Chinese" (Ratnam and Milne, 1967: 372–73).

I have discussed earlier the districting policy in Ceylon that has produced relatively homogeneous districts and has given minority ethnic groups a proportionate share of districts dominated by them. As a consequence the political parties are sensitive to the claims of these groups for representation: "With few exceptions, the first consideration in candidate selection is that the nominee be of the same ethnic community, caste, and religion as the majority of the constituency residents" (Kearny, 1973).

There is little research on the political tactics or voting of minority groups in African countries with problems of minority integration. This results in part from the lack of party competition in some African countries and in part from the shortage of accurate election data, survey research work, and detailed analyses of elections in most of Africa. Studies of Nigeria in the 1950s and early 1960s have demonstrated that each of the major political parties drew its support overwhelmingly from areas dominated by a particular tribe or group of tribes, evidence strongly suggesting that the party and tribal loyalties of many voters were parallel. This fact contributed heavily to the disintegration of the nation and the resulting civil war (Schwartz, 1965; Rivkin, 1969).

There are, of course, more studies of elections and voting behavior in Western countries, but survey research efforts have usually been concentrated on national samples, and American surveys have focused more on presidential than congressional elections. Consequently there are not as much data as would be desirable concerning how minority groups vote in legislative elections and why they vote that way. In the United States there is sometimes very cohesive voting by blacks in support of or in opposition to particular candidates. (The black preference for Johnson over Goldwater in 1964 is a familiar example.) But such bloc voting certainly does not occur in every election. At the congressional and legislative level there are very little survey data on black voting, but the increase in black legislators results directly from the increasing number of districts with a black majority. The race of candidates is apparently important to many voters, black and white, just as the religion and nationality background of candidates used to be to many voters in the United States earlier in the century.

There is enough evidence from a number of countries to demonstrate that information about political tactics and voting behavior is essential to a study of minority representation, but in most countries there is still a shortage of such information. Leaders of minority groups have usually followed the tactic of trying to form coalitions except where there have been local majorities, but in some countries they have followed several tactics simultaneously. Parties dominated by majority groups have sometimes slated minority candidates and formed coalitions with them. The larger and more powerful the minority group, the greater the necessity of such tactics by majority-dominated parties. When minorities are large and powerful, however, the majority-dominated parties may feel more threatened and may drive a harder bargain in negotiations. We know least about how minority voters think and act, but it would be unwise to assume they always identify with their minority group in voting or that they consistently engage in bloc voting.

ROLES AND BEHAVIOR OF LEGISLATORS

Most of the studies that pertain to the representation and integration of minorities describe formal systems of representation, political parties, and elections. In some countries there is reasonably accurate and complete information concerning the selection of legislators who belong to, or who are elected by, minority groups. But there is very little information about how such minority legislators act once they get elected. Several explanations for this vacuum can be offered. Until very recently scholars have neglected legislatures in developing countries, at least in comparison with political parties and other institutions. In some countries where minority representation is an important topic, such as Malaysia, the legislature has appeared to be so weak and so dominated by other institutions that it was not worth careful study. Even where more research has been done on the legislative process, there has been little attention to minority legislators as individuals or as a group.

An agenda for research concerning those legislators chosen by or from a minority group should include at least the following questions:

1. Are these members different from other legislators in terms of education, experience, occupation, and the other pertinent socioeconomic characteristics?

2. What are the role perceptions of these members? Are they significantly different from those of other legislators? Do they perceive themselves as representatives of the minority—perhaps specifically as intermediaries between the people and the government? (see Weinbaum 1974, on Afghanistan). What are their role orientations regarding leaders of the minority group outside the legislature?

3. What types of communication do they have with their minority constituents? Are they familiar with the needs and demands of these persons and groups?

4. Do these minority legislators act as a bloc in terms of communications, caucuses, voting, or other activities?

5. Do minority legislators have loyalties—to party or to legislative subgroups—that supercede or compete with loyalties to their minority group?

6. What are their relationships with legislators who do not belong to the minority group? How much interaction do they have? How are they perceived by these other legislators? Is their representation of minority interests considered a legitimate role by nonminority legislators?

Among the very few scholars who have raised these questions about minority legislators are several who have written about the legislative process in India. One study (Chauhan and Chopra, 1969) compared the members elected to reserved seats for scheduled castes and tribes and those elected to general seats in the Lok Sabha for four elections, 1952–67. It showed that those elected to reserved seats were more likely to be male, were considerably younger, had less education, and were less likely to be lawyers and more likely to work in agricultural occupations. Studies (Mohapatra, 1971: 82; Sisson and Shrader, 1972: 9, 13) of the state assemblies in Orissa and in Rajasthan show that the upper castes are overrepresented in the legislature, an indication that the scheduled castes and tribes would be underrepresented without a policy of reserved seats. In the Rajasthan assembly, as in the Lok Sabha, members belonging to scheduled castes and tribes were less likely to be lawyers and more likely to have agricultural or other lower-status occupations. The Orissa study provides one small bit of evidence about the power of members holding the reserved seats. They were much less likely than other legislators to serve as cabinet members or as chairmen of committees in the assembly (Mohapatra, 1971: 84).

One study by Wright (1964) provides a profile of Muslim legislators at the national and state level in India. They come primarily from medium-sized cities, are relatively well educated with an emphasis on law degrees among the college educated, and are more likely than other legislators to be engaged in law or business and less likely to be engaged in agriculture. Wright provides many other details of background and experience in this study and in another study (1966a) he has provided an excellent analysis of the effectiveness of Muslim representation in India. He notes several factors that limit the effectiveness of Muslim legislators, in addition to the previously emphasized point that most represent districts where Muslims are not a majority. Many of them have difficulty maintaining contact with constituents and interest groups and determining what their needs and grievances are. Muslim legislators in the Congress Party may be more successful in getting individual grievances taken care of, but they have to be cautious in making policy demands on the government in behalf of Muslim constituents.

Although the characteristics and behavior of minority legislators (both lower-caste and Muslim) have received more attention in India than in other countries, there is not any systematic or comprehensive study of these groups in either the Lok Sabha or a state legislative assembly. There is no evidence demonstrating whether either group of minority legislators acts in a coordinated or cohesive fashion, or whether caste or religious loyalties compete with party loyalties, generally regarded as the strongest groups in the Indian legislative bodies. The studies of Indian minority legislators may, however, suggest types of analyses that could be conducted in other countries with significant minorities.

THE EFFECTS OF LEGISLATIVE OUTPUTS ON MINORITIES

In the last analysis we cannot determine whether and how a legislature contributes to the integration of a plural society without studying the outputs of the legislative process. Many studies of the problem have suggested implicitly that methods of districting which increased the representation of minorities would benefit these groups, but little specific attention to outputs has been given. One reason presumably is that these outputs are difficult to measure, and the perceptions of minority groups concerning legislative outputs are even more difficult to assess.

Some of the studies already referred to in this chapter provide impressionistic evidence or examples of outputs, but there seem to be no systematic studies of legislative outputs as they affect particular minority groups. In his study of the effectiveness of Muslim representation in India, Wright (1966a) demonstrates a concern for outputs and provides examples concerning specific policy questions. Studies of the Indian government's policies regarding the scheduled castes and tribes do not relate these to the activities of the legislators representing these groups who hold reserved seats (Dushkin, 1967; Desai, 1969; Isaacs, 1965). One study (Grossholtz, 1970) of Malaysia emphasizes the ineffectiveness of Chinese legislators in influencing the policies of the government, which has maintained policies that benefit the Malay population in general and only a portion of the Chinese community but which refuses to recognize as legitimate the demands for additional rights and benefits of the Chinese community in general.

Students of Northern Ireland (Budge and O'Leary, chap. 5 in this volume; Lakeman, 1970: 238–42) have argued that the districting system in that country has contributed to the polarization of politics along religious lines and has also denied Catholics a proportionate share of seats in the legislative body. The districting system is seen as a tool that has enabled the Protestant government to maintain its domination over the Catholic minority.

There have been no detailed studies of the legislative outputs in Lebanon that would make it possible to evaluate the consequences of reserving seats for religious sects. Writers on Lebanon disagree in their more general assessment of the consequences. Some conclude that the reserved-seat policy leads to deadlock in the legislature, a decline in legislative power, and general stagnation in the country (Hudson, 1968). A more positive conclusion is that the policy has contributed to integration in Lebanon, an integration built on a recognition of the need for diversity in that highly plural society (see Baaklini, chap. 7 in this volume).

The recent growth of scholarly interest in legislative outputs has led to a number of studies that are systematic and quantitative, but these studies have been confined primarily to the American states and a few European countries, and they have not been focused on outputs that benefit particular minorities.[4] In order to determine what difference minority representation makes, we must find out what tangible results minority legislators have been able to produce for their groups. These might include the passage of legislation protecting their rights, the expansion of economic benefits or the development of projects serving group needs, or the allocation of various kinds of patronage to the group. They might include the success of legislators in mediating individual minority grievances with administrators (see Weinbaum, chap. 3 in this volume). In countries where minorities lack proportionate or effective representation, it is necessary to find out whether governmental policies, and specifically legislative policies, discriminate against these minorities. Many of the policies affecting minority groups, positively or negatively, are difficult to measure in quantitative terms. The best opportunity for studying outputs probably occurs when there is some change in representation that permits us to measure outputs before and after the change. (The studies of legislative outputs in American states have generally concluded that the degree of malapportionment has little effect, but some have detected effects on certain policy outputs, and it should be noted that only a few of the studies have compared outputs in the same states before and after reapportionment). In studying the effects on outputs, we should examine not only changes in formal systems of representation but also changes in party tactics, minority voting patterns, and the behavior of minority legislators. By considering all aspects of minority representation we can improve our chances of determining which aspects have the greatest effect on legislative outputs.

THE LEGISLATURE, SUPPORT, AND NATIONAL INTEGRATION

Studies of support (Boynton, Patterson, and Hedlund, 1968) usually distinguish between specific and diffuse support, both of which are expected to contribute to the support that the public, or segments of the public, give to a political system. We would expect minority groups to be more supportive of political institutions if they are satisfied with the specific outputs of the legislative process. Their diffuse support may depend in part on their perceptions of how the legislative process works. We need to know what these perceptions are. Do these groups derive satisfaction from the fact that the formal system of representation and/or the operation of the party system enable them to have a certain proportion of members in the legislature? If these legislators have an opportunity to take part in debate, introduce resolutions, and question cabinet members, do these activites fulfill in part the demands of minority groups? In short, does the process of representation, and not just the tangible results of representation, enhance support for the system by minority groups? It is, of course, much easier to pose such questions than to answer them with evidence. It may be necessary to study legislative debates and statements of groups leaders, and to interview legislators, other elites, and rank-and-file minority citizens in order to provide answers to such questions. But the absence of such data should not blind us to the possibility that the symbolic outputs are meaningful and that any efforts to change the system of representation may have important political repercussions because of the symbolic implications of such a change. It may also be possible to measure changes in diffuse support that are associated with, and may be a consequence of, changes in the system of representation.

Support for a political system by minority citizens should contribute to national integration. Such citizens should be willing to accord legitimacy to the national government, and under these conditions the government should have the capacity to carry out its policies in areas dominated by minority groups. The final step in this analysis must be to determine whether political systems in which minorities have equitable legislative representation are well integrated, whether such representation can overcome disintegrative and secessionist movements. Have changes in representative systems to make them more equitable been successful in preventing disintegration? Alternatively, it is possible that the equitable representation of minorities, by providing them with a political base in the legislature, will enhance the influence of disintegrative forces within a minority group and will exacerbate differences between the minority group and other forces in the political system. There is no reason to suppose that the representative system is the only, or the most important, factor that may affect integration in a plural society. But we need to study all of the aspects of representation, and not just formal electoral systems if we are going to understand the relationships between representation and national integration.

NOTES

1. This analysis of federalism as a device for protecting minorities is based largely on LaPonce (1960: 67–78) and Milnor (1969: 136–42).

2. For a more detailed description, see Great Britain Parliamentary Papers (1971).

3. My calculations are based on the data in Chandidas, Morehouse, Clark, and Fontera (1968).

4. See particularly, Dye (1966), Sharkansky (1967), Hofferbert (1966), Sharkansky and Hofferbert (1969), Pulsipher and Weatherby (1968), and Bicker (1971).

REFERENCES

AHMED, B. (1970) "Caste and electoral politics." Asian Survey 10 (Nov.): 979–92.

BAXTER, C. (1969) District Voting Trends in India. New York: Columbia Univ. Press.

BICKER, W. (1971) "The effects of malapportionment in the states—a mistrial." In Reapportionment in the 1970's, ed. N. W. Polsby. Berkeley: Univ. of California Press. Pp. 151–200.

BOYNTON, G. R., S. C. PATTERSON, and R. D. HEDLUND (1968) "The structure of public support for legislative institutions." Midwest Journal of Political Science 12 (May): 163–80.

CALLARD, K. (1957) Pakistan: A Political Study. New York: Macmillan.

CHANDIDAS, R., W. MOREHOUSE, L. CLARK, and R. FONTERA (1968) India Votes. New York: Humanities Press.

CHAUHAM, D. N. S., and S. L. CHOPRA (1969) "A comparative study of the socio-economic background of the members of the Lok Sabha elected from the reserved and the general constituencies." Journal of Constitutional and Parliamentary Studies 3 (Apr.-June): 94–100.

CROW, R. E. (1962) "Religious sectarianism in the Lebanese political system." Journal of Politics 24 (Aug.): 521–44.

CZUDNOWSKI, M. M. (1970) "Legislative recruitment under proportional representation in Israel: a model and a case study." Midwest Journal of Political Science 14 (May): 216–48.

DERFNER, A. (1972) "Multi-member districts and black voters." Black Law Journal 2 (Summer): 120–28.

DESAI, C. C. (1969) "Reservation of seats in the House of the People and state legislative assemblies for Scheduled Castes and Scheduled Tribes and nomination of Anglo-Indians thereto: case for extension of the period." Journal of Constitutional and Parliamentary Studies 3 (Apr.-June): 86–93.

DUSHKIN, L. (1967) "Scheduled caste policy in India: history, problems, prospects." Asian Survey 7 (Sept.): 626–36.

DYE, T. (1966) Politics, Economics, and the Public. Chicago: Rand McNally.

Great Britain Parliamentary Papers (1970) Report of the Fiji Constitutional Conference 1970. Cmnd. 4389. London: H.M.S.O.

———— (1971) Rhodesia: Proposals for a Settlement. Cmnd. 4835. London: H.M.S.O.

GROSSHOLTZ, J. (1970) "Integrative factors in the Malaysian and Philippine legislatures." Comparative Politics 3 (Oct.): 93–113.

GUPTA, S. K. (1962) "Moslems in Indian politics, 1947–1960." Indian Quarterly 18 (Oct.-Dec.): 355–81.

HOFFERBERT, R. (1966) "The Relation between public policy and some structural and environmental variables in the American states." American Political Science Review 60 (Mar.): 73–82.

HUDSON, M. C. (1968) The Precarious Republic: Modernization in Lebanon. New York: Random House.

ISAACS, H. R. (1965) India's Ex-Untouchables. New York: John Day.

JEWELL, M. E. (1969) Metropolitan Representation: State Legislative Districting in Urban Counties. New York: National Municipal League.

KEARNY, R. (1973) Unpublished manuscript, MacKenzie Univ.

LAKEMAN, E. (1970) How Democracies Vote. London: Faber & Faber.

LANDAU, J. M. (1961) "Elections in Lebanon." Western Political Quarterly 14 (Mar.): 120–47.

LaPONCE, J. A. (1960) The Protection of Minorities. Berkeley: Univ. of California Press.

LOEWENBERG, D. (1967) Parliament in the German Political System. Ithaca, N.Y.: Cornell Univ. Press.

MacKENZIE, W. J. M. (1954) "Representation in plural societies." Political Studies 2 (Feb.): 54–69.

MEANS, G. P. (1970) Malaysian Politics. London: Univ. of London Press.

MELLOR, N., and J. ANTHONY (1968) Fiji Goes to the Polls. Honolulu: East-West Center Press.

MILNOR, A. J. (1969) Elections and Political Stability. Boston: Little, Brown.

MOHAPATRA, M. K. (1971) "Intervener and non-intervener: a study of legislators' administrative role orientations in an Indian state." Ph.D. dissertation, Univ. of Kentucky, Lexington.

MORRIS-JONES, W. H. (1957) Parliament in India. Philadelphia: Univ. of Pennsylvania Press.

PULSIPHER, A. G., and J. L. WEATHERBY, JR. (1968) "Malapportionment, party competition, and the functional distribution of governmental expenditures." American Political Science Review 62 (Dec.): 1207–19.

QURAISHI, Z. M. (1968) "Electoral strategy of a minority pressure group: the Muslim Majlis-e-Mushawarat." Asian Survey 8 (Dec.): 976–87.

RATNAM, K. J. (1965) Communalism and the Political Process in Malaya. Singapore and Kuala Lumpur: Univ. of Malaya Press.

_____, and R. S. MILNE (1967) The Malayan Parliamentary Election of 1964. Singapore: Univ. of Malaya Press.

RIVKIN, A. (1969) Nation-Building in Africa. New Brunswick, N.J.: Rutgers Univ. Press.

SCHWARTZ, F. A. O. (1965) Nigeria. Cambridge, Mass.: M.I.T. Press.

SHARKANSKY, I. (1967) "Economic and political correlates of state government expenditures." Midwest Journal of Political Science 11 (May): 173–92.

_____, and R. HOFFERBERT (1969) "Dimensions of state politics, economics, and public policy." American Political Science Review 63 (Sept.): 867–79.

SISSON, R. (1972) The Congress Party in Rajasthan. Berkeley: Univ. of California Press.

_____, and L. R. SHRADER (1972) Legislative Recruitment and Political Integration: Patterns of Political Linkage in an Indian State. Berkeley: Univ. of California Center for South and Southeast Asia Studies.

SMITH, D. E. (1963) India as a Secular State. Princeton, N.J.: Princeton Univ. Press.

_____ (1966) "Emerging patterns of religion and politics." In South Asian Politics and Religion, ed. D. E. Smith. Princeton, N.J.: Princeton Univ. Press. Pp. 21–48.

STULTZ, N. (1970) "The National Assembly in the politics of Kenya." In Legislatures in Developmental Perspective, ed. A. Kornberg and L. Musolf. Durham, N.C.: Duke Univ. Press. Pp. 303–33.

VASIL, R. K. (1965) "The 1964 general elections in Malaya." International Studies 7 (July): 20–65.

WEINER, M., and R. KOTHARI, eds. (1965) Indian Voting Behavior: Studies of the 1962 General Elections. Calcutta: Firma K. L. Mukhopadhyay.

WRIGHT, T. P. (1964) "Muslim legislators in India: profile of a minority elite." Journal of Asian Studies 23 (Feb.): 253–67.

_____ (1966a) "The effectiveness of Muslim representation in India." In South Asia Politics and Religion, ed. D. E. Smith. Princeton, N.J.: Princeton Univ. Press. Pp. 102–37.

_____ (1966b) "The Muslim League in South India since independence: a study in minority group political strategies." American Political Science Review 60 (Sept.): 579–99.

_____ (1969) "Muslims as candidates and voters in 1967 general election." Political Science Review 8 (Jan.-Mar.): 23–40.

Chapter 2

SOCIAL REPRESENTATION AND POLITICAL INTEGRATION IN AN INDIAN STATE: THE LEGISLATIVE DIMENSION

R I C H A R D   S I S S O N
L A W R E N C E   L.   S H R A D E R

In the achievement of political integration one must assume at a minimum that either structural or value conditions exist within a political society which enable collective decisions to be made and applied on behalf of that society. How integration comes about and how it is maintained, of course, is not new to social and political inquiry. In analyses of Western societies it has received unusual scholarly attention and has assumed public importance since the industrial revolution; in the changing societies of the new states the problem of integrating culturally plural societies is continuously significant. In the politics of these societies as well as in those first modernized, integration involves not only the association of different cultures in a common arena, but it also involves the forging of links that are conducive, at a minimum, to effective governance and to communication between political elites and mass society. It is our intention to explore the character of elite-mass relations and their salience for political integration in an Indian state. We shall do so by focusing upon members of the state legislative assembly (MLAs) in the Indian state of Rajasthan and the various forms of their association with their social and political environments.[1]

PLURALISM AND POLITICAL INTEGRATION:
SOME THEORETICAL CONSIDERATIONS

Studies of political development in the new states have commonly focused upon the "gap" between elites and the larger society and its impact upon political integration.[2] Indeed, the "gap" between elites and mass society has been advanced as a condition of political instability and decay. Without penetrative and vital institutions the exercise of effective authority by elites is severely constrained. Without channels of communication and without an effective network of political linkages, the socialization of mass publics into the norms and rules of the political format is uneven, frequently distorted, and of limited intensity (LeVine, 1963; Langdon, 1969). The values and symbols which affirm a national political community and sustain legitimate public authority are submitted to harsh questioning and their efficacy is often diluted. Demands for entry into elite positions, for political mobility, and for participation in effective control disrupt fragile institutional relationships. Where channels are not open or where they are not known, the probability that clamorous demands for collective mobility will arise is increased. Such demands left unsatisfied, it has been strongly suggested, frequently result in the rejection of community and regime and in the rise of political violence and commitment to the creation of a new community, a new regime, or both.[3] It has been further suggested that where society has undergone only limited mobilization, and/or where the rate of mobilization has been controlled or slow, the disruptive consequences of demands for participation are muted. Crisis arises where these conditions do not prevail or where, if they do, a segment of the elite feels that existing elite-mass distinctions and patterns of political control are morally unacceptable and act to effect change in a radical manner.

While in our conception integration entails both normative and structural attributes, our present analysis concentrates principally upon the structural, and we do not propose to examine here the critical issues concerning the degree to which shared values about the fundamental bases of its collective life exists in Rajasthani society.[4] We do maintain, as part of our general theoretical conception, that the political system exhibits a degree of collective affirmation that the society should resolve its public disputes in common; that there is functional agreement on the political form that community life should assume and on the rules and spirit by which the community is to be governed; and that there is—if in a general or diffused way—a conception of the scope of human behavior that is to be judged in the political marketplace and governed by public law. Furthermore, we recognize that the salience of these norms varies greatly along the elite-mass continuum and may be latent or even nonexistent among nonmobilized segments of a society. Indeed, an important aspect of political mobilization is the public salience of these norms for groups that had not previously considered them beyond the scope of their primordial associations or traditional authority structure.

While a degree of value consensus is critical, structural relationships give form to integration. Political integration in structural terms requires, first of all, a formal association of governmental structures and territorial units, whether these are the federal relationships in a sovereign state or the cross-national institutions of an international region. Second, it must have formal linkages among positions of public authority—a set of reciprocal rights and obligations legally defined. Third, it requires the existence of informal linkages between rulers and the ruled. This entails interpretations of rights and obligations, judgments of performance, and channels of communication, access, and control. Finally, political integration demands formal and informal linkages among citizens as well as among elites. That is to say, it requires the capacity to organize in contractual manner for the pursuit of common goals.

In this conception, then, political integration undergoes continual testing. This is true in any society, but it is particularly true in those where elementary political mobilization is still in process. Furthermore, as mobilization proceeds, the more critical become the structural conditions noted above. That is, not only are community and legitimacy tested with the entry of new cultural groups into the political marketplace and with changed configurations of class interest, but the logic of public numbers and the proliferation of public interests makes more relevant the social scope that political life is to assume and makes more critical the development of informal linkages between and among leaders and citizens.

In an important sense, too, democratic government rests upon the assumption of political integration. The classical model of individualistic liberal democracy assumes the existence of political community, as does the corporate conception of democracy, the difference resting principally in the conception of the role that the representative is to play and in the conception of the basis upon which he is to make his public judgments and be governed in his public acts (Fairlie,

1940; Eulau, 1959; Beer, 1958). Whether our reference is Locke's disquisition on representation or Burke's "Speech to the Electors of Bristol," democratic theory has emphasized the importance of structural linkages which assure citizens access to the centers of decision making and control over those who govern. Democratic theory has thus assumed the existence of value and community integration in vertical terms. Our concern is to explore the character and quality of structural integration in a new state with a democratic format.

CULTURAL PLURALISM AND LEGISLATIVE ROLE IN RAJASTHAN

India provides an illuminating and fascinating case for the study of political integration at both the state and national levels. Indian governments both past and present have been extremely sensitive to the problem of protecting cultural minorities and associating them with the larger political community. Several strategies pursued at the national level have been discussed in Chapter 1, by Malcolm E. Jewell, in this volume. The structure of relationships among minorities at the national level is also found in microcosm in a number of the Indian states.

One of the most culturally plural states of India is Rajasthan.[5] This tradition of cultural pluralism has historic roots and has been expressed through several institutional forms. Before independence and the subsequent formation of the state of Rajasthan, this area of India was composed of some 22 semisovereign princely states, many of which traced their lineage from medieval times. Each of the major states served as a center of a distinctive culture which found expression in such ways as language and derivative dialects, art forms, literature, dress, and in some cases dietary habit. Primary kinship and marriage ties were also largely confined to the territory of the state in all but some families of aristocratic castes.

A second form of cultural difference in Rajasthan is found in the social structure. While the institution of caste is pervasive in Rajasthani society just as it is in other areas of India, the particular constellation of castes in given areas varies immensely. The social structure of the northern and western desert regions of the state, for example, is quite different from that found in the eastern plains which border the Hindi-speaking areas that were a part of British India before 1947. The social structure of the southern region of the state was different still, given the sizable numbers of tribal populations that live there.

Together with these differences in culture and social organization there was also a low level of political mobilization in these princely states prior to independence. The nationalist movement was restricted, partially by necessity, partially by design, to the British provinces. The only impact the movement had in the states of Rajputana was among the educated elites in urban areas and among certain trading families with social ties to the commercial centers in British India. Popular movements devoted to the creation of representative government in the Rajputana states did develop, but they were as confined to each state in their activities as were the people before whom their cases were dramatized. In addition to urban-based movements for political reform, peasant movements developed on a small scale in several states and were committed to the rationalization and liberalization of rules having to do with land tenure and revenue. These movements were also limited in their activity and support to individual states and in most instances were divided on a territorial basis within these states as well. In conjunction with these modes of political participation, we should finally note that there was minimal experience with legislative institutions prior to independence. Indeed, the first responsible legislative body to exist in this area was created with the first general elections held in 1952.

At the time of the creation of legislative institutions in Rajasthan, therefore, there were several different dimensions of cultural pluralism in the state which eventually assumed important political salience. These included historic territorially based cultures, regional variations in social structure, differential levels of political mobilization among various castes, and a legacy of minimal cooperative endeavor among aristocratic elites in the traditional order as well as among the counter-elites which were eventually to displace them and manage the state after independence.

The forces of cultural pluralism have fundamentally affected the politics of Rajasthan in several ways. The first instance concerned the process of state integration whereby the various princely states of Rajputana were merged step by step into a larger political entity within the Indian Union. Regional sentiment continued in the politics of coalition formation and institution building within the state legislative assembly as well as within major political party organizations. It was particularly important with respect to the political divisions which developed with the rise of peasant caste groups demanding an expanded share of political power and a new formula for the distribution of political goods. Integration was also at issue in the attempts of the national Congress party leaders to inhibit the displaced aristocratic elites, which enjoyed extensive mass support in rural areas, from becoming an alienated and atavistic political force, and to absorb them into the state Congress party. The state legislative assembly was an important arena in which these problems of political integration were confronted.

It must also be noted that legislative assemblies in the Indian states have come to be extremely important institutions, and their incumbents are a critical segment of India's political elite. In those areas that formerly constituted British India legislative assemblies at the provincial, now the state level were progressively granted effective power, particularly after World War I. Since independence states in the Indian federal system have enjoyed considerable power through constitutional stipulation. The state legislator participates in the exercise of power over important sectors of public life. He participates in the making and unmaking of governments as he does in the making of law. He also has the ability, albeit not by constitutional fiat, to influence the "Raj"—the bureaucracy—an image and repository of power with ancient and historic roots. In these activities the MLA often performs communication and brokerage functions in the political process and helps to make comprehensible powers that often appear to the citizen as distant, impersonal, and impervious to social control.

The state legislative assemblies are extremely attractive institutions for those who aspire to a political career. And they are no less attractive to those social groups within Rajasthan that are experiencing or aspiring to rapid social mobility. The assembly provides local visibility and better access to strategic positions of power than does the national parliament (Lok Sabha). The legislator also has access to locally important resources and agencies of economic planning and social control, i.e., to state and local administrative agencies whose decisions impinge upon the common man more than do those of the central government and which are charged with the distribution of local welfare and developmental resources. The MLA is located in a political milieu with which the citizen is familiar.

In pursuing our larger theoretical concerns, we propose, first, to address the following questions. To what extent do state legislators constitute links between elite and mass society? What form of association exists among these linkage roles? To what extent are legislators representative of important social collectivities? (see Eldridge, Introduction to this volume). This we shall do by exploring

(1) the patterns of change in the profile of legislative representation, (2) the extent to which new social and territorial groups are finding representation in the legislative assembly, and (3) the extent to which new political generations are distinct from the old in terms of socioeconomic status.

Second, we shall explore the relationship of the legislator to his constituency. This we propose to do by using both structural and attitudinal data. What is the relationship between the location of the legislator's constituency and his ancestral home? If parochial ties are indeed salient in legislative selection, we would expect to find constituency location and ancestral home to be fairly coincident. Given the occupational demands of the legislator, what proportion of his time is spent in work as an MLA and what proportion is spent in his constituency? What, we shall then ask, is the legislator's perception of the interests that are most salient in defining his representational role? In short, what interests does he feel he represents? What does he perceive as the most important point of reference in his role as state legislator?

Third, what is the effective form of linkage and association between legislative cohorts? What is the character of the legislator's political association in the formal organization of the legislative assembly and in the infrastructure of parties and groups at the state level? Are his political ties, whether in formal organizations or informal factional groups, based primarily upon caste, upon region, upon political generation, upper class, or what? In the case of major political disputes in Rajasthani politics, from whom does the legislator take his cue? While these questions and the data they elicit cannot close the case on elite-mass relationships, they can give us some important indications of the legislator's place in the linkage system within the Indian federal framework and of the extent to which parochial ties affect legislative behavior.

LEGISLATIVE REPRESENTATION OF SOCIAL GROUPS: RECRUITMENT AND CAREER PROFILES

We shall commence our analysis of the elite-mass gap in Rajasthan with an examination of the relationship between the MLA and his society along the vectors of social stratification, social mobility, and political generation. While such an analysis does not resolve the question of the degree of representativeness of the legislative assembly, it does locate the MLA within the social matrix of his society.

The social stratification system defined in terms of caste and community is of pervasive importance in Indian society. To a greater degree than in most societies, the social group defines one's status and role in India and hence is an important source of identity. Because the legislator's socialization and the ceremonies of his life cycle are derived from and are defined to a substantial degree in terms of selected ascriptive groups, an analysis of the social background of legislators is important. It is important not only, nor necessarily, in terms of the legislator's perception of his world and the way he behaves politically, but in the way relatively self-contained social groups have customarily related to the political process and to the larger community of which they are a part.[6]

Social background is also important as a gauge of political aspiration and acceptance in legislative institutions. By establishing a social profile of elites over time and comparing this with the larger society, we can make tentative projections concerning the types of participation which might be anticipated in the future. By comparing profiles of elites at different times, we can determine rates of political mobilization. More important, an analysis of the organization of legislative parties, cliques, and groups can enable us to determine the extent of the development of new intrainstitutional linkages that cut across traditional social categories and the conditions of the formation and maintenance of these linkages.

To do this, it is not necessary to assume that political organization will be based upon primordial units or that an elite structure must, by some "natural order of things," be a microcosm of the larger collectivity. The structure of participation may, of course, be organized in many ways. What we are suggesting is that political mobilization augurs for a changed social profile of varying orders of magnitude which, in turn, is dependent upon the permeability of institutions and the predilections of their managers at critical times. Social background indices are useful in analyzing these changes.

Table 2.1 compares the caste distribution in Rajasthani society with that of legislators in the first three legislative assemblies in the state. The state's caste structure is highly fragmented and no caste exceeds 10% of the total population. The 1931 census—the last in which caste information was given—distinguished 393 castes and tribes for the Rajputana States, although this wide dispersion is lessened somewhat in that 42 castes and tribes accounted for 84% of the total population. Table 2.1 further simplifies the caste structure in Rajasthan by placing the numerous *jatis* of some major caste

TABLE 2.1

CASTE COMPOSITION OF ASSEMBLY AND SOCIETY
(IN PERCENTAGES)

Caste	State Population[a]	First Assembly (1951–57)	Second Assembly (1957–62)	Third Assembly (1962–67)
		(N=126)	(N=166)	(N=176)
Brahman	8	17	15	17
Rajput	6	44	19	20
Mahajan	7	9	11	11
Peasant	18	11	18	18
Jat	(9)	(11)	(11)	(16)
Other[b]	(9)	–	(7)	(2)
Scheduled castes	14	11	16	16
Scheduled tribes	11	4	13	13
Other[c]	35	4	8	5

a. Source: Government of India, Census of India, 1931 (Rajputana Agency), vol. 27 (Meerut: Government of India Press, 1932).

b. Other peasant castes are Sirvi, Vishnoi, Gujar, and Ahir.

c. This category includes Muslims, Kayasths, and Sikhs.

groups under their *varna* designation. While such a procedure may violate the meaning of caste in its strictest "anthropological" sense, it does not do so in terms of the political significance of caste.[7]

As shown by Table 2.1, four castes—Brahman, Mahajan, Jat, and Rajput—have consistently been overrepresented in the assembly in relation to their respective proportions of the population. Although they represent only about 30% of the population, they account for 64% of the MLAs. Their preponderance is even greater if we exclude from our calculation the scheduled castes and scheduled tribes, which are guaranteed proportional representation by the reservation of assembly seats. Furthermore, between 1957 and 1967 the proportion of MLAs from each of the four major castes was stabilizing. Rajputs have stabilized at approximately 20% of the legislative assembly, Brahmans at between 15 and 17%, and Mahajans at slightly more than 10%. Jats show an increase from 11 to 16%, while the overall peasant representation has tended to stabilize at 18%. While the overall representation of the peasant castes is proportional to their population in the state as a whole, the Jat caste is overrepresented and has clearly become one of the four political elite castes in the state. The tendency for the four major political castes to stabilize their positions in the assembly is even more impressive when we consider that the electoral fortunes of political parties have varied widely.

Even though the data give evidence of elitism and growing stabilization of representation patterns, considerable change has occurred. Membership turnover in each assembly has been 50% or more; thus, the general social representation pattern has remained more constant than have the holders of legislative office. Furthermore, in comparison with the traditional preindependence political systems of the state, dominated as they were by the Rajput princely order, a much more broadly based political elite has emerged to reflect more accurately the social structure of the state. It is particularly significant, and a sign of the degree to which the political order has been transformed, to have members of peasant castes, scheduled castes, and scheduled tribes occupying key political offices in the state. This is true not only for legislative representation, but for ministerial representation as well.[8]

The MLAs are distinguishable not only by their social origins but also by their personal life styles and experiences. To pursue this point, we must ask whether the MLAs are established members of their communities, drawing heavily upon their traditional status and influence, or whether they are "new men" who have forged ahead in recent decades on the basis of achievement, drive, and attitude. In short, are they traditional men following old ways, or are they drawn significantly from the socially mobile men of the more modern elements of the society?

In a predominantly illiterate society, education is one hallmark of modern attitudes, change, and social mobility. Western education in India has also meant intellectual socialization in the assumptions and procedures of liberal democratic thought and practice. By 1962 in Rajasthan, 85% of the population was illiterate and only 1% had received a high school education or more. Yet, as shown in Table 2.2

TABLE 2.2
LEVEL OF EDUCATIONAL ACHIEVEMENT OF MLAS (IN PERCENTAGES)

Educational Level	First Assembly	Second Assembly	Third Assembly
	(N=121)	(N=154)	(N=176)
None	7	11	5
Primary	21	8	8
Middle	4	19	21
High School	12	16	15
College	30	19	25
LL.B	26	28	26

the MLAs are immensely more educated than the population they represent. Some 66% of the MLAs in the third assembly had at least graduated from a higher secondary school, 25% had attended college, and another 26% had received law degrees.

Education also expanded the geographical scope of many MLAs' experiences. Sixty % of the MLAs in the third assembly, for example, left their district to acquire an education and, of these, nearly two-thirds attended an educational institution outside Rajasthan. In fact, many legislators first became involved in politics as students in British India, where fewer constraints were placed on political particip-ation than in the princely states and where the nationalist move-ment was much more socially pervasive and intense.

The MLAs' high level of education has also affected their com-munication patterns. Sixty-eight % of all legislators in the third assembly reported that they spoke and read English. That English is used extensively by a substantial proportion of MLAs in gaining political information about national affairs is indicated by the fact that 44% reported that they depend "considerably" on English-lan-guage newspapers for political news. Although Hindi-language news-papers scored higher (63%) as a source of information, the English media rank significantly high.

The thesis that the MLAs are not only "new men" but upwardly mobile gains support when we compare their education with that of their fathers (Table 2.3). For example, whereas 51% of the MLAs received at least a college education, 61% of the fathers had received no education at all. Only 4% had attended college. Fourteen % of the

TABLE 2.3
COMPARISON OF FATHER'S
EDUCATION WITH EDUCATION OF
MLAS IN THIRD ASSEMBLY
(IN PERCENTAGES)

Educational Level	MLAs	Fathers
	(N=176)	(N=74)
None	5	61
Primary	8	11
Middle	21	9
High School	14	4
College	25	3
LL.B	26	1
Traditional Schooling	0	11

legislators had graduated from a higher secondary school, while only 4% of the fathers had done so.

By comparing the occupations of the MLAs with those of their fathers, the degree of social mobility experienced by the MLA is even more apparent. As shown in Table 2.4, the highest proportion (47%) of MLA fathers were agriculturalists, followed by social and political workers (16%) and by rulers and *jagirdars,* landlords in the traditional order (again, 16%). Business and trade occupations accounted for 14%, and low status occupations for 6%. Only 1% were advocates and government servants.

It is also clear that the new occupations of the MLAs break radically with the traditional norms of the society. There is a strong relationship between caste and traditionally prescribed occupation among the fathers, while for the MLAs this relationship is quite weak. Among the fathers, nearly all those of peasant caste were agriculturalists; Rajputs were almost entirely either rulers, jagirdars, or farmers; and 82% of the Mahajans were businessmen. In marked contrast, only 31% of the peasant caste legislators are farmers, while 41% are advocates, 14% government servants, and 11% social and political workers. Clearly the large majority are involved in the modern occupational sector of Rajasthani society. Compared with the peasant caste MLAs, Rajputs have remained more heavily agricultural, although law, business, social and political work, and government service have attracted 45% of the Rajput legislators. Mahajan MLAs contrast most sharply with their fathers in that only 26% are engaged in business pursuits while 42% are lawyers and 21% are social and political workers. While business occupations overall have remained a relatively stable category, accounting for 11% of the MLAs and 14% of the fathers, the MLAs' generation includes a large number of businessmen who do not come from the traditional business and trading category.

Legislators in Rajasthan have also experienced considerable geographic mobility. Ninety-one % of the MLAs were raised in either villages or towns; only 9% grew up in large cities. Today, only 40% of the MLAs still live in villages, whereas 36% live in cities of at least 50,000 in population. A comparison of the MLAs with regard to current residence and place of rearing in terms of caste reveals a major shift to the cities among the four political elite castes but only a slight increase among scheduled castes and tribes. Peasant caste MLAs show the largest shift.

Although 97% of the peasant caste MLAs were born in villages,

TABLE 2.4
COMPARISON OF OCCUPATIONS OF MLAS AND FATHERS BY CASTE
(IN PERCENTAGES)

												Occupations				Jagirdar and		
Caste	Advocate		Business		Agriculture		Social and Pol. Work		Low Status		Govt. Service		Other	Ruler	MLAs	Father
	MLA	F	MLA	F	MLA	F	MLA	F	MLA	F	MLA	F	MLA	Father	N=174	N=146
Brahman	30	0	17	18	7	45	27	0	0	36	0	0	20	0	30	11
Mahajan	42	0	26	82	11	12	21	0	0	6	0	0	0	0	19	17
Peasant castes	41	0	0	0	31	94	16	0	0	3	9	3	3	0	32	32
Rajput	14	0	6	0	49	29	11	0	0	0	14	6	6	65	35	34
Scheduled tribes	0	0	4	5	57	73	9	14	0	9	22	0	9	0	23	22
Scheduled castes	0	0	18	8	21	12	11	77	36	4	11	0	4	0	20	26
Other	43	25	14	25	14	50	14	0	0	0	14	0	0	0	7	4

only 31% now reside there; 46% live in cities. An impressive shift has also occurred among the Rajput MLAs: with 71% born in villages, only 29% now reside there and 44% live in cities. Brahman MLAs are the most urbanized, with the 62% living in cities representing nearly three times the number born there. Surprisingly, Mahajans show the least degree of urbanization among the political elite castes, the majority living in neither villages nor cities but in the middle-sized towns of the state.

There is also impressive evidence which suggests that many MLAs do not come from the "best families" of their respective communities. Legislators from the Mahajan castes, for example, come primarily from families of medium economic resources in communities that are noted for their immense wealth. They are drawn from families of small traders in small towns and villages. Brahman MLAs also come from less urban and less educated backgrounds than might be expected and from families in which traditional occupations tended not to be followed. When the value of education for Brahmans is considered, it is most surprising that no Brahman fathers received more than a primary school education and that 78% received no education at all. Their lack of any association with the princely houses in Rajputana, their village or small-town birthplaces, their subsequent rapid rise in education and urbanization, and the improvement in their families' economic conditions all suggest that these Brahman MLAs represent a mobile group *within* their caste and that they have succeeded in competing with more prestigious families within their own community through political activity.

Another indicator of the mobility of MLAs within their respective ascriptive social groups is the economic history of their families. When the MLAs were asked whether their families were better off, worse off, or had remained the same as ten years ago, 61% responded that their families were better off, 25% that they were worse off, and 14% that their families' positions had remained the same. Of those MLAs who believed that their families were worse off, 63% were Rajput MLAs who also scored the highest on such economic variables as land holding and income. Clearly, this former ruling caste was expressing a sense of relative, rather than actual, deprivation. Most MLAs responded as socially mobile men would be expected to respond—they reported that their families were better off.

Legislators in Rajasthan are highly educated men in a largely illiterate society and highly mobile men in a relatively immobile society. They are the first generation to have experienced high

education, mobility, occupational change, and substantial urbanization, and some MLAs have used political activity as a means of
intragroup mobility. Rajasthan is therefore governed by an elite
which is modern in outlook and much more capable of handling the
complex problems of administration and planning than are members
of the general society. Although the MLAs have experienced substantial change and mobility, their local ties have not been destroyed.
Their early socialization and life experiences were rural, like those of
the vast majority of the society, and despite the significant measure
of urbanization and occupational change, 89% of the MLAs own
agricultural land. Most holdings are within the "middle peasant"
range of 10 to 20 acres. But perhaps the best indication of the MLAs'
continuing ties with their region of origin is that they tend to
represent their constituency of birth in the legislature. In contrast to
the general society, the MLAs represent transitional men who have
been socialized in both a traditional and a modern culture. Their role
as links between the more traditional general society and the more
modern political system derives in part, then, from personal transitional experience, and, as W. H. Morris-Jones (1963) has suggested,
the MLA tends to be skilled in both the traditional and modern
idioms of politics.

Timing has been a vital element in the political careers of many
MLAs, for political mobilization is closely linked to the nationalist
movement of preindependence India. Such major events as the non-
cooperation movements of the 1920s and 1930s, the Quit India
Movement launched in 1942, and the final phases of the independence struggle reached deeply into Indian society and increased the
level of political participation and the rate of political recruitment. It
is not strange that such men as we have described were drawn into
the vortex of these historic and dramatic events. Since independence
elections have been major political events; it is at these times that
political awareness has been heightened and politics have penetrated
the society most thoroughly. The political system's expanding scope,
its rising saliency with a growing institutionalization and differentiation, and its growing capability to distribute resources vital to the
maintenance or improvement of status, power, and welfare have
increased the appeal of politics for a growing proportion of the
state's society. The historic waves of the nationalist movement come
periodically, as do elections, and political recruitment has been in
terms of political generations which, at times, overshadow mere age
as the crucial recruitment factor. All MLAs recruited before the 1942

movement are designated Old Nationalists, while MLAs who entered politics between 1942 and 1947 are termed New Nationalists. The period between 1947 and the first General Elections in 1952 was of greater importance in Rajasthan than in many Indian states, for it was then that the state was created and the future political order took definite form. Thus this period is treated separately, and those who entered politics at the time are termed Early Entrants. Finally, those who have entered since 1952 are termed Recent Entrants. The data in Table 2.5 suggest that the Rajasthan Assembly contains important representation from the four most significant political periods in the state's history and that the scope of experiences and attitudes within the assembly is broad. Old Nationalists comprised 33% of the third assembly, New Nationalists 20%, Early Entrants 14%, and Recent Entrants 33%. While the representation of preindependence recruits is still considerable, these data indicate a progressive recruitment of activists who have entered politics since independence.

The data also indicate, however, that the general configuration between generations is skewed when time of entry into politics is analyzed in terms of caste. The Brahman and Mahajan MLAs make up the great bulk of Old and New Nationalists, and only 17% of the Brahman MLAs and 16% of the Mahajan MLAs have been recruited since independence. On the other hand, 56% of the Peasant MLAs, 83% of the Rajput MLAs, and 65% of the scheduled tribe MLAs entered politics since independence. Of the lower castes, only the scheduled castes had a slight majority of MLAs recruited in the preindependence period.

TABLE 2.5
CASTE AND POLITICAL GENERATION OF MLAS IN THIRD ASSEMBLY (IN PERCENTAGES)

Caste	Old Nationalists	New Nationalists	Early Entrants	Recent Entrants	(N=174)
Brahman	43	40	10	7	30
Mahajan	53	32	11	5	19
Peasant	28	16	22	34	32
Rajput	11	6	17	66	35
Scheduled tribes	17	17	17	48	23
Scheduled castes	39	18	11	32	28
Other	72	29	—	—	7
Total sample	33	20	14	33	

The variation between caste and political generation is due to the differential rates of political mobilization, and these reflect important aspects of the state's political history. As early as the 1920s, Brahmans and Mahajans tended to be the leaders of the nationalist movement and headed most of the Praja Mandals in the state.[9] Being better educated and more urban than members of other castes, they more easily became politically aware and active. The fact that 57% of the scheduled caste MLAs are either Old or New Nationalists is in part testimony to the effectiveness and extent of the social uplift work led by many of the same Brahmans and Mahajans who have served as state legislators. Although members of the Jat caste (the main representative of the peasant castes) organized Kisan Sabhas [10] in the 1930s, and although some Jats participated in the Praja Mandal movements in the eastern portion of the state, most (57%) of the Jat MLAs are either Early or Recent Entrants. They represent the highly educated political leaders who emerged out of the earlier caste reforms and educational institutions established by the Kisan Sabhas of the state. Jat MLAs are among the most mobile, energetic, and purposeful members of the state assembly and have maintained a strong peasant orientation. Since both the nationalist movement and the peasant movements of the preindependence period were directed against the princely order and the traditional political system, it is not surprising that most Rajput MLAs did not participate in these movements but entered politics after 1952 when the new political order was clearly established. By 1962 few Rajput MLAs were senior representatives of the princely order; most were either sons of former jagirdars or from second-line Rajput families.

There are several reasons for this which throw some light on political career patterns in Rajasthan and indicate the type of impact and adjustments stimulated by the introduction of a new political system into a traditional order. The older members of the princely order are more deeply committed to the traditional political system and its values and are thus more reluctant to participate in the "new politics" than are the younger members, who are often sons of jagirdars. Many of the senior members of the princely order, although successful in the first elections, have found electoral politics demeaning, having had to plead and make compromises with those over whom they formerly wielded authority. Most younger Rajputs did not experience this transformation of the political system and thus find in politics a way to protect traditional status and participate in the new society. Rajputs also realize that they can maximize their influence if the former rulers and jagirdars remain inactive in the new political system and continue their style of life, thus retaining a maximum amount of their traditional legitimacy. Younger members can draw on their senior's prestige and legitimacy, which increase their political power in the new political system even while minimizing the risk of compromising their traditional status. Younger representatives of the traditional political aristocracy have also been schooled in the ways of modern politics. They are able to work better with political leaders from other castes, who do not react with such suspicion and distrust as they do with a number of the men against whom they had rebelled. Younger Rajput MLAs are, therefore, strategically placed to play an important role in linking the old and new political systems and their differing values.

Although the Rajasthan Assembly contains broad social representation and a balanced representation of political generations, some signs of strain are evident. Of particular note is the drastic reduction in the rate of recruitment of Brahman and Mahajan MLAs, which contrasts so markedly with mobilization patterns of other major castes. This suggests that a major change in the balance of social representation will occur in the 1970s unless younger elites from these two important groups appear soon. If the role of the MLA becomes more secular, less linked to primordial identities and interests, a "balanced" social representation will not be so important, of course, and broader identities and interests such as class or region may replace the more traditional linkages among the state's significant sociocultural groups and their representatives.

THE LEGISLATOR AND HIS CONSTITUENCY: STRUCTURAL AND ATTITUDINAL LINKAGES BETWEEN ELITE AND MASS

We have established above that the MLA is a highly mobile man in a relatively unmobilized society. He is educated, often highly so, and his education has taken place away from his home and place of birth. He tends to have a "modern" occupation and an autonomous source of income. He is well traveled, he receives immense flows of information from the mass media, and, if he is like most MLAs, speaks English. He is, as he was before his election, an active participant in the modern sector of Indian society.

Our next set of questions, then, concerns the relationship between the MLA and his electoral constituency. To what extent, we ask, does the state legislator have personal or familial ties with the area of his constituency, whether those ties be ancestral or generated through birth or rearing? If the MLAs were to score high on this scale, we would infer that local and cultural linkages exist and that they are important for political success. We would also infer that the successful candidate—for the state assembly, at least—is attentive to these local primordial bonds.

Our inquiries indicate that most legislators in Rajasthan have close social and cultural associations with the area of their constituency (Table 2.6). Most were born and raised in the district in which their constituency is located. A majority (69%) were born and raised within the territorial confines of their constituency itself. The larger majority of those born and raised within the district of their constituency, but not in their constituency, were reared in areas geographically contiguous with the constituency they represent. This observation is enhanced by the character of the MLAs' generational ties. Our data also indicate that the majority of MLA fathers (64%) were born in the constituency from which their sons were elected. All but 12% were born in the district in which their sons contested. Since the geographical mobility of the population in Rajasthan is low, we can reliably infer that the social linkage of the MLA and his constituency is of long standing.

This pattern of affinity between legislator and constituency is further indicated by continuity of contest. The successful candidate for the state assembly tends to contest from the same constituency in subsequent elections. In the third assembly, for example, only 17% of the incumbents had previously contested elections from constituencies other than the one they represented at the time. It should be noted that of those who contested from another constituency, almost all (84%) stood for election in the district in which their current constituency was located. All those who did contest from other constituencies were important members of their respective parties, 77% having been successful in their previous efforts.

Another indication of the legislator's affinity is suggested by what

TABLE 2.6
PLACE OF REARING AND RESIDENCE OF STATE LEGISLATORS
(IN PERCENTAGES)

Residence	Constituency	District	Outside	(N=)
Born and raised	69	15	16	162
Permanent residence	54	23	24	147

TABLE 2.7

PERCEPTION OF MOTHER TONGUE BY LEGISLATORS
(IN PERCENTAGES)

Party Affiliation	Local Dialect	Hindi	Other	(N=79)
Congress	67	33	0	39
Swatantra	53	47	0	15
Jan Sangh	0	100	0	7
Other	72	22	6	18
Total sample	59	39	1	

he considers to be his mother tongue (Table 2.7). This is a particularly useful test, given the wide variation of local dialects in Rajasthan. We might first note, however, that 68% of the MLAs in the third assembly were at least minimally conversant in English, the highest proportions occurring among members of the Congress and leftist parties. Yet, as the data in Table 2.7 indicate, the majority of Rajasthani legislators consider their mother tongue to be the dialect spoken in the area of their constituency, only 39% claiming Hindi as their native language and none English. Furthermore, 10% of the respondents come from Hindi-speaking areas that border on Uttar Pradesh. If this is taken into account, then only 30% of the legislators claim as their mother tongue a language other than that spoken in their local area. This is an important indication of the affinity that MLAs, largely highly "modern" men, have retained for the culture of the area they represent.

This pattern of close social linkage between the MLA and mass society is paralleled by the way the legislator spends his political time. Most MLAs, for example, spend the bulk of their time within their constituency and/or in fulfilling the obligations associated with their office. Of those legislators interviewed, 67% spent over half their time within their constituencies (Table 2.8) while 81% indi-

TABLE 2.8

TIME SPENT IN CONSTITUENCY BY MLAS
(IN PERCENTAGES)

Party Affiliation	0–24%	25–49%	50–74%	75–100%	(N=80)
Congress	21	24	42	13	38
Swatantra	19	25	31	25	16
Jan Sangh	14	0	43	43	7
Other	5	11	58	26	19
Total sample	17	17	45	22	

cated that they spend more than 60% of their time fulfilling the duties of an MLA (Table 2.9). Interestingly, opposition MLAs spend more time in their constituencies than do Congressmen. While only 55% of Congress legislators spend over half of their time in their constituencies, 78% of the Opposition MLAs do. This profile is generally true for all Opposition parties.

There are several interesting variations concerning time spent in politics in terms of party affiliation and constituency location. The Congress legislator spends more of his time in the work of legislation, intercession with administrative agencies, and just plain "politicking" than does his Opposition counterpart. While most MLAs spend most of their time engaged in political life, Congress legislators are more likely than others to pursue politics as a vocation. For example, 87% of the ruling party's legislators spend at least 60% of their time in political work, while "only" 70% of Opposition MLAs do. Differences in terms of location of constituency are not great, although city and rural MLAs spend somewhat more of their time fulfilling the duties of an MLA than do those from rural towns.

The above analysis demonstrates the close relationship between the legislator and his constituency in Rajasthan. The MLA has close social links of long standing in his area. He tends to contest from that same area. We have also established that he gives continual attention to legislation and other forms of political work, much of which is

TABLE 2.9
TIME SPENT IN FULFILLING DUTIES OF MLA
(IN PERCENTAGES)

	0–19	20–39	40–59	60–79	80–100	(N=80)
Political generation						
Old nationalist	0	13	6	25	64	16
New nationalist	0	9	4	13	74	23
Early entrants	0	9	13	13	65	23
Recent entrants	0	11	17	22	50	18
Party affiliation						
Congress	0	3	11	21	66	28
Swatantra	0	19	13	19	50	16
Jan Sangh	0	14	0	14	71	7
Other	0	16	11	11	63	19
Constituency location						
Rural	0	8	9	17	66	53
Town	0	17	17	28	39	18
City	0	11	0	0	89	9
Total sample		10	10	18	63	

within his constituency. He maintains a local "presence" and availability to monitor public wants. In view of relatively late and continuing political mobilization taking place in the Rajasthani countryside, it is particularly significant that rural MLAs spend the bulk of their time in political activity. Finally, Congress legislators tend to be more mobile than their Opposition counterparts and to spend less time in their constituencies, but they spend more time fulfilling the duties of an MLA than do most members of the Opposition.

We proposed at the outset that an important attitudinal linkage in the Indian political system is the MLA's perception of what interests he represents. Whom does he feel he represents? To what locus of interest or opinion does he feel most responsive? What level of the political system is most salient in his perception of his role as representative? Does he see ideological and programmatic prescription as most salient or some form of material interest? We are interested in addressing these questions in terms of political generation, party affiliation, and the location of the constituency from which the legislator was elected.

The data presented in Table 2.10 indicate that the large propor-

TABLE 2.10
LEGISLATORS' PERCEPTIONS OF THEIR CONSTITUENCIES
(IN PERCENTAGES)

	Constituency Interest	State and Regional Interest	National Opinion	Ideology	Social Background	(N=76)
Political generation						
Old nationalist	29	21	29	21	0	14
New nationalist	33	24	29	14	0	21
Early entrants	57	13	22	4	4	23
Recent entrants	50	22	17	0	11	18
Party affiliation						
Congress	47	17	19	8	8	36
Swatantra	53	27	20	0	0	15
Jan Sangh	43	0	29	29	0	7
Other	56	0	33	11	0	18
Constituency location						
Rural	55	12	22	8	4	51
Town	41	12	35	6	6	17
City	37	25	13	25	0	8
Total sample	50	13	24	9	4	

tion of Rajasthani MLAs conceive constituency interests to be their principal point of reference.[11] Exactly 50% of our respondents indicated that constituency interests had the most significant influence on their role as representative. The proportion noting state and regional interests was low—only 13%. Given the presumed importance of social groups in a highly status-oriented caste society like India's, we might predict that a large proportion of legislators would perceive their constituency in terms of their social group. This, however, did not prove to be the case: only 4% of our sample perceived their role in terms of social group. The proportion of those indicating national political opinion and ideology as most important was 33%, considerably more than for state and regional interests.

Perception of representational role varies in terms of political generation, party affiliation, and constituency type. The "nationalist" political generations are much more oriented toward national public opinion and party ideology than are the more recent recruits into the legislative process. Constituency and state interests as well as social background, on the other hand, are much more significant for those recruited into politics since independence.

We also find several striking differences with respect to party affiliation. National opinion and ideology are more salient for Jan Sangh and leftist party members than for Congressmen and members of the Swatantra; none of the Swatantra members listed party ideology as important in their conception of their legislative role. Congress and Swatantra MLAs, on the other hand, indicated that constituency and state interests were primary.

There are also discernible differences between representatives from urban and rural constituencies. Rural legislators appear to be much more attuned to the interests of their constituents than their urban counterparts are, the latter reflecting a closer relationship with the larger political system. Urban legislators are more concerned than rural ones with state and regional interests and with ideology.

Although we have shown, through the use of a broad range of socioeconomic, cultural, educational, and mobility indicators, that the MLA is clearly an elite and distinctly separate from the general society, we have also clearly demonstrated that he has a close cultural and residential linkage with his constituency. Furthermore, he is a local man not only in fact but also in his perception of his role as legislator, and this role consumes the bulk of his time and energy. Distinct he clearly is, but isolated he is not. To the degree that an elite-mass gap exists in Rajasthan, it seems more likely to be due either to breaks in the linkage system below the constituency level or to attitudinal differences within the mass public concerning judgment of governmental performance.

DIVISION AND COHESION IN THE LEGISLATIVE SYSTEM: PATTERNS OF INTRAELITE LINKAGE

We have analyzed the close historical, physical, and political relationships that exist between the MLA and his constituency together with the MLA's orientation toward constituency opinion and interest. We have suggested that legislators constitute an important institutional linkage between electors and the larger political system in both formal-legal and informal terms. But there are other dimensions to be addressed. How, precisely, does the legislator relate to the larger political system? What is the character of this linkage? With whom does he operate? How does he, and how has he, related to the party system?

One of the basic assumptions of democratic pluralism is the existence of an interlocking web of crosscutting associational ties within society.[12] Such a profile of linkages, it has been maintained, is conducive to the muting of political conflict and serves as a structural regulator in the number and intensity of demands made upon the state. This is particularly critical with respect to those who are active and articulate in the political marketplace. The character of linkages between legislators and different organized groups within a society is therefore an important consideration in the analysis of elite-mass relationships. We turn now to a brief investigation of this form of linkage in the case of Rajasthan.

It should be noted from the outset that the infrastructure of active voluntary associations and political interest groups in Rajasthan is not complex. The number of such groups is small; their activities are limited. Furthermore, the participation of MLAs in those associations that do exist is quite low. For example, only 11% of our respondents are or have been members of a trade union, only 14% claim association with a religious or cultural organization, only 17% are members of a bar association (although 26% have earned a law degree), and only two percent are members of associations of commerce and trade. Those who do participate in secular associational life tend to be affiliated with organizations dedicated to improving the welfare of depressed castes, with community associations within their own caste, or with governmental organizations and economic cooperatives.

The pattern of these associational linkages has changed with the

TABLE 2.11

PARTICIPATION AND LINKAGE WITH INSTITUTIONAL ENVIRONMENT
(IN PERCENTAGES)

	Panchayats	Cooperatives	Social Uplift Associations	Caste Associations
Party affiliation				
Congress	27	51	52	45
Swatantra	21	38	37	68
Jan Sangh	7	29	29	56
Other	28	59	28	24
Political generation				
Old nationalist	17	8	53	39
New nationalist	19	16	54	39
Early entrants	38	41	35	63
Recent entrants	25	35	24	59

emergence of new political generations since independence. Thus, as Table 2.11 indicates, the "nationalist" generations are particularly active in social welfare organizations, a form of public activity that constituted an important moral imperative for political activists during the preindependence period. Members of postindependence generations, however, tend to be more active in either governmental and quasi-governmental organizations or in caste associations, although the latter and MLA participation in them have diminished in importance during the past decade.

This configuration suggests the increasing importance of governmental and government-supported institutions as channels of communication and access between the state and society. The institutions of Panchayati Raj, for example, have provided a new avenue for political mobility in the rural areas and small towns of Rajasthan, and they have at their disposal economic resources for assisting rural development. Indeed, these institutions were created with the express purpose of associating mass man more intimately with the modern political and economic system in the state. Particularly important in the rationale was the encouragement of mass participation in the process of planned change. Emphasis was placed upon local participation and local control of local development problems. Political entrepreneurs have come to use these institutions for purposes of political mobility, and the *panchayats* have become important links between the state political system and mass society. The cooperative societies, licensed and partially funded by the state, were created to provide another means to the same ends. They, too, provide for local participation and control, operate in a milieu that is understandable to the local society, and provide services that are economically important. Both panchayats and cooperative societies have been important in political mobilization and are more important than voluntary associations as channels of political access.

Another critical segment of the institutional environment in which the state legislator operates is the party system. While interparty mobility of legislators in the third assembly was considerable, the majority had been associated with their current party for some time. By the time of their election in 1962 exactly 60% of the MLAs had been members of their current political party for at least five years, and just under 50% had been members for ten years or more. A noticeable proportion, however (32%), had joined their party less than one year before election. Mobility is higher for opposition MLAs than for those of the Congress, 70% of whom had been members of their party for at least one decade. The Congress Legislative party, therefore, was not a party of recent political recruits but of incumbents who have spent years within it.

Furthermore, interparty mobility has been conducive to the creation and maintenance of channels of communication between the ruling party and the opposition. Departees from the Congress party through 1967 did not include major Congress leaders at either state or district level.[13] Many who have departed to the opposition continue to identify with the Congress, and some, having proved their electoral prowess and power, await the call to return to the fold.

The final focus of our inquiry into the linkage system of the state legislator and political integration in India is the organization and social base of party factions. Much has been made of factionalism in Indian politics—particularly its destabilizing consequences in terms of party loyalty and its proposed violation of the principles of secular representation. Factions do in fact pervade Indian political life. They are found at all levels of politics; they are found in all parties; they are found in all states.[14] They have also been found to rest upon religious bases, upon caste, upon personalities, upon region, upon political generation, and upon the basis of shared ideological commitment. Whatever their basis might be, however, the role of factions in the informal organization of the elite linkage system is immensely important. It should be particularly noted that the creation of effective linkages across primordial social categories is important in the creation of communities and in the maintenance of secular party institutions, whether the linkages are coalitions between self-contained units or connections between constituent units within a larger organization (Rose and Urwin, 1969; Lipset and Rokkan, 1967).

Rajasthan at the time of independence was India in miniature. It was composed of territorially bounded regional cultures distinct in language, diet, social organization, agricultural practice, and political tradition. Unlike the provinces of British India, however, there were no political institutions serving to link these areas. The Congress party was created in 1946 by contract among the various urban-based protest organizations that had arisen during the preindependence period, each having separate leaders and cadres, each with a distinct set of shared political experiences. Peasant movements, the Kisan Sabhas, were absorbed into the Congress en masse in 1951.[15]

At the time of its founding and for several years afterwards, the effective organization of power within the Congress party was based on regional and/or caste factions, with a relatively simple web of association of low intensity connecting groups from the smaller former princely states with those of the larger. Dissident factions within each state searched for external association both from necessity and for convenience. Coalitions of these primordially based political groups were struck at the state level, with competition for support and the vagaries of elections resulting in changes in the composition of factions as well as in the structure of their alignments.

The segmentary organization of political power which has existed within the Congress system since its founding in Rajasthan has tended to encourage continual competition for political support. [16] This struggle involves all aspects of a faction's environment. It is directed first of all toward those groups which are already mobilized and active within a particular area of conflict, but it is relevant also with respect to all other potential resources, whether mobilized or not. Thus, factional competition has been conducive to the recruitment of new political resources into the Congress system. Although new leaders and groups may be supported by, and tend to become associated with, a particular faction, associations can change; this is more likely to happen in the case of relatively new political recruits with autonomous clienteles than it is with either the old units of the institution or new units that have been coopted and owe their political position in some measure to that center of power by which they were coopted. This process has resulted in the secularization of recruitment into factions and the social pluralization of factional composition.

The data in Tables 2.12 and 2.13 indicate the changing complexion of factional composition in the Congress Legislative party in each of the first three legislative assemblies. The changes are indeed significant. Factions at the state level have been relatively stable in terms of leadership, but the support base of each has become increasingly pluralized in both regional and social composition.

Immediately evident is the rise of state-level factions organized around dominant competitors for control over the state ministry and the diminution in number and importance of autonomous factions, all of which were exclusively regional in their recruitment. While subfactional identity in certain cases has continued, bonds with the larger factional coalition have progressively assumed increasing importance for the legislator.

The composition of these state-level factions reflects important changes in the structure of political linkage in Rajasthani politics during the last two decades. Regional pluralization in dominant coalitions has been pronounced. For example, the faction led by the chief minister of the state from 1954 to 1971, Mohanlal Sukhadia, not only expanded in size but has become increasingly plural in its base of recruitment. In the first assembly 80% of the faction was recruited from the chief minister's "home" region, Udaipur Division, but in the third assembly this proportion decreased to 40%. The new factional members were recruited from Jaipur and the quasi-desert areas of Shekhawati and Jodhpur. It is essential to note that Sukhadia successfully maintained the integrity of his faction in his home region. This is indicated by the few Udaipuris found among the members of the Vyas and Kumbharam coalitions. It must also be noted that Sukhadia was quite successful in seeing to the election of candidates who were receptive to his leadership—a form of success enjoyed in lesser measure by his major opponents.

It is important to examine shifts in the other two coalitions as well. While the immediate base of support for the Vyas faction was initially concentrated in the Jodhpur region, all but one of the representatives of this faction were defeated in that region in the first General Elections. This severe setback at the hands of candidates from the traditional ruling aristocracy had a permanent impact, not only on the Vyas faction, but on the larger arena of Rajasthani politics. From the outset, therefore, Vyas's coalition in the Congress

TABLE 2.12

REGIONAL DISTRIBUTION OF STATE FACTIONS IN CONGRESS LEGISLATIVE PARTY
(IN PERCENTAGES)

Region	Sukhadia	Vyas I[a]	Kumbharam	Shoba Ram	Paliwal	Vyas II[a]	Rajput	Shastri
First Assembly (1952–57)	(N=24)	(N=25)	(N=16)	(N=7)	(N=16)	(N=3)	(N=25)	(N=3)
Matsya	8	32	0	100	0	0	0	0
Jaipur	0	12	0	0	81	100	8	0
Kotah	8	12	0	0	0	0	24	0
Udaipur	80	4	0	0	0	0	20	0
Shekhawati	4	8	25	0	19	0	12	100
Jodhpur	0	20	31	0	0	0	32	0
Bikaner	0	12	44	0	0	0	4	0
Second Assembly (1957–62)	(N=43)	(N=39)	(N=22)	(N=2)	(N=6)	(N=5)		
Matsya	0	26	9	100	0	0		
Jaipur	14	18	5	0	67	80		
Kotah	7	18	0	0	33	20		
Udaipur	63	5	0	0	0	0		
Shekhawati	5	13	14	0	0	0		
Jodhpur	12	10	50	0	0	0		
Bikaner	0	10	23	0	0	0		

Third Assembly (1962–67)	(N=47)	(N=17)	(N=21)
Matsya	2	6	5
Jaipur	19	6	14
Kotah	2	41	0
Udaipur	40	6	0
Shekhawati	13	6	5
Jodhpur	15	24	67
Bikaner	6	12	10

Note: The figures in this table represent factional dispersion at the first sitting of the assembly after each of the first three general elections with the exception of the first assembly, which was calculated after the entry of opposition Rajput MLAs into the Congress Legislative party. Marginal changes take place in factional association during the course of an assembly.

a. Vyas I refers to the faction led by Jai Narain Vyas, the eminent preindependence leader from Jodhpur. Vyas II refers to a localized faction led by Damodarlal Vyas from Tonk District in Jaipur Division. This faction worked quite closely with Paliwal until 1955, after which it became increasingly associated with Sukhadia. It has maintained a certain autonomy largely because of the dynamism and ability of its leader.

TABLE 2.13

CASTE DISTRIBUTION OF STATE FACTIONS IN CONGRESS LEGISLATIVE PARTY (IN PERCENTAGES)

Caste	Sukhadia	Vyas I	Kumbharam	Shoba Ram	Paliwal	Vyas II	Rajput	Shastri
First Assembly (1952–57)	(N=24)	(N=25)	(N=16)	(N=7)	(N=13)	(N=3)	(N=25)	(N=3)
Brahman	25	36	0	0	54	33	4	0
Mahajan	17	20	0	29	23	33	0	33
Peasant	4	8	75	29	0	0	0	0
Rajput	0	4	0	0	0	0	96	0
Scheduled castes	8	8	6	14	8	33	0	67
Scheduled tribes	29	0	0	0	8	0	0	0
Other	17	24	19	29	8	0	0	0
Second Assembly (1957–62)	(N=43)	(N=39)	(N=22)	(N=4)	(N=6)	(N=5)		
Brahman	26	15	0	25	33	60		
Mahajan	14	8	5	0	0	0		
Peasant	0	10	63	50	0	0		
Rajput	14	23	0	0	17	0		
Scheduled castes	14	26	18	0	17	20		
Scheduled tribes	19	0	14	0	33	0		
Other	14	18	0	25	0	20		

Third Assembly (1962–67)	(N=47)	(N=17)	(N=21)
Brahman	32	0	0
Mahajan	9	11	0
Peasant	17	0	62
Rajput	6	53	0
Scheduled castes	13	6	19
Scheduled tribes	17	6	14
Other	6	24	5

Note: As in Table 2.12, the figures in this table represent factional dispersion at the first sitting of the assembly after each of the first three general elections with the exception of the first assembly, which was calculated after the entry of opposition Rajput MLAs into the Congress Legislative party. For the meaning of Vyas I and Vyas II, see Table 2.12.

Legislative party was composed principally of supporters from regions other than Jodhpur. While the faction increased in size during the second assembly, largely because of the absorption of members of the Paliwal and Rajput factions, Vyas's support subsequently diminished, and by the fourth General Elections in 1967 the integrity of his faction had dissipated. This faction, like Sukhadia's, however, became interregional in composition.

The faction led by Choudhry Kumbharam Arya, the able populist Jat leader from Bikaner, began as a coalition of peasant caste MLAs, primarily Jat, from the desert regions of Bikaner, Jodhpur, and Shekhawati. The composition of this faction did not become as regionally dispersed as that of others, although it did attract supporters from nondesert regions of the state. Through the mid-1960s the faction was a most important force in Rajasthani politics and had important links with Opposition MLAs. Striking, however, was the progressive decrease of its MLAs from Bikaner and the dramatic increase in its proportion of members from Jodhpur—a change that eventually led to intense strain within the coalition and was partly responsible for Kumbharam's departure from the Congress before the fourth General Elections.

Change in the regional composition of state factions has been accompanied by changing configurations of caste representation. The highest degree of pluralism in social representation is to be found in the Sukhadia faction. While the Brahman and scheduled tribe elements have been pronounced, the faction has been successful in attracting recruits from both peasant and Rajput castes. The Vyas coalition, initially dominated by Brahmans, Mahajans, and Kayasths—almost all of whom were from cities and large towns—expanded its social base considerably in the second assembly. This socially cosmopolitan character diminished during the third assembly, however, with the demise of the faction in state politics. The Kumbharam faction demonstrated the smallest magnitude of social change, remaining throughout largely a peasant caste faction, although it successfully developed support among important political aspirants of the scheduled castes and scheduled tribes.

The foregoing data indicate the extent to which pluralized secular institutions have replaced primordially based ones as the effective informal linkages in state politics. State-level factions within the Rajasthan Congress have changed in both regional and caste composition, each constituting a linkage system that includes representation from almost all regions of the state and from all strata of the caste hierarchy. It should be further noted that factional conflict within a segmentary organization of power, such as has characterized the Rajasthan Congress and the state of Rajasthan since their founding, is conducive to the development and maintenance of plural axes of political conflict. This has been true of the Congress institution itself as well as the political society in which it functions. The process of coopting new political resources into the party—resources which in themselves do not have the capacity for establishing or maintaining control over the power apparatus of the state—has tended to divide corporate social groups. This has been true particularly in the case of the dominant peasant and Rajput castes. In the case of the factional system, competition and the desire for increased mobility on the part of subordinate political leaders in factions recruited at one point in time—primarily from primordial groups—have given rise to a new system of alliances which have cut across these lines of social cleavage. This has made both the Congress party and the factional coalitions of which it consists a qualitatively new system of linkages which has given cohesion to a highly pluralistic and segmented political community. It has also tended to reduce the intensity of conflict both in the larger political system and in the Congress system itself.

The system of competition and segmentation which we have described has given rise to the integration of political groups and the creation of both vertical and horizontal linkages within the Congress party organization. These linkages have been encouraged not only by the segmentary organization of political power at given points in time but also by the competition and political responsiveness made mandatory by the quest for political influence and control. Lateral association has been important with respect both to the alliances forged between important political peers at each level of conflict and to the types of associations which have connected the Congress system with its political environment. Elite recruitment within the party, however, has rested principally on vertical mobility. These political connections within the autonomous environment have been linked primarily through the various factions within the Congress system. They have, in many cases, been employed on the part of one Congress faction against others. Factional competition has also, however, encouraged a cooperative posture between the Congress system as a whole and the political environment because of the access which important political units in the Opposition have enjoyed through connections with, and sometimes membership in, Congress coalitions. In many sectors there is a desire for entry into the party, and this has tended to maintain divisions within the organized political opposition of the Congress. This factor has facilitated the working of the factional system by affording the possibility of alliances, the making of deals, and the existence of conflict without the necessity of drawing closed lines of conflict within the confines of a set field of political units. It must be noted, however, that this characteristic of the factional system has been, and will continue to be, tested by the results of the fourth General Elections, where the Opposition tended to break those lateral ties with the Congress system. The development of a more cohesive opposition would place a higher premium on containing conflict within the Congress system and would reduce the effectiveness of working on the margins of the system to influence the organization of power within the party. This would perhaps be conducive to the erosion of important groups on the periphery of the Congress system.

CONCLUSIONS

Our analysis of Rajasthan's legislative elite establishes a pronounced asymmetrical relationship between legislators and mass society. The legislator is quite distinct from his society in several important ways. He is much more highly educated, he is mobile, and he has an occupation that reflects his close association with the modern sector of Indian society. While proportional representation for scheduled castes and scheduled tribes has been assured by reserved constituencies, legislators elected from General Seats tend to be recruited from social groups that enjoy privileged ascriptive social status.

State legislators in Rajasthan are distinctive in yet another way. Compared with their fathers' generation, we find that MLAs have achieved considerable mobility. We further find that Brahman and Mahajan MLAs tend to come from marginal families within their castes. The political vocation for these men provides a new avenue of social mobility. Rajput legislators tend to come from families with small traditional agricultural holdings or to be the sons of those who ruled before independence. With a few notable exceptions, those who enjoyed the perquisites of power in the traditional political order have not continued in public life since the early fifties. In these terms, then, there is a marked "gap" in Rajasthan between society and political elite.

Longitudinally, however, legislative representation has become increasingly socially plural. The legislature has served as a forum for bringing into public life social groups which had previously been at best petitioners of government rather than participants in the decisions of government. While those from a number of small and marginal castes have found their way into the legislative assembly, expanded representation has been most impressive in the case of the larger peasant castes who had been deprived of representation in the traditional polities which existed before independence. Representation in the legislative assembly as well as across party lines within the assembly has consistently included a sizable contingent of Rajputs and reflects the acceptance and the accommodation of this former ruling elite caste into the authority structures of the modern state. These are important indications of social integration in public life.

While a social "gap" clearly distinguishes the legislative elite from mass society in Rajasthan, we have found a number of important forms of horizontal integration between elite and mass. While members of the legislative assembly tend to be "modern" men, they have close associations with the constituencies they represent. Most have close familial and ancestral ties; most spend considerable time in their constituency; most spend most of their time actively engaged in politics. The language which most legislators consider to be their mother tongue is that spoken by their constituents. Furthermore, a large proportion of MLAs perceive constituency interests and opinion as the primary factors in their definition of their role as representative. Constituency reference has tended to be more salient for the more recent generations of legislators than for the older ones; and it is more salient for legislators from rural constituencies than for those from urban ones.

We have also explored the network of structural linkages between legislators and constituents through formal groups and organizations. Participation of legislators in voluntary associations turned out to be extremely low. It was high, however, in institutions of rural government and in cooperative societies. This is particularly significant given the fact that these associations in almost all cases are located in the MLA's constituency or district. Most legislators have also held positions of authority in their party organization, a large proportion before their election to the assembly. Legislators from rural constituencies and of more recent political vintage tend to participate more in Panchayati Raj and cooperative societies than in party organizations, while urban representatives tend to participate more in the latter.

There are also important linkages between and within political parties. The Congress party, we found, has supplied a large proportion of the Opposition legislators, many of whom maintain their ties with factions of the ruling party. Within parties, but particularly noteworthy in the Congress, factional linkage is the most important form of organization and control. This system of factions, however, has changed immensely since independence, the state-level factional coalitions constituting, as does the parent organization, a web of connections that cut across traditional social and regional categories. Faction, like party, constitutes a form of intersocial linkage unknown in preindependence Rajasthan. It has been a major form of political integration.

There are, of course, important questions which have gone unexplored. The present analysis has been confined largely to structural elements of integration and of legislative-environmental relationships. It does not get at important attitudinal questions concerning value consensus in the community with regard to the quality of its collective life. We do not know with much precision the extent to which cognition of collective life exists. We have analyzed with some thoroughness the linkage system that defines the relationship of the state legislator to his immediate environment; we have not, however, investigated linkage patterns within constituencies at the interstices where party and state institutions blend with local society. Our perspective has been from the elite looking out, rather than from mass publics and certain institutional environments looking in. What characterizes mass linkages with secular associational life? Where are the nexuses, if they do exist? What characterizes mass perceptions of representational role, real and ideal? What are mass judgments of legislative and governmental performance? What are the mass predilections concerning sustained and organized collective action? Do mass publics perceive a linkage system? Do they see this system as open and responsive? Nor have we considered legislative-bureaucratic relationships, of which too little is known.

Finally, the existence of linkages in a structural sense does not constitute integration or institutionalization; it does not assure political stability or ordered change. We can, however, make inferences about integration and institutionalization given the continuity of certain structural relationships over time and the demonstrated capacity of institutions to expand incumbencies and/or to augment and redistribute resources for newly mobilized, expectant, and assertive groups. Men surrounded by structures which encourage and reward participation and coordinated effort may develop orientations that help to sustain such activity as a behavioral mode and to sustain those particular structures in which such orientations were molded and assumed value. This question is particularly important with regard to existing elites; it will also assume importance when the reservoirs of elite recruitment are considered.

NOTES

1. Useful general studies of this dimension of legislatures include Packenham (1970) and Jewell (1968 and 1971). In terms of institutionalization see Polsby (1968) and Sisson (1973).

2. Our concern here is guided by the general considerations of Shils (1962), Pye (1962), Huntington (1968), and Nettl (1967). For explorations of this genre in the Indian case see Weiner (1959 and 1965b).

3. For a concise inventory of propositions concerning this question, see Gurr (1970, appendix) and Eckstein (1964), especially the essays of Feldman, Janos, Kornhauser, and Pye.

4. Important general considerations of this conceptual problem include Jacob and Teune (1964), Weiner (1965a), and Binder (1964). Useful in the Indian case are Weiner (1967) and Sisson (1972).

5. The data upon which this analysis is principally based were collected in Rajasthan from August 1963 to November 1964. An effort was made to collect SES data for all MLAs elected in each of the first three General Elections. These data, while not complete for all variables in all cases, were obtained from several sources. These include the Biographical Files maintained by the secretariat of the Rajasthan Legislative Assembly, the Constituency Files maintained by the Rajasthan Pradesh Congress Committee, and through interviews. The state office of the Rajasthan Jan Sangh also supplied biographical information for legislators of that party elected in 1962. Attitudinal data and those concerning career patterns and mobility were acquired through a questionnaire administered to all MLAs elected in 1962 to the third legislative assembly. The return was 46%.

6. See Seligman (1964). Striking in the Indian situation has been the rise of caste and community associations for the engagement of traditional social groups with the secular world. For a discussion of the Indian case see Rudolph, 1965; Hardgrave, 1969; Kothari and Maru, 1965; and Sisson, 1969.

7. The concept of *varna* refers to the four-fold categorization of society set forth in the ancient Hindu scriptures. The highest category, Brahmans, were traditionally priests. The Kshatriva were warriors and rulers; Rajputs constitute this category in our case. The Vaishya included men of commerce and trade, colloquially referred to as either Mahajan or Bania. The Shudra included peasants and artisans. The untouchables, herein referred to as sched-uled castes and scheduled tribes, are outside this classical conception of caste Hindu social organization. It should be emphasized that varna and *jati* are distinct categories, the former being a general order of status and including large numbers of the latter, social collectivities, most of which do not take meals together, intermarry, or participate in common life-cycle ceremonies. For an excellent consideration of jati, see Fox (1967).

8. For an elaboration, see Shrader (1968).

9. Praja Mandals, literally "peoples' Societies," were organizations of political protest that were formed in the princely states of Rajputana before independence. They merged in 1946, and in 1948 became the Rajasthan Congress party.

10. The Kisan Sabhas, literally "Peasant Societies," agitated for land reform during the preindependence period. They were formed primarily in the desert states of Rajputana.

11. This configuration is strikingly similar to that found for U.S. representatives by Dexter (1957). In this regard also see Kornberg (1966).

12. For a provocative test of this common assumption of group theory, see Verba (1965).

13. For example, 52% of the rural legislators, but only 40% of the urban ones, had been members of cooperative societies of some kind. Similarly, while only 17% of the urban MLAs had served either as a *pradhan* of a *panchayat samiti* or as a *pramukh* of a *zila parishad,* 28% of the rural MLAs had done so. (The latter institution is the district-level body in the *panchayati raj* system, while the former is located between the village and district levels. Pradhan and pramukh may be freely translated as "president.")

14. The highest incidence of party defection in Rajasthan, as in most other states, occurred prior to the 1967 elections. This was the first instance in which major leaders of the Congress party in Rajasthan defected and formed a new opposition party. It is important to note, however, that those who did leave were unable to take with them all the faction members who had customarily supported them within the Congress party. Thus these leaders found themselves without their customary base of support. As a result of the elections, which witnessed electoral coalitions on the part of some opposition parties, the Congress party found itself two members short of a legislative majority. It was eventually able to form a government after several opposition MLAs, all former Congress party members, were enticed back into the fold.

15. The empirical literature in this regard is fairly extensive. See, for example, Brass (1965), Wallace (1966), Roy (1966), Rosenthal (1966), and Miller (1965).

16. The development and organization of party factions in Rajasthan are matters too complex to deal with here. For a detailed treatment, see Sisson (1972) and Shrader (1965), chap. 7.

REFERENCES

AKE, C. (1967) A Theory of Political Integration. Homewood, Ill.: Dorsey Press.

BEER, S. H. (1958) "Group Representation in Britain and the United States." Annals 309 (Sept.): 131–40.

BINDER, L. (1964) "National Integration and Political Development." American Political Science Review 58 (Sept.): 622–31.

BRASS, P. (1965) Factional Politics in an Indian State: The Congress Party in Uttar Pradesh. Berkeley: Univ. of California Press.

DEXTER, L. A. (1957) "The Representative and His District." Human Organization 16 (Spring): 2–13.

ECKSTEIN, H., ed. (1964) Internal War. New York: Free Press.

EULAU, H. (1959) "The Role of the Representative: Some Empirical Observations on the Theory of Edmund Burke." American Political Science Review 53 (Sept.): 742–56.

FAIRLIE, J. A. (1940) "The Nature of Representation," American Political Science Review 34 (Apr.-June): 236–48, 456–66.

FOX, R. G. (1967) "Resiliency and Change in the Indian Caste System: The Umar of U.P." Journal of Asian Studies 26 (Aug.): 575–87.

GURR, T. (1970) Why Men Rebel. Princeton, N.J.: Princeton Univ. Press.

HARDGRAVE, R. L. (1969) The Nadars of Tamilnad: The Political Culture of a Community in Change. Berkeley: Univ. of California Press.

HUNTINGTON, S. P. (1968) Political Order in Changing Societies. New Haven, Conn.: Yale Univ Press.

JACOB, P. E., and H. TEUNE (1964) "The Integrative Process: Guidelines for Analysis of the Bases of Political Community." In The Integration of Political Communities, ed. P. E. Jacob and J. V. Toscano. Philadelphia: Lippincott. Pp. 1–49.

JEWELL, M. E. (1968) "Comparative Research in State Legislative Politics." In American Legislative Behavior: A Reader, ed. S. C. Patterson. Princeton, N.J.: Van Nostrand. Pp. 397–411.

_____ (1971) "Linkages Between Legislative Parties and External Parties." In Legislatures in Comparative Perspective, ed. A. Kornberg. New York: David McKay. Pp. 203–34.

KORNBERG, A. (1966) "Perception and Constituency Influence in Legislative Behavior." Western Political Quarterly 19 (June): 285–92.

KOTHARI, R., and R. MARU (1965) "Caste and Secularism in India." Journal of Asian Studies 24 (Nov.): 33–50.

LANGDON, R. P. (1969) Political Socialization. New York: Oxford Univ. Press.

LEVINE, R. A. (1963) "Political Socialization and Cultural Change." In Old Societies and New States, ed. C. Geertz. New York: Free Press. Pp. 280–303.

LIPSET, S. M., and S. ROKKAN (1967) "Cleavage Structures, Party Systems, and Voter Alignments: An Introduction." In Party Systems and Voter Alignments, ed. S. M. Lipset and S. Rokkan. New York: Free Press. Pp. 1–64.

MILLER, D. F. (1965) "Factions in Indian Village Politics." Pacific Affairs 38 (Spring): 17–31.

MORRIS-JONES, W. H. (1963) "India's Political Idioms." In Politics and Society in India, ed. C. H. Philips. London: Allen & Unwin. Pp. 133–54.

NETTL, J. P. (1967) Political Mobilization: A Sociological Analysis of Methods and Concepts. London: Faber & Faber.

PACKENHAM, R. (1970) "Legislatures and Political Development." In Legislatures in Developmental Perspective, ed. A. Kornberg and L. Musolf. Durham: Duke Univ. Press.

PYE, L. (1962) Politics, Personality and Nation Building: Burma's Search for Political Identity. New Haven, Conn.: Yale Univ. Press.

POLSBY, N. (1968) "The Institutionalization of the U.S. House of Representatives." American Political Science Review 62 (Mar.): 144–68.

ROSE, R., and D. URWIN (1969) "Social Cohesion, Political Parties and Strains in Regimes." Comparative Political Studies 2 (Apr.): 7–67.

ROSENTHAL, D. B. (1966) "Factions and Alliances in Indian City Politics." Midwest Journal of Political Science 10 (Aug.): 320–49.

RUDOLPH, L. I. (1965) "The Modernity of Tradition: The Democratic Incarnation of Caste in India." American Political Science Review 59 (Dec.): 975–89.

ROY, R. (1966) "Intra-Party Conflict in the Bihar Congress." Asian Survey 6 (Dec.): 706–15.

SELIGMAN, L. G. (1964) "Elite Recruitment and Political Development." Journal of Politics 26 (Aug.): 612–26.

SHILS, E. (1962) Political Development in the New States. The Hague: Mouton.

SHRADER, L. L. (1965) "Politics in Rajasthan." Ph.D. dissertation, Univ. of California, Berkeley.

_____ (1968) "Rajasthan." In State Politics in India, ed. M. Weiner. Princeton, N.J.: Princeton Univ. Press. Pp. 321–98.

SISSON, R. (1969) "Peasant Movements and Political Mobilization: The Jats of Rajasthan." Asian Survey 9 (Dec.): 946–63.

_____ (1972) The Congress Party in Rajasthan: Political Integration and Institution Building in an Indian State. Berkeley: Univ. of California Press.

_____ (1973) "Comparative Legislative Institutionalization: A Theoretical Exploration." In Legislatures in Comparative Perspective, ed. A. Kornberg. New York: David McKay. Pp. 17–38.

VERBA, S. (1965) "Organizational Membership and Democratic Consensus." Journal of Politics 27 (Aug.): 467–97.

WALLACE, P. (1966) "The Party System of Punjab State (India): A Study of Factionalism." Ph.D. dissertation, Univ. of California, Berkeley.

WEINER, M. (1959) "Some Hypotheses on the Politics of Modernization in India." In
    Leadership and Political Institutions in India, ed. R. Park and I. Tinker. Princeton, N.J.:
    Princeton Univ. Press.
_____ (1965a) "Political Integration and Political Development." Annals 358 (Mar.): 52–64.
_____ (1965b) "India: Two Political Cultures." In Political Culture and Political Develop-
    ment, ed. L. W. Pye and S. Verba. Princeton, N.J.: Princeton Univ. Press. Pp. 199–244.
_____ (1967) Party Building in a New Nation: The Indian National Congress. Chicago: Univ.
    of Chicago Press.

Chapter 3

THE LEGISLATOR AS INTERMEDIARY: INTEGRATION
OF THE CENTER AND PERIPHERY IN AFGHANISTAN

M A R V I N   G.   W E I N B A U M

LEGISLATURES IN THE MIDDLE EAST

Legislatures in the Middle East are seldom credited with an active role in national integration. Although most parliaments in the region were born in a constitutional or independence movement founded on a broad societal coalition, few escaped an early domination by provincial notables and an urban bourgeoisie intent on employing representative democracy to perpetuate economic and class privilege. Aside from the suppression of successionist or dissident national elements, parliaments were usually neither concerned nor competent to deal with regional, religious, ethnic, and tribal cleavages. The recognition of subnational communities and the mechanisms to resolve intergroup conflict improved only slightly where revolutionary and populist regimes replaced older elites with representatives of the salaried middle class and occasionally with peasants and urban workers. Lacking institutional autonomy, these legislatures bowed to charismatic leaders, mass parties, and military cadres in the task of building a national consensus and identity.

The burden of this chapter is to describe a process through which many parliaments in the Middle East, both revolutionary and conservative, make their only measurable contribution to national integration. Individual legislators, regardless of their performance as lawmakers, often serve as intermediaries in a communication network that links a nation's periphery with its center. The legislator is frequently the sole mediator between constituents and national policy elites. Legislators may carry and interpret commands from policy makers, or they may inform and sensitize national leaders to the demands and attitudes of local elites and mass publics. In transmitting national goals and symbols, legislators often can hardly compete with electronic and print media and party apparatus. Legislators are also nearly everywhere subordinate to security police and party workers in intelligence functions. But the member of parliament does best in dealing with particular demands which constituents, organized and unorganized, make of a national bureaucracy. Though party and local officials often share this mediating role, legislators are customarily unsurpassed for their effectiveness as middlemen. Typically, no other set of national actors has a better defined clientele, and few are perceived as more accessible and legitimate ombudsmen.

Legislators as intermediaries are essentially preoccupied with ombudsmenlike tasks—aiding constituents in obtaining the redress of grievances against alleged administrative improprieties and arbitrariness—as well as with other personal petitions. Their interventions are no less consequential, however, because they do not regularly raise issues of broad public policy. For the activities of elected representatives that help satisfy even unmomentous demands cannot be negligible where, as in much of the Middle East, central governments remain remote and suspect for large segments of the population. Any routinization of communications with national administrators that brings familiarity and increases trust becomes a suitable, if necessarily gradual, means of loosening deep-rooted parochial and sectarian allegiances.

The Afghan parliament (*shura*) resembles many others in the Middle East for its ineffectiveness as a legislative and deliberative body. Nonetheless the Afghan legislature is not a modal type, and its members are hardly prototypic. The strong tribal and ethnic allegiances of Afghan legislators are not unique in the region, but only the Lebanese deputy is perhaps more locally oriented or a better spokesman for a family or clan. The Afghan parliament is striking, moreover, for its combativeness with a national executive and for the government's highly selective interference in parliamentary elections. But the sharpest regional contrast is the Afghan legislators' freedom from any parliamentary discipline and their virtual ignorance of ideology. Indeed, with political parties illegal, and economic and other voluntary associations still largely inchoate, members of the Afghan shura often monopolize the popular linkages to national elites. Accordingly, a study of the Afghan deputy (*wakil*) permits a direct assessment of the potentials and limitations of legislators as intermediaries. Moreover, the depth and persistence of social cleavages in Afghanistan provides a worthy test of the role of legislatures in fostering a national identity in a developing society.

This chapter first describes the highly fragmented social context for contemporary Afghan politics. A brief overview of the structure and origins of the Afghan parliament follows, after which the ethnic and tribal constraints that have shaped the legislature's operating norms and influenced the social composition of members of the lower house, the Wolesi Jirgah (House of the People) are identified. The chapter next describes in detail the constituent-legislator-administrator nexus. The cultural bases for this relationship are pointed out, and the various strategies and resources available to the legislator as a mediator of demands are delineated. These observations are then summarized by positing four legislative role orientations. A concluding section considers how Afghan parliamentary democracy has helped to institutionalize provincial and regional claims against national authority. The intermediary behavior of legislators is identified as a prime manifestation of this process.

THE SOCIAL SETTING

The diversity of Afghan society defies any easy description. Racial types are overlapping; ethnic distinctions are usually oversimplified; linguistic varieties are numerous and usually mixed; and tribal origins are often unclear. To add to the complexity, the most salient social cleavages do not align neatly, and nearly all cut across class and economic lines. Still, at first glance, Afghan society does not seem remarkably heterogeneous or especially disjunctive. An estimated half or more of the country's 15 million inhabitants are thought to be Pashtun, a people of probable Aryan ancestry.[1] Nearly all Pashtuns speak Pashto, one of two official languages and alone designated as the national language. Afghans seldom question the status of Pashtuns as the ascendant national group; indeed, the terms "Afghan" and "Pashtun" are on occasion used synonymously. The heavy representation of Pashtuns among the national elites, especially in coveted ministry and military posts, is seldom contested. And for two centuries two clans of a single Pashtun subtribe have furnished the nation with all its royal families.[2]

The Pashtuns and at least 80% of the population adhere to the Sunni branch of Islam. The rest, aside from a small Sikh community and a scattering of other non-Muslims, are Shi'a Muslims, mainly of the Imami (Twelvers) sect. A common Islamic heritage, buttressed by the unshaken orthodoxy of most Afghans, is an obvious point of departure for any appeals to Afghan nationalism. Culturally, the nation seems no less of one fabric. Tribal mores and structures are common to much of Afghan society, often transcending distinctions of wealth and social class. The bases of political authority are broadly agreed upon, and at least one tribal institution, the *jirgah* (council), would seem to predispose most Afghans to democratic government. The jirgah's stress on equality and individual expression and its use of consultation and compromise in settling intratribal rivalries and in mitigating the power of traditional leaders establish it as a likely model for a national representative assembly (see Newell, 1972: 25).

The dominance of one ethnic group and the bonds of religion, language, and tribal culture in fact disguise the real fragmentation of Afghan society. First, it is only an article of political faith that Pashtuns constitute a numerical majority. Afghanistan has never conducted a national census; nor is a comprehensive count likely while some doubt exists that Pashtuns are more numerous than all other Afghans combined. Afghanistan's ethnic mosaic includes at least 15 easily identifiable elements. They range from the geographically dispersed Tajiks, who may number one-third of the population, to such groups as the small and regionally isolated Brahuis (of Indian subcontinent origin) and the Nuristanis (nineteenth-century converts to Islam of uncertain descent). The Tajiks themselves include two or three distinct ethnic types. One set of Tajiks is indigenous to the mountains of the northeast; a larger number, the Farsiwan, are inhabitants mainly of the western plains. The Farsiwan are largely Sunni, but the mountain Tajiks are commonly Shi'a. Although Tajiks are likely descended from the area's aboriginal Iranian people, they are now a strong mixture of Caucasian and Mongoloid types. Most Tajiks are sedentary and urban, with strong family ties having replaced tribal modes of social organization.

The Hazaras, the country's third most salient group after the Pashtuns and Tajiks, are in the main Shi'a and of essentially Mongol lineage. Traditionally the inhabitants of an infertile area of central Afghanistan known as Hazarajat, their population is sometimes estimated as high as one million. Many Hazaras have migrated to the cities, but their meager skills and heretical religious beliefs have relegated them to menial jobs and the lowest social rank. Two other ethnic minorities, the Uzbeks and the Turkomans, stand out from several groups of Turkic origin for their size and their integral role in the Afghan economy. Both are Sunni in practice and are typically Mongoloid in appearance. Concentrated in the more fertile northern provinces, the Uzbeks number upwards of 900,000, and the Turkomans probably under 250,000. Many Turkomans have strong tribal ties across the Soviet border. Although traditionally they have formed highly independent nomadic tribes, both they and the Uzbeks are now more sedentary, engaged in cultivation and sheep breeding.

Though Pashto is the first language of the largest number of Afghans, the language which comes closest to a *lingua franca* is Dari (Persian), which, like Pashto, is of Indo-European origin. Much to the annoyance of many Pashtuns, Dari rather than Pashto serves as the working language of government ministries and is spoken in the royal court. Few non-Pashtuns, aside from those with formal schooling, have much facility with Pashto. Dialects of Persian are the primary language of the Tajiks and the Hazaras, while other ethnic groups, including the Pashtun, have some acquaintance with Dari. Besides Dari and Pashto, there are at least 20 other languages and major dialects commonly spoken in the country.

A small Dari-speaking group, the Qizil-Bash (descended from an administrative class left by an eighteenth-century Persian conqueror), have commonly gravitated to the civil service and urban professions, and Tajiks are also well represented in the bureaucracy. Otherwise, Pashtun political hegemony, noted above, is real enough. Their preeminence, however, has been less a force for unity than a source of suspicion and resentment by non-Pashtuns. Pashtun ascendence does not extend nearly so much to the economic and religious realms, where, the successful merchant and influential *mullah* (cleric) are drawn from all major ethnic groups. It is also misleading to view the Pashtuns as a monolithic people. The ten or so major Pashtun tribes, the numerous minor ones, and the scores of subtribes and clans, many of them still nomadic, are with few exceptions fiercely proud and independent social units. As with most Afghans, obligations to tribe and family take precedence over an individual's loyalty to the more abstract notion of ethnic community. Intra-Pashtun tribal and family conflicts have been historically bitter and enduring. Finally, Pashtun allegiance to the Afghan state is itself ambiguous.

Most Pashtuns cling to the irredentism of a greater state of Pashtuni-stan which, if created, would encompass the bulk of what is pres-ently northwest Pakistan. Where Afghanistan's Pashtuns, especially the large border tribes, would then rest their loyalty is not entirely clear.

Religion and culture are also subject to qualifications as bases for national unity. Despite the large areas of doctrinal similarity between the Sunni and Shi'a sects, religious animosities have often reinforced ethnic and regional separatism. Afghan rulers were able to expand the scope of their political authority during the nineteenth century by rallying Sunni tribesmen against so-called heretics and infidels in raids on Hazaras, Sikhs, and Nuristanis (Kafirs). While discrimination against the Shi'a has waned, suspicion of their possibly divided loyalty, in particular to the Shi'a majority of Iran, still persists. Neither the Sunni nor the Shi'a, however, has nurtured a leadership or set of orgnizations that could readily assume a national role. The influence of the *ulema* (clergy) in matters of justice, education, and conventional wisdom is substantial, but locally focused. Few reli-gious figures have a broad reputation, and none has created a disci-plined political following. On the several occasions when mullahs have been roused as a political force, it has been to challenge the authority of the central government. The puritanical character of the clergy's Islamic interpretations is a further source of disunity. Mul-lahs' demands for individual piety and worth offer "nearly limitless opportunities for invidious comparisons between the moral standards of one tribe and another, one village and another, or one region and another" (Newell, 1972: 24).

In similar fashion, the common tribal frame of reference of most Afghans has probably heightened rather than diminished parochial-ism. Those traditional values of cooperation and collective responsi-bility, which seem so promising as ingredients for nation building, are also the mainstays of tribal and family self-sufficiency—assuring the survival of small independent social units under ordinarily difficult physical and human conditions (see Newell, 1972: 19–20). And Pashtunwali, the comprehensive, widely observed tribal code that condones individual acts of retribution, mitigates against the transfer of legal and political authority to larger units (Gregorian, 1969: 41). Even the democratic ethos of the tribal jirgah makes a questionable contribution to national unity. Although the institution has a na-tional counterpart in the Loya Jirgah (a constituent assembly of tribal chiefs, religious leaders, and ethnic notables called together in periods of national crisis), the jirgah has never entirely transcended its tribal origins. The notion that all participants have equal competence and are entitled to unrestricted self-expression has left unfortunate precedents for a contemporary parliament. All in all, the culture's insulating and often divisive values, when added to the nation's ethnic cleavages and its physical and educational barriers to communication, place formidable obstacles to the emergence of a modern Afghan state.

THE AFGHAN PARLIAMENT

THE LEGISLATURE

The Afghan shura captures the highest aspirations of the liberal constitution promulgated by King Mohammad Zahir in 1964. As conceived by a committee of progressives and approved by a broadly representative Loya Jirgah, the shura was intended to be the capstone of a system that would both assure ample protection to the nation's plural interests and induce a consensus on national goals. The framers dispersed powers among a bicameral legislature, an independent judiciary, and an executive answerable to elected deputies. The document further promised competitive political parties, a free press, and the creation of meaningful provincial councils. While significant powers were retained in the monarchy, the reforms signaled the royal family's willingness to share their once cautiously guarded governmental authority. The 1964 constitution is all the more remarkable for its initiation by a traditional monarchy acting not under popular duress, but in anticipation of the needs of a modern state and readiness to experiment with democratic institutions.

Afghans were already acquainted with a parliament. A 1931 constitution given by King Mohammad Nadir had authorized a two-house legislature—an upper chamber of up to 45 members appointed by the king for life and a lower house of initially 120 members elected to three-year terms. An accompanying election law permitted nearly universal male suffrage and invited competition for office by all literate males. Specially created jirgahs were prescribed to administer a secret ballot, though in practice local notables, under a mandate to elect reputable people loyal to the regime, usually designated deputies in open jirgahs. With small inclination or opportunity for coordinated candidates, it hardly mattered that political parties were barred. The scant publicity given to the election process by the government and the public's usual indifference testified to the shura's impotence: it was called upon to do little more than to dutifully accede to the government's legislative requests. Between the king and his upper house, any unsanctioned action of the lower chamber faced certain veto.

To run his governments, King Zahir, who had succeeded to the throne on his father's assassination in 1933, turned to his uncles and later his first cousins. Often skillfully, but usually autocratically, they managed the affairs of state as a family fief. Only once, in 1949, did the regime allow relatively free elections and give critics in the parliament and press a wide berth. This brief liberalization period ended abruptly in 1953 with the jailing of the most politically outspoken, including several prominent legislators. There survived, however, the more traditional means of bidding for national support—the convening of a Loya Jirgah. Attended by tribal chieftains and ethnic leaders, these meetings brought together the first line of Afghanistan's provincial power elite.[3]

The shura inaugurated in October 1965 reflected both a continuity and a break with the past. The lower chamber, the Wolesi Jirgah, reapproved as prime minister the commoner, Dr. Yousef, who two years earlier had been the king's choice to prepare the way for constitutional reforms.[4] About 30% of the 216 wakils were veterans of a previous parliament, and the new chamber resembled the old in its high proportion of traditional leaders and local notables (Dupree, 1971a: 4, 11). By contrast to the members of the first 11 Afghan parliaments, those elected to the lower house in both 1965 and 1969 experienced minimal intervention by government authorities.[5] Only a handful of the legislators were directly beholden to the government in Kabul for their victories. The overwhelming number of wakils were free, as never before, to dedicate themselves to the well-being of local, sectarian, and personal interests. Legislators readily grasped the opportunities for uninhibited debate and the utility of their parliamentary office in seeking favors from the government ministries.

Members of the Wolesi Jirgah are elected to serve four-year terms, as are a third (28) of the upper house, the Meshrano Jirgah (House of Elders, or Senate). Another third of all senators are appointed by the king for five-year terms, and seats for a final third have remained vacant, to be filled by provincial councils which have yet to be created. The 1964 constitution grants wakils and senators wide parliamentary immunities and permits them to establish the procedures for their respective houses. The document specifies that members of the shura be able to read and write, though the scarcity of literate individuals in the provinces—in a nation where less than 10% have had any formal schooling—obliges the lower house to overlook the doubtful literacy of many members. Aside from several legislators who represent Afghanistan's two million nomads and a large eastern border tribe, the Shinwari, candidates for the Wolesi Jirgah run in single-member districts drawn with little concern for the principle of "one man, one vote." Thus Kabul province, with the largest estimated population of 1.3 million, had the same number of deputies (13) elected to the lower house in 1969 as did Paktia province with 732,000 inhabitants and Herat province with only 680,000. In Parwan province the (1964) constitution required a population of 880,000 to elect five wakils, while in Nimroz province, 120,000 inhabitants were sufficient to elect an equal number.[6] In general, the population imbalances exaggerate the already enormous disadvantage in representation felt by the nation's modest urban and educated population. Moreover, the apportionment, as we observe more closely below, most benefits those areas with heavy Pashtun majorities.

The Wolesi Jirgah badly defaults as a legislating body. The constitution calls for the shura to be in session for at least seven months of the year; in recent years, however, the lower house has seldom managed to aggregate more than a month's time at work. Members either remain in the provinces, engaged in constituency and personal business, or are preoccupied with the same matters in Kabul's government offices. By contrast with the Meshrano Jirgah, whose appointed members usually assure the upper chamber a quorum and reasonably focused discussions, sessions of the Wolesi Jirgah are regularly bogged down in procedural questions and personal squabbles. Chances of drawing a quorum—which requires two-thirds of the membership in the lower house—improve with the scheduled appearance of the prime minister and his cabinet for a question hour. Otherwise, only the introduction of a motion of no confidence or a discussion of alleged government intimidation of a member is likely to attract many wakils to a plenary session (see Weinbaum, 1972: 63).

The same lopsided legislative majorities that have on six occasions confirmed the king's designate for prime minister assume an adversary role once the government has taken office. Most wakils resent the prerogatives of high government officials and are suspicious of executive intentions to subvert the powers of the legislature. The executive has found few legislators who will openly rise to its defense in the chamber or who will commit themselves as a bloc to the government. At best the prime minister musters what influence he has with wakils to deny a quorum when the lower house appears on the verge of a debate or vote embarrassing to the government. The Afghan cabinet expects little more from the shura each year than the passage of a budget and approval of pending foreign loan agreements. For the few pieces of major legislation that require prompt enact-ment, the prime minister relies on the king's constitutional power to issue decrees while the shura is in formal recess. Even this route can be obstructed if the Wolesi Jirgah chooses later to amend decrees—a fate suffered by vital education and municipal government legislation in the late 1960s.

The failure of the lower house to develop the cohesion and institutional norms necessary for orderly legislative processes is often attributed to the absence of political parties. A law legalizing parties was passed by both houses in 1969 but remains unsigned by the king. Recent governments and the royal court are openly apprehensive that incipient parties of Marxist youth, ultranationalists, and reac-tionary mullahs will profit most from a law permitting direct appeals to Afghan voters. The regime at first had pinned its hopes for a democratic party system on the appearance of one or more mod-erate, nonideological groups which could, once parties were legalized, rally voters and deputies to the government's view. An attempt by a former prime minister, Mohammad Maiwandwal, to build a person-ally loyal government party ran into bureaucratic resistance and the king's displeasure. In general, encouragement by the government of middle-of-the-road groups has been inconsistent and ineffectual. The difficulty lies not so much in the weak organizing skills of middle-class intellectuals as in the lack of national issues and incentives adequate to override traditional divisions and personal interests. Many progressives believe that the regime has delayed too long in implementing the party law. The expectation that a partisan-led shura might reduce the present anarchy of the lower chamber and stimulate organization by urban interests has been replaced by the fear that a multifactional system will transform the presently uncoor-dinated maneuvering of wakils for political favors into an open competition for scarce resources among historically antagonistic so-cial and ethnic elements. The Wolesi Jirgah has performed remark-ably well in deflecting these factors. Periodically, issues do emerge that expose the tenuous agreements and even threaten to upset the delicate formulas. Political parties could provide the vehicle that would finally overwhelm the shura and other national institutions with the country's unresolved ethnic and tribal problems.

ETHNICITY IN THE WOLESI JIRGAH

The practices of the lower house often seem guided by the doctrine of the concurrent majority. While no major national constituency has the right of a veto, the vital interests of the larger ethnic and regional groups are granted safeguards. The formal and informal procedures of the Wolesi Jirgah are, moreover, intended to assuage intergroup conflict, even at the price of legislative immobilism. The norms of the lower chamber permit members to act as staunch advocates of regional or sectarian causes, but at the same time inhibit any suggestion of incompatibility between subnational elements. Even though debates are often intemperate, particularly when the chamber is challenged by one of its two avowed Marxists, the deputies carefully avoid direct references to members' social origins. The sensitivity to regional and ethnic balance is also reflected in the lower house's requirements that each of the 28 provinces be represented on the credentials committee and that seats on any of the chamber's 15 standing committees be open to any province's wakils. In practice only the more prestigious committees, such as Legislation and Legal Affairs, Finance, Education, and International Relations, draw close to their full complement of legislators, but the chamber leaves it to the wakils from each province to decide who among them will stand for election to particular committees.

The formal rules provide that resolutions and proceedings be recorded in both Dari and Pashto. Yet speeches in the chamber are not simultaneously translated, helping to maintain the fiction that no Afghan legislator is ignorant of the national tongue. (In fact the number of wakils with no working knowledge of Pashto probably runs higher than 70). The impractical quorum rule is perhaps the best instrument of the concurrent majority. Besides assuring that no legislation can pass without broadly representative support, the quorum rule grants any sizable minority in the Wolesi Jirgah the power to bring legislative business to a halt. The practical effect, then, is to deny the Pashtun majority an opportunity to enact bills without appreciable non-Pashtun backing. Thus, undisputed Pashtun preeminence in the lower house provides no assurance of Pashtun legislative control.

TABLE 3.1

WOLESI JIRGAH REPRESENTATION BY ETHNIC GROUP: TWELFTH–THIRTEENTH PARLIAMENTS

	Twelfth Parliament	Thirteenth Parliament
Pashtun	139	131
North	58	51
South	81	80
Tajik	35	17
Hazara	10	15
Farsiwan	3	2
Qizil-bash	2	4
Aimaq	7	10
Uzbek	4	15
Turkoman	1	3
Baluch	2	3
Nuristani	1	1
Pashai	1	1
Shugni	1	
Sayyid		5
Khawaja		2
Ismailiya		2
Moghol		1
Sikh		1
Total for which ethnic data available	206	213
	(10 missing)	(3 missing)
	Non-Pashtun total: 67	Non-Pashtun total: 82

Source: Dupree (1971b: 15). Reprinted by permission of American Universities Field Staff Reports.

Wakils identifiable as Pashtuns account for almost 62% of those elected in 1969 to the thirteenth Shura. As Table 3.1 indicates, however, the 131 constitute an absolute decline from the twelfth Shura, most of it occurring in the northern provinces. The largest gains in 1969 were registered by the Uzbek, the Aimaq, and the Hazara groups. Several smaller ethnic and sectarian communities also added wakils or were newly represented in the lower house. Tajiks suffered the sharpest decline in membership, from 35 to 17 legislators. Dupree interprets the Tajik loss as resulting from the election of many Pashtun tribal chiefs who were no longer content to have Tajiks speak for them in Kabul (Dupree, 1971a: 6). A seat in the Wolesi Jirgah has understandably grown in attractiveness to local notables as the possible benefits of direct intervention with central authorities have become more visible. This same new awareness may explain the increased spread in ethnic representation, although at least in some cases in 1969 a contender identified with a smaller ethnic minority owed his victory to a bare plurality in a heavily crowded field of aspirants.

Figure 3.1 depicts the sectional character of Pashtun representation in the Wolesi Jirgah during the thirteenth Shura. (The shaded areas are intended to show the proportion of Pashtun and non-Pashtun representation and not their geographic concentration in each province.) Aside from Nimroz Province, at least two-thirds of all wakils in the 10 southern provinces—for a total of 80 of the region's 89 seats—were held by Pashtuns; and two neighboring northern provinces, Kunar and Laghman, had nearly exclusive Pashtun representation. Overall, Pashtuns held a strong edge in seats throughout the north; in only four provinces of this region were Pashtuns absent.[7]

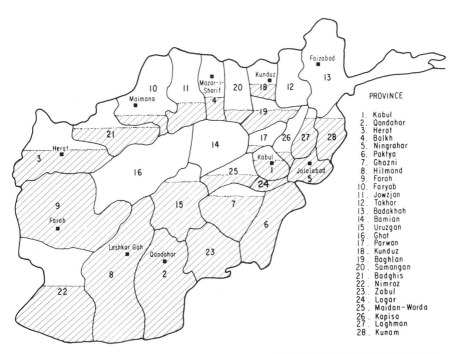

PROVINCE

1. Kabul
2. Qandahar
3. Herat
4. Balkh
5. Ningrahar
6. Paktya
7. Ghazni
8. Hilmand
9. Farah
10. Faryab
11. Jowzjan
12. Takhar
13. Badakhah
14. Bamian
15. Uruzgan
16. Ghot
17. Parwan
18. Kunduz
19. Baghlan
20. Samangan
21. Badghis
22. Nimroz
23. Zabul
24. Logar
25. Maidan-Warda
26. Kapisa
27. Laghman
28. Kunam

Figure 3.1: THE PROPORTIONAL DISTRIBUTION OF PASHTUN AND NONPASHTUN DEPUTIES BY PROVINCE

Key: The shaded portions indicate the percentage of Pashtun representation.

One basis for a possible overrepresentation of Pashtuns is the apportionment bias, described above, that favors more thinly populated provinces. However, an examination of representation in all 28 provinces seems to negate this proposition. Assuming, for the purposes of analysis, that districts within each province are reasonably equal in population,[8] Pashtun wakils represent an average of 69,000 constituents and non-Pashtuns roughly 65,000. This finding of a slight *under*representation of districts that chose Pashtun legislators is perhaps not surprising since Pashtun wakils are elected in some of the nation's heaviest as well as most sparsely populated provinces. But even when the 10 least populated provinces are isolated, the pattern is unchanged. Districts that averaged 40,000 people elected 23 non-Pashtun legislators, while 39 districts that chose Pashtuns had an average of 46,000 constituents.

Any advantage to the Pashtuns in the apportionment of seats for the lower house must be a sectional bias. The 10 southern provinces, plus Laghman and Kunar provinces, areas believed to have the highest proportion of Pashtun settlement, embrace an estimated total population of 5.85 million as against the rest of the country with 9.7 million. Leaving aside the nondistricted nomadic and Shinwari tribal wakils, the 93 legislators elected in 1969 from the 12 mainly southern provinces represented an average of 63,000 people. The remaining 123 deputies from 16 provinces were elected in districts that averaged an appreciably more numerous 79,000 constituents. Even in the absence of reliable ethnic population figures, it is probably safe to conclude that Pashtuns are numerically better represented in the Wolesi Jirgah.[9]

The data on ethnic backgrounds assembled by Dupree's research team also points up the heterogeneity of Pashtun membership in the lower house. At least 39 different Pashtun tribes and subtribes could be identified (Dupree, 1971a: 17). Most prominent were several divisions of the Durrani and Ghilzai tribes, Afghanistan's royal tribes and the prime competitors for national ascendance since the eighteenth century. Better than two of every three legislators elected in 1969 who could be linked to a Pashtun tribe belonged to one of these two groups.

Because Afghanistan's several major ethnic and tribal groups have been largely content with their local suzerainty, their representatives have typically shrunk from tampering with the status quo. The Wolesi Jirgah has managed to ignore or finesse most potentially divisive ethnic questions. Bills approved by the lower house that were likely to shift power, such as laws affecting municipalities and provincial councils, won the acceptance of wakils only because both pieces of legislation promised common gains at the expense of the Kabul government. Similarly, little opposition was heard in the lower chamber during a 1970 debate on an election law amendment—like the municipal and provincial council laws still awaiting the king's signature—that would further diminish the proportion of seats in the Wolesi Jirgah going to Kabul, Herat, and other population centers. Naturally, most wakils welcomed a provision that would augment the representation of more conservative areas. Should the central government's resources grow and its ability to implement policies in the provinces improve, tribal and ethnic groups are certain to find increased value in legislative office.

The Wolesi Jirgah departed most radically from its cautious ethnic policies in an amendment to the civil service law in mid-1972 (passed two years earlier in a royal decree) that proposed to deny government employment to those who could not speak *both* Dari and Pashto. If enacted, the provision would immediately slow the recruitment of non-Pashtuns and give a decided advantage to bilingual Pashtuns who have not in recent years kept pace with the rising number of educated members of other ethnic groups entering the bureaucracy.[10] Afghan governments have regularly drawn criticism in the shura for their alleged indifference to the popularization of the Pashto language. What set the language controversy of 1972 apart from earlier debates was the participation of the chamber's most respected wakils and the clear division it drew on an issue that raises awkward questions—not only about the meaning of a national language but about the essence of Afghan identity. Only once before, during the 1949–53 parliamentary term, had legislators sorted themselves out along linguistic lines, a development that no doubt hastened the demise of that first liberalization period.

The executive at first welcomed and—some suspect—instigated the civil service amendment in the hope of distracting the lower house from mounting criticisms of government policies—on Pashtunistan, in the wake of Pakistan's loss of its eastern territory, and also on food distribution policies following a disastrous year of drought and floods. The wakils were also conspiring to remove the shura's confidence from two ministers. Because the language issue pitted wakil against wakil, it broke a pattern of recent years where legislators had regularly closed ranks against the executive. Before long, however, the government was obliged to block a quorum in the Wolesi Jirgah in order to quiet acrimonious debate that had encouraged ethnic chauvinists outside the shura. It required a parliamentary summer recess and a government fiat prohibiting continued discussion of the issue in the press—in the name of national unity—to return the language question to its customary political limbo.

Specific complaints of regional, ethnic, and linguistic discrimination cannot be similarly eschewed from parliamentary debate. No occasion has proven more propitious for their presentation than the extended speeches that until 1972 preceded the confirmation of every government. Legislators had regularly taken the opportunity, made especially appealing by nationwide radio coverage, to allege government abuse of power and neglect of constituency problems. Deputies typically have spoken with conviction of inadequate educational and public health facilities or the slow pace of local economic development. But rarely have their remarks touched on pending or probable legislation. To the extent that wakils dealt with demands made against the central government, it was almost wholly of a personal and particular nature, requiring their intercession as brokers or advocates rather than as lawmakers.

FUNCTIONS OF LEGISLATURES

LEGISLATORS AS MEDIATORS

Afghan tradition reserves a valued place for those who serve the community as middlemen. The notion that elders of the family or tribe should accept responsibility for mediating interpersonal conflicts is well established in the practices of tribal jirgahs. In a similar vein, individuals who are anxious to approach those in high authority, particularly agents of a central government, are expected to seek the intercession of designated persons, typically the natural leaders of their family and community. Wide differences of status and function are seen as most easily bridged by individuals adept at routinizing and personalizing petitions. To disregard their good offices is to invite uncertainty and to chance embarrassment. Thus, a citizen who acts entirely on his own behalf runs the risk of rejection or, worse still, having his actions interpreted as disrespect for those in authority.

The Afghan legislator has seized claim to the role of intermediary with the Kabul government and provincial officials. His social position and the opportunities inherent through the parliamentary system make him a logical choice. Dupree estimates that at least two-thirds of the legislators in the lower house are members of a local elite (Dupree, 1971a: 4, 11). All but a few wakils are identifiable (see Appendix, page 121) as *khan* (tribal chief), *malik* (village head), religious leader, prosperous merchant, teacher, and minor government official—all roles traditionally suited to mediating activity. As one deputy observed: "People make little distinction between their wakil and other local influentials. He may be someone who is feared and disliked, but he is needed and is willing to be helpful—for a price."[11]

To aspire to the position of wakil is in itself evidence of prestige and wealth. A campaign gives the candidate ample opportunity to demonstrate his largesse by the purchase of voters' meals, transport, and even ballots. Legislators are accustomed to requests to intercede where constituents have run afoul of the law or to help settle family quarrels. Ultimately, however, it is by the deputy's actions in the national parliament that he best validates his claims as community broker and advocate. In the view of a deputy from Kabul: "Most of my colleagues are already locally prominent in their cities and villages. But they become something more when they can call themselves 'wakils.' For they are then informing their constituents that they have friends in high places in Kabul."

A wakil is expected to treat petitioners cordially and, where called for, to extend his hospitality by offering food and temporary lodgings. Legislators are prepared to find constituents camped in their courtyard or their business establishment and to be accosted in any public place. Speaking of the steady stream of petitioners who approach legislators, one wakil insisted: "The people have a right to ask their deputies for help, and deputies have a similar right to go to [government] offices to assist people. This will continue to be necessary until laws are enforced equally for everyone without discrimination."

Another wakil commented: "I am the most obvious person for people to come to—and they hound me. There are other channels— the governors, the ministries, and the parliamentary petitions committee—but the deputy is the most useful man if he is on your side."

Those constituents who attempt a direct appeal to government offices or who use the mediation of a shura committee are almost inevitably drawn into a protracted process of case review. Not infrequently, an administrator will bluntly inform a petitioner to send his wakil (the term also means "barrister" in Persian) or to return with a letter of introduction. A high-level bureaucrat admitted: "We will politely hear out individuals who come in without their wakil. In all honesty, though, the man who has his wakil as a sponsor has a better chance of getting what he wants and far more speedily."

A legislator's success in facilitating contacts and satisfying requests naturally enhances his reputation locally and creates individual and family debts that can be redeemed at any time—notably in a reelection effort. But many wakils also insist on more immediate and material compensation for their services. Fees and salary kickbacks may be demanded in payment. And it is not uncommon for a wakil to insist on a share in any monetary gains realized through his intercessions in Kabul or elsewhere. According to a veteran legislator: "Typically the deputy is for himself. He takes a cut of most of the favors he does for constituents and he, in turn, must share it up the line. Few deputies are truly concerned with legislation and policy; most have not the slightest interest."

In broad terms, the wakils' mediations on behalf of constituents fall into three classes. The first involves the transmission to the national level of adjudications that have either been unresolved locally or that have not been settled to the satisfaction of the deputy or his client. Legislators are drawn into attempts to overrule judgments of provincial courts, and the rulings of local administrators are in effect appealed to higher authorities, as familiarly occurs in disagreements over tax levies. On occasion, a Kabul ministry may be asked simply to remove a decision from the hands of a provincial official. A second but related category of pleadings involves efforts to win special consideration for petitioners. Legislators are regularly asked to assist in a promotion or transfer of a government employee or to help arrange a military reassignment. Requests to expedite a business transaction with a government agency are common; indeed, legislators are asked to deal with requests for exemptions from virtually every kind of government regulation. Third, the deputy appears as a constituency advocate, championing its cause in the constant competition for attention and scarce resources. He is expected to plead the constituency's case publicly and to prod the appropriate ministers privately for approval, for example, for a new school, an improved road, or a water supply system. The plea of one deputy is not atypical: "We have a responsibility to the people to improve their health condition. In Bamian there had been no medicine for six months. The friendly foreigners finally provided some. In

Kabul there is medicine, but in Bamian we practice blood-letting and dress ourselves in special animal skins to cure our diseases."

Although legislators usually insist that their time is consumed in all three classes of interventions, the pursuit of general benefits is seldom carried on with the same perseverance as the quest for individual gain.

Wakils find easy access to the highest levels of officialdom in the capital. A request to meet with the prime minister is rarely refused, though it warrants an appointment through his parliamentary liaison secretary. Visits to other cabinet officials require no prior notice; a wakil merely announces himself at the office of the minister and waits to be seen. The legislator's normal refusal to bring petitions before subordinate officials is understandable in a bureaucracy where significant authority is infrequently delegated and insecure lesser officials often shun responsibility. The provincial elite status of most legislators also discourages contacts with secondary officials, many of whom are the poorly paid sons of upwardly mobile urban families. Furthermore, only government ministers are directly accountable to the shura. Rudeness and obvious indifference to wakils' demands invite certain retaliation. Legislative approval of a budget allows vindictive deputies to eliminate ministry jobs and programs and to deny pay raises and equipment—including such items as new office furniture and cars. Offended deputies will harangue ministers during a question hour and in several cases have introduced motions of no confidence.

The ministers' often solicitous attitude toward legislators is a natural consequence of the government's precarious position in the shura. Lacking a dependable majority, the executive branch has little choice but to try to curry support with favors. In the view of an elected leader of the lower house: "The government constantly complains that deputies keep them from their work and are a general annoyance. But the fact is that many government officials prefer to have them around in order to create obligations." A deputy was quoted in the press as saying: "Officials intentionally create problems for the people so that their deputies must go there asking for help" (Daily Caravan, March 23, 1970).

Recent prime ministers have deliberately chosen their cabinets on a regional basis in the hope that ministers would develop a legislative clientele—a policy that seeks to capitalize on the affinity many wakils feel for administrators of like ethnic or regional background. The same commitment to a strategy of personal persuasion is reflected in the prime minister's willingness to hear the appeal of every legislator who believes he has been wronged by a minister.

Despite all its efforts, the government is forced to settle for fickle ad-hoc legislative alliances. While the executive repeatedly overestimates the pliability of wakils, its ministers have not proven adept in extracting promises from them. Government offices fail to keep systematic records of favors dispensed or to report them to the prime ministry. Endemic bureaucratic practices account for much of the communications breakdown, but ministers are also naturally disinclined to reveal agreements with wakils where they have mutually profited. And the cabinet's few technocrats are no more anxious to disclose concessions that so often blatantly compromise rationally conceived policies.

Political expediency and even personal gain cannot entirely explain the Afghan administrator's generous accommodation of the legislator. Despite complaints about the distractions of petitions and the shura's inertia, most government officials acknowledge the legitimacy of a wakil's activities. Policy makers grudgingly admit that the aggressive, independent legislator is an unavoidable antidote to a weakly coordinated and often unresponsive administrative structure. The executive has few illusions about the limits of legislators' commitment to constituency interests. But in the absence of more sensitive monitors of national demands and reliable checks against administrative injustices, the regime tolerates a breed of legislator whose motives and legislative styles assure that the Wolesi Jirgah will be unsuitable as a law-making institution.

LEGISLATIVE ORIENTATIONS

The Wolesi Jirgah owes much of its reputation to the presence of between 75 and 90 members who are best described as the "entrepreneurs." As conceived by these wakils, shura credentials are an invitation to come to Kabul for the purpose of doing business—especially of a self-serving nature. Accordingly, the entrepreneur feels little compulsion to attend sessions of the lower chamber. His affairs take him to the ministries and elsewhere in the capital, or prompt his frequent return home. At heart the entrepreneur is a provincial and apolitical creature. He learns little of parliamentary practices and conceives of his vote as a negotiable commodity. The joining of entrepreneurs with other members to criticize government actions is intended to remind officials of the shura's power to punish. Almost to a man, the entrepreneurs are a conservative lot, anxious to preserve the web of relationships and the privileged status that have enabled them to profit handsomely under the 1964 Constitution.

The "institutionalists" represent a sharply contrasting legislative type. Numbering no more than six to eight members in the present chamber—fewer than in the previous parliament—their behavior as wakils often seems patterned after Western models. Though members of this group vary in their attentiveness to local problems and their personal interests, they all view themselves as representative of a national as well as a local constituency. The ranks of the institutionalists include members of the lower house with the most extensive educations and the widest contacts within Kabul's foreign community. Nearly all have won election from urban constituencies. They comprise the most active and efficient element in parliamentary debates and on committees. Colleagues have named institutionalists to serve in the Wolesi Jirgah's secretariat and to chair its major committees, though more in recognition of their parliamentary skills than in agreement with their political views, for most institutionalists are moderate socialists, advocates of economic reforms and pluralistic democracy. Understandably, then, the frustrations of a shura that can neither enact general legislation nor advance their national ambitions has left the institutionalists without a meaningful political role.

Another set of wakils can rightly be labeled the "ideologues." Besides the chamber's two Marxists, they include eight to ten mullahs and religious zealots and a somewhat larger number of ultra-nationalists. For all of them, the Wolesi Jirgah offers a useful but far from ideal platform from which to bring pressure on policy makers and educate the public. Most ideologues participate energetically in debates and are at the forefront in attacks against the executive. At least several have considerable familiarity with Western parliamentary practices. Yet few if any ideologues are instrumentalists; their demands for legislation are largely intended to raise the level of doctrinal awareness outside the shura rather than work for legislatively produced change. Like the institutionalists, they speak to a national constituency, and much of their time is shared with giving direction to political movements and protoparties of the left or right. While none would disclaim a responsibility for looking after his electoral constituency, ideologues have frequently been criticized on these grounds.

A fourth category of wakils, the "agents," resemble the chamber's entrepreneurs in their dedication to parochial concerns and in their evasion of a programmatic role. Nevertheless, agents are, at least by degree, distinguishable from entrepreneurs by the priority they give to representational activities on behalf of individuals and groups. As such the agents, who account for from 40% to 50% of the Wolesi Jirgah's membership, most nearly qualify as full-time intermediaries. Although not disdainful of the petitions of ordinary citizens, agents are preoccupied with mediations on behalf of locals of higher status than themselves or as spokesmen for families, tribes, and their constituencies. Legislators have also been cultivated by the nation's few urban economic and professional groups. But regardless of the client, the stakes in administrative decisions typically overshadow those in legislative actions. Agents and entrepreneurs alike appreciate that their leverage with the bureaucracy rests on the existence of a freely elected parliament, but not necessarily an active one.

The Wolesi Jirgah's largely distinctive role orientations follow neither ethnic nor regional lines. Agents and entrepreneurs are found among wakils of every origin, and ideologues and institutionalists come from more than a single group. Aggressive and opportunistic legislators are identifiable in all four types, though the focus of ambition for entrepreneurs and agents is more localized. Formal education and an urban background appear to set apart the small contingent of institutionalists, but not from the chamber's Marxists. Both institutionalists and ideologues are influenced, moreover, by imported ideas and values. More significantly, the divergent orientations point up motivational differences that help to explain the shura's sluggish and often confusing behavior. At the same time, the orientations illustrate the convergent interests of the great majority of legislators and the nation's provincial elites. Only incidentally do wakils also appear as intermediaries for the nonelite.

CONCLUSIONS

Afghanistan's democracy has never delivered its promised full freedom of the press and the right to assemble. All the same, the regime's decisions to relax controls over elections and to widen the scope of permissible dissent have brought two profound changes in the nation's politics. One has been the radicalization of an expanding student population and early signs of mobilization in other sectors of the society; the other has been the entry of provincial notables into decisional realms once reserved for minions of the royal family. The first development is potentially more destabilizing, though probably not threatening as long as it remains confined to the major cities and is free of serious interference from foreign powers. However, the sharing of national authority with the nation's local centers of power, institutionalized in the Wolesi Jirgah, has already resulted in decision processes which cast doubt about the system's capacity for planned social and economic growth.

A liberal, representative system has created a paradox for Afghanistan which it shares with many other developing nations that have resolved to work within a democratic framework. The very parliamentary freedoms that appear requisite to the building of a legitimate, authoritative state release forces that are largely resistant to a change in national goals. In the presence of a weakly integrated society, parliamentary democracy in the Middle East has always allowed the ascendance of the least progressive, most privileged classes and interests.

The formation of a largely open electoral system in Afghanistan was not inevitable. The royal court could have indefinitely maintained its paternalistic reign, hand-picking its parliaments and stifling its critics. However, what the regime could not expect to accomplish by retaining the status quo was to extend its power to govern effectively beyond the major population centers, or to transform a traditional society. For two decades Afghan governments have encouraged the migration of talented and progressive people to the capital. The absence of just such a clientele in the 1920s had doomed the plans of King Amanullah to force a Westernization of the nation. By the 1960s a sizable modernizing elite in Kabul assured King Zahir of a sympathetic bureaucracy and a likely source of ideas and leadership. He could rely on his Soviet-trained and equipped army to bar an insurrection from the provinces such as toppled Amanullah in 1929. But after nearly a decade under the new constitution, it remains clear that any pervasive reforms initiated from the center require the passive approval, if not the active cooperation, of tribal, ethnic, and religious leaders.

The constitution's framers calculated that the responsibilities of legislative office and an exposure to national leadership would impress provincial notables and their surrogates with the potential benefits of collaboration in national development. A noncoercive approach to breaking down localism may have been, in any case, impossible. But the regime's refusal to authorize political parties removed what little chance there may have been to evolve a parliamentary leadership or to generate incentives for nontraditional political alignments. Once wakils were given time to style legislative roles that compensated them generously for individual efforts in mediation and enterprise, there was little likelihood that they would submit to parliamentary discipline and accept the distractions of law making. Moreover, the regime's hesitation to implement several pieces of legislation considered integral parts of the constitutional reform convinced many wakils that the government had no serious intention of allowing the shura to operate freely. Members of the lower house found it easier to influence policy formation by frustrating government legislative designs, including the holding of bills in ransom for favors in the ministries. Most wakils have concluded that a legislative moratorium works no special disadvantages to their community or personal interests. The irony of it all is that recent improvements in education and communications and the sufferance of a shura that articulates local grievances and fears has apparently set back the cause of national integration. In the presence of a series of indecisive governments and an often aloof king, the changes set in motion in 1964 have reinforced the allegiances of most subnational elements. While this assertion of ethnic and regional loyalties and sensitivities is perhaps only a transitional stage in a process of discovering a national identity, the usually slow pace of social change in Afghanistan suggests a lengthy period of disunity.

This chapter reveals the Afghan legislator as the prime actor in the modus operandi that has emerged since 1964. Without question, the wakil best embodies the local elites' penetration of national decision arenas, and he has carried most of the burden of communications between the periphery and center. His activities, we find, have attracted notable societal and interinstitutional supports. And yet the parliamentary system which promotes the legislators' roles is highly fragile and its survival in doubt. The constitution is endangered only secondarily from the heavy backlog of demands that await legislative action because Afghanistan appears to have a remarkable capacity to leave problems unresolved without passing on to national crises. Undoubtedly, low political participation extends the reaction time available to decision makers, but this may be changing as the Afghan masses gradually gain an awareness that their personal hardships can have political solutions. More in a feudal than a revolutionary way, however, nonelites are initially likely to vent their anger against distant authority rather than to hold local notables accountable. If the curtain falls on Afghan parliamentary democracy, it will probably be executed after a sober decision by the royal family, the military, or both in concert. In order to constrict the influence now enjoyed by local influentials, the new system will of necessity be a highly repressive one—with no immediate use for a parliament. A failure of the Afghan shura and the experiment it represents will still leave students of parliaments uncertain, however, whether failure results from an incomplete test—that is, the absence of legalized political parties and the want of adroit national leaders— or whether the legislature was an inappropriate institution in which to entrust any responsibilities for national integration and modernization.

NOTES

1. Fairly comprehensive demographic figures are contained in Wilber (1962: 36–65) and Gregorian (1969: 25–43). However, the enormous discrepancies in population estimates for Pashtuns and other ethnic groups suggest that all population statistics are at best educated guesses. For example, the Afghan Ministry of Planning estimates that the nation's total population in 1972 was 17.8 million while most foreign experts working in Afghanistan insist that it runs between 12 and 15 million. Official government figures place the Pashtun population at 65.5% of all Afghans. The Soviet Academy of Sciences in 1960 estimated the number of Pashtuns at 50%, and a briefing book for employees of USAID (1970: 1) gives the total as 35–45%. Statistics for the Tajiks, Hazaras, and other groups vary widely, depending on the author's definition of ethnic boundaries. Probably the most widely quoted set of estimates is provided by Arez (1970); his figures are the basis for analyses in this essay.

2. The birth of a modern Afghan state is usually placed at 1747, the year when a chief of the Durrani tribe won the allegiance of most of the region's leaders in a loose tribal federation. Prior to this time the area had been repeatedly subjugated and ravaged by foreign invaders. During the nineteenth century the British managed the nation's foreign affairs and kept many tribes subservient to its interests through regular subsidies. Amir Abdur Rahman Khan brought a degree of centralization to the country at the end of the century with raids against dissident tribal and ethnic elements. Only once, however, did the Durrani tribe relinquish control of the monarchy. A Persian-speaking bandit, Bacha Saquo, riding the wave of conservative discontent with the projected reforms of the reigning King Amanullah, seized the crown for nine months during 1929.

3. King Nadir had approved a law that specified that only a Loya Jirgah could amend the constitution. Nadir also gave formal assurances to tribal leaders that they would be asked to approve any new taxes, modernization plans, or radical departures in foreign policy. It was further agreed that a Loya Jirgah should be convened every four years. Of necessity the royal family consulted regularly with tribal chiefs, but King Zahir failed entirely to honor the promise that the Loya Jirgah would meet on a regular basis. The Loya Jirgah remained alive as an institution, however, both for its value in time of national emergency (as occurred at the beginning of World War II) and, as one scholar observes, because it "served to institutionalize the supremacy of the Afghan [Pashtun] ethnic element over the non-Afghan elements" (Gregorian, 1969: 305).

4. The second Yousef government lasted only three days. It was brought down by student rioting in protest over the alleged corruption of holdover members of the new cabinet. The king then named Mohammad Hashin Maiwandwal, a former ambassador to the

United States, to head a new government. Under the 1964 Constitution, members of the royal family are prohibited from assuming parliamentary or government offices.

5. A vivid description of the conduct of the 1969 elections in the provinces is found in Dupree (1971b: 10–15). The author documents the outright interference of government agents in one district where former Prime Minister Maiwandwal attempted unsuccessfully to make a political comeback through election to the Wolesi Jirgah.

6. Elections to the lower house in 1969 were never held in one district of Nimroz province and canceled in single districts of Qandahar and Kapisa provinces, all as a result of tribal feuding (Dupree, 1971a: 10).

7. Identification of wakils by ethnic and tribal origins (Dupree, 1971: 10) was obtained for all but three members of the Wolesi Jirgah by a team of Afghans supervised by Dr. Dupree. The data was acquired with great difficulty, since official reference sources are badly incomplete and many wakils are reluctant to divulge ethnic information.

8. This mode of analysis is necessitated by the absence of reliable data on district (woleswali) size. That there is relative population equality among districts in the same province is not an unreasonable assumption, however. The available information indicates that interprovince variance among districts is customarily greater.

9. The tendency for government agencies to exaggerate the number of people in Pashtun-dominated areas probably means that the bias is in fact understated by the figures presented here.

10. One Pashtun nationalist claims that only 15,000 of about 70,000 civil servants are Pashtun and that Pashtuns hold inferior positions in the ministries. While his statistics are unsupported by any documentation and are disputed by most observers, this commentator's conclusion that only a small portion of government officials have a good knowledge of Pashto is probably correct (Ulfat, 1972: 2–4). In the Ministry of Education, Ulfat claims, neither of the two deputy ministers and only 3 or 4 of the 78 director generals can speak Pashto with any fluency.

11. This statement and those following are taken from interviews conducted during 1970 with a sample of incumbent and former legislators. The four legislative role categories presented in the next section are based on the full set of interviews and were refined in additional interviews with legislators, ministry officials, academicians, and journalists in the summer of 1972.

REFERENCES

AREZ, J. A. (1970) The Kabul Times Annual. Kabul: Government Printing House.
      The Daily Caravan. Kabul.
DUPREE, L. (1971a) "Comparative profiles of recent parliaments in Afghanistan: 1971." American Universities Field Staff Reports 15, 4 (July): 1–35.
——— (1971b) "Afghanistan continues its experiment in democracy." American Universities Field Staff Reports 15, 3 (July): 10–15.
GREGORIAN, V. (1969) The Emergence of Modern Afghanistan. Stanford, Calif.: Stanford Univ. Press.
NEWELL, R. S. (1972) The Politics of Afghanistan. Ithaca, N.Y.: Cornell Univ. Press.
ULFAT, A. (1972) Commentary. Kabul: Afghan Millat. Also in Caravan Translations (July 29): 2–4.
U.S. Agency for International Development (1970) Briefing Book. Kabul: Communications Media Office.
WEINBAUM, M. W. (1972) "Afghanistan: nonparty parliamentary democracy." Journal of Developing Areas 7 (Oct.): 57–74.
WILBER, D. (1962) Afghanistan. New Haven, Conn.: Human Area Files.

APPENDIX
AGE/OCCUPATION PROFILES: TWELFTH–THIRTEENTH PARLIAMENTS: WOLESI JIRGAH (LOWER HOUSE)

Age

	25–35	36–45	46–55	56–65	66+
12th	41	79	28	12	3
13th	39	77	38	13	2

Occupation

	Religious Leaders	Education Admin.	Teachers	Kabul U. Teachers	Government Admin.	Newspaper Publisher	Provincial Officials	Tax Collectors	Mayors	Asst. Mayors	Senator	Municipal Officials	M.D.	Judges	Police	Military (Rtd.)	Business	Cabinet Minister	Journalist	HAVA[a]	Banker	Provincial Consult.[b]	Total for which Data Available—Age	Total for which Data Available—Occupation
12th	25	5	7	4	5	1	2		3	2			1	1	1	4	4		3	2	1	2	163	70
13th	21	3	8	3	9		6	2	4	2	1	2		1	1	4	10	1	1	2	1	4	167	87

Source: Dupree (1971b: 13). Reprinted by permission of American Universities Field Staff Reports.

a. Hillmand-Arghandab Valley Authority.

b. An appointive position, the local adviser to the provincial governor, usually a member of the local power elite.

Chapter 4

CONFLICT MANAGEMENT AND POLITICAL INSTITUTIONAL-
IZATION IN SOCIALIST YUGOSLAVIA: A CASE STUDY
OF THE PARLIAMENTARY SYSTEM

LENARD J. COHEN

In December 1968 the Yugoslav regime enacted a series of constitutional amendments assigning the Federal Assembly a major role as a political arena for the representation of the country's diverse nationality and regional interests. Nominally the Yugoslav state had been operating under a federal system since the formation of the Communist regime in 1945 and had experimented earlier with various institutional arrangements for the formal representation of nationality groups and regional territorial units within the governmental structure. The new constitutional measures, however, represented the first attempt to give the parliamentary system any genuine responsibility for the consideration of internationality and interregional matters. In part, the 1968 amendments gave institutional expression and legitimacy to the reemergence of the "national question" as a major political issue in Yugoslav society.[1] Equally important, the new constitutional provisions reflected the growing importance of the parliamentary system as a center for political decision-making. In the following pages we will attempt to describe and evaluate the operation of the Yugoslav Federal Assembly as a setting for the expression and resolution of ethnic and regional conflicts, focusing particular attention on the operation of the Chamber of Nationalities between 1968 and 1971. In order to do so, however, it is essential to understand the changing significance of the parliamentary system and the nationality issue in the Yugoslav political process.

THE "NATIONAL QUESTION" AND PARLIAMENTARY DEVELOPMENT

In considering the role of the Yugoslav parliamentary system with respect to nationality and regional affairs, it is useful to delineate three broad periods of development. The different character of each period has been shaped primarily by the changing significance of the "national question" in the Yugoslav political process. During the first period from 1945 to 1953, the federal legislature was assigned a largely symbolic function. While serving as a site for the formal representation of nationality groups and the territorial units of the Yugoslav federation, the parliamentary system at this stage was devoid of any real influence on political decision making. In the second period, from 1953 to 1967, the formal responsibilities of the Federal Assembly relating to nationality and regional problems were sharply curtailed, although there was a gradual expansion of parliamentary influence in other areas. The next period, from 1968 to 1971 and the one with which we are most concerned in this chapter, witnessed a significant increase in parliamentary management of ethnic and regional conflicts.

THE FIRST PERIOD: 1945-53

One of the chief claims made by the Communist leadership that assumed power at the end of World War II was its success in having found a solution to the "national question." Skillfully tapping a reservoir of dissatisfaction among Yugoslavia's various ethnic groups which had been generated by the policies of the interwar regime, the Communist party had succeeded in attracting considerable multinational support for the wartime partisan struggle against the Germans and their domestic allies. Centering their appeal around concepts such as equality, brotherhood, and the unity of the Yugoslav peoples, as well as the more tangible promise of a federal system after the war, Tito and his fellow revolutionaries had endeavored to convince the various ethnic groups that the realization of their respective "national" aspirations were linked to a social revolution led by the Communist party. Thus, once having acquired political authority, the Yugoslav Communists attributed their success, with considerable justification, to a correct treatment of the nationality problem.[2]

The constitutional system adopted by the Yugoslav leadership in the early postwar years was designed to demonstrate its achievements in the field of internationality relations. As part of the new federal system, the Constitution of 1946 established a bicameral federal parliament, the People's Assembly, composed of a Chamber of Nationalities, in which each republic had an equal number of representatives, and a second house, the Federal Chamber, elected on the basis of population. The adoption of laws required a simple majority vote in both chambers of the Assembly, the Council of Nationalities formally having equal status with the Federal Chamber. The equal representation of republics in the federal legislature was alleged to express the equality and unity of the Yugoslav nationalities.[3]

It has become almost an axiom of political theory that constitutional documents and formal institutional arrangements are generally better indicators of officially acceptable beliefs and intentions than of the actual way a political system operates. Yugoslavia's federal system and legislative assemblies during this period were no exception. Closely modeled on Soviet institutions and Stalinist practice, the parliamentary system operated essentially as a transmission belt for the ratification of decisions made in the upper echelons of the Communist party and implemented by a highly centralized state apparatus. From 1946 to 1953 the members of the People's Assembly met only twice annually, for extremely short periods, in which they unanimously ratified an enormous number of laws and administrative decisions prepared earlier by the party and state bureaucracies.[4] Those questions which touched upon nationality questions during the period were handled outside of the legislative institutions formally entrusted with these matters. Despite the weakness of the parliamentary system, however, it should be stressed that the structure of governmental institutions at this stage of Yugoslav political development was intended primarily to contrast with the unitary system and ethnic imbalance of the preceding regime. In this respect, the equal representation of the republics and provinces in the Chamber of Nationalities performed an important symbolic function for the new regime (see Pijade, 1950).

THE SECOND PERIOD: 1953–67

During the second period of parliamentary development (1953–67), the formal role of the federal legislature was reduced considerably with respect to nationality affairs. The major reasons for this change can be traced to the general reexamination of goals and methods by the Yugoslav leadership which followed its 1948 rift with the Soviet Union. In an effort to buttress national unity and reaffirm its ideological credentials against pressure and charges of revisionism from the other Communist party states, the Yugoslav regime attempted to downgrade the pluralistic and potentially divisive aspects of its society, emphasizing instead the alleged unity of its class structure. As a result, beginning in the early 1950s party policy, and consequently constitutional theory, stressed the socialist character of Yugoslav society rather than its federative native and multinational composition (Shoup, 1968: 184–89).[5]

In the realm of parliamentary development this change in policy was expressed in the complete reorganization of the Federal Assembly. Under the Constitutional Law of 1953 the position of the Chamber of Nationalities as an independent house of the federal legislature was eliminated. The republics and provinces still sent a fixed number of representatives to the federal legislature (10 from each republic, 6 from Vojvodina, and 4 from Kosovo), but instead of constituting a separate chamber the 70 regional delegates now were merged with 280 other legislators directly elected on the basis of population to form a single house, the Federal Chamber, within the Federal Assembly. Under this encapsulated chamber-within-a-chamber arrangement, the Chamber of Nationalities was to operate as an ad hoc committee of the Federal Chamber for the protection of ethnic and regional rights. The new constitutional provisions authorized the representatives of the republics and provinces in the Federal Chamber to convene separately as a "Chamber of Nationalities" only when the rights of Yugoslavia's nationalities or republics might be threatened, an occurrence which the Yugoslav leadership portrayed as a highly unlikely possibility. In addition to the reorganization of the Chamber of Nationalities, and perhaps more important for subsequent parliamentary development, the Constitutional Law of 1953 established an entirely new federal legislative body, the Chamber of Producers, elected on the basis of economic activity. This last innovation, which preserved the bicameral structure of the legislature, was designed to link the system of workers' councils, established in economic enterprises during the 1950s, directly to the federal structure. As one Dutch observer noted, "the 'working people' made their appearance on the constitutional stage, in competition with the 'peoples' " (Hondius, 1968: 388).

In practice the 1953 reorganization of the federal legislature resulted in the complete atrophy of the Chamber of Nationalities as a political institution.[6] While the Chamber of Nationalities before 1953 had been at least formally independent, having a symbolic function with respect to nationality and regional interests, it was now relegated to a completely secondary position as the Yugoslav leadership began to experiment with various forms of economic representation. According to official Yugoslav policy in this period, the national question had fundamentally been solved, and any problems which might develop in this area would be dealt with more effectively without excessive public attention. The existence of separate ethnic and regional identities was regarded as a vestige of the past which, although likely to persist for some time, would ultimately be erased by the impact of economic change. Over the next 15 years the parliamentary system was used primarily as a forum for the representation of "producers," a strategy aimed at stimulating integration by strengthening bonds of economic interdependence. This is what Yugoslav authors meant in referring to the "integration of the self-managing structure" within the Federal Assembly (see Gerskovic, 1955 and 1967).

It is important to note that despite the curtailment of parliamentary functions in the field of internationality affairs between 1953 and 1967 this second period also witnessed a gradual increase in the overall importance of the Federal Assembly within the political system. The Constitutional Law of 1953 expanded the brief semi-annual meetings of the Federal Assembly into sessions held on a continuous basis throughout the year and significantly broadened the scope of parliamentary activity. The real take-off stage of parliamentary development did not occur, however, until the adoption of a new constitution in 1963. In addition to reorganizing completely the structure of Yugoslav governmental institutions, the changes initiated by the Yugoslav leaders in 1963 represented a serious effort to upgrade the status and influence of the Federal Assembly.[7] A glance at some empirical indicators of change in the activity and composition of the Federal Assembly (Table 4.1) reveals the significant impact of this policy. The most noteworthy features in terms of legislative institutionalization included (1) the increasing scrutiny and control of executive and administrative behavior by parliamentary committees and individual deputies, (2) a greater share of legislative activity by the assembly relative to the executive organs, and (3) the growing specialization of federal legislators in parliamentary affairs. These factors, together with the introduction of multicandidate electoral contests for legislative assemblies and increasing public concern with the activity of parliament reflected the new position of the Federal Assembly as a significant part of Yugoslavia's emerging socialist pluralism.[8]

The most important impetus to the emergence of the parliamentary system as a center for political decision making, however, was the new role of the Yugoslav Communist party in the political process. The transformation of the party after 1952 from a command-oriented revolutionary movement into an "ideological guiding force" (reflected in its new designation as the League of Yugoslav Communists) contributed to the growing institutional autonomy of the parliamentary system. The removal of the League from operational control over broad areas of social and economic activity made the Federal Assembly a focal point for the active consideration of questions which had previously been handled exclusively by top party bodies.[9] Moreover, the devolution of influence to the various republican and provincial organizations within the League of Communists severely limited the party's capacity to act as an integrative mechanism; while Tito and a small number of truly "Yugoslav" political functionaries still provided a cohesive force within the party, the influence of the central party apparatus on the republican and provincial organizations was diminished considerably.[10] It is not surprising, therefore, that when the national question once again assumed serious political importance, the Yugoslav leadership should turn to the parliamentary system as a device through which to channel and contain intergroup conflict.

The mid-1960s witnessed a rapid deterioration in the relationship among Yugoslavia's national and regional groups. The national question reappeared primarily because of the divisive tensions and anxieties released by the process of rapid modernization and the highly uneven pattern of social and economic development among the various regions and nationalities. These difficulties were compounded by the centrifugal pressures of decentralization which accompanied Yugoslav political and economic reforms. The combined impact of these factors, coupled with a history of ethnic controversy, proved to have a more decisive influence on internationality relations than the short-lived solidarity of the wartime liberation movement or the Communist party's effort to manufacture a new, supranational Yugoslav identity in the postwar period. As a consequence, rivalry among the republics and provinces over the distribution of funds for economic investment, disputes about the powers and composition of

TABLE 4.1
POLITICAL INSTITUTIONALIZATION OF THE YUGOSLAV FEDERAL ASSEMBLY: SOME EMPIRICAL INDICATORS

	Jan. 1953–Dec. 1957		Jan. 1958–1963		1963–1967–68	
	No.	%	No.	%	No.	%
I. Parliamentary activity						
A. Sessions of the Federal Assembly	214		140 (Apr. 1963)		376 (Oct. 1968)	
B. Legislative output: Laws, decisions, and other acts adopted by the Federal Assembly	254	15.6	435	28.6	993	55.2
Decisions and regulations adopted by the government (federal Executive Council)	1,373	84.4	1,085	71.4	805	44.8
Total	1,627	100.0	1,520	100.0	1,798	100.0
C. Parliamentary control						
Questions posed by federal deputies to the executive and administration	59		243 (Apr. 1963)		498 (Dec. 1967)	

II. Parliamentary composition

	1953 %	1958 %	1963 %	1965 %	1967 %	1969 %
A. Educational background of federal deputies						
Elementary school or less	46.1	38.0	9.1	7.3	4.3	2.6
Secondary and vocational schools	30.3	31.8	24.6	22.1	20.6	15.1
Higher schools/university faculties	23.6	30.2	66.3	70.6	75.0	82.3
Total	100.0	100.0	100.0	100.0	100.0	100.0
(number)	(554)	(587)	(670)	(670)	(670)	(670)
B. Professionalization: percent of federal deputies who previously served in federal, republican, and provincial assemblies						
Political chambers[a]	66.0	59.8	71.0	78.4	82.6	83.3/69.2[c]
Functional chambers[b]	10.0	18.1	21.7	19.4	21.7	36.7
Total Assembly	45.4	43.3	35.7	36.1	39.0	53.4

Sources: Dokumentacija Savezne skupstine (1953–68); Savezna Narodna Skupstina (Belgrade: "Kultura," 1955); D. Tozi and D. Petrović, "Politički odnosi i sastav skupstina društveno-politikih zajednica," Socijalizam 11 (1969): 1594; Statistički bilten; Predstavnička tela društveno-politickih zajednica: izbori i sastav, Numbers 266, 372, 491, and 590 (Belgrade: Savezni zavod za statistiku, 1964–69).

a. Political Chamber(s): 1953–68, Federal Chamber including the Chamber of Nationalities; 1969–73, Chamber of Nationalities and the Socio-Political Chamber.

b. Functional Chamber(s): 1953–63, Chamber of Producers; 1963–73, Economic Chamber, Social-Health Chamber, Educational-Cultural Chamber, and (until 1969) Organizational-Political Chamber.

c. The data on the professionalization of deputies in the "political chambers" of the Assembly is divided between the Chamber of Nationalities (83.3%) and the Socio-Political Chamber (69.2%). Nineteen hundred sixty-nine was the first year the Chamber of National- ities had a separate identity as as branch of the Assembly. The Socio-Political Chamber had succeeded the Federal Chamber as the popularly elected house in the Federal Assembly.

central political institutions, and disagreements over various linguistic and cultural questions—all familiar problems to the student of inter-war Yugoslavia—once again came to dominate political life. In the light of these developments, statements by both Yugoslav and for-eign observers about the Communists' success in having found a permanent solution to the national question appeared to indicate bad judgment or wishful thinking.[11]

THE THIRD PERIOD: 1967–71

One consequence of the change in internationality affairs was a significant change in the structure and functions of the parliament. Faced with the prospect of increasing ethnic and regional conscious-ness, the Yugoslav leadership began seriously to reevaluate the role of the federal legislature as an integrating force. Thus, during the third stage of parliamentary development, from 1967 to 1971, the Federal Assembly's Chamber of Nationalities was given a key role in dealing with the national question. The changing attitude of the Yugoslav political elite toward the parliamentary system is well illustrated by some selected quotations from speeches made by Edvard Kardelj in 1964 and 1967. As a high-ranking party functionary and close associate of Tito since the wartime revolutionary struggle, Kardelj played an important role in shaping the organization of Yugoslav governmental institutions. Addressing the Federal Assembly as its president in February 1964 (Kardelj, 1965: 39), he suggested the possibility of broadening the role of the Chamber of Nationalities, but emphasized that

> in the practice of the Federal Assembly to date, none of its decisions have been at variance with the constitutional rights of the republics and therefore the Chamber of Nationalities has had no need to convene in order to deliberate on problems of this kind. I believe that it will have no need to do so in the future either. The mere presence of the Chamber of Nationalities is a guarantee that every proposal before being submitted to the Assembly for final deliberation, is thoroughly examined beforehand from the standpoint of whether it is in accordance with the constitution and the constitutional rights of the peoples and republics.

Three years later, speaking at a symposium of legal scholars and political functionaries considering changes in the constitutional sys-tem, Kardelj was somewhat less sanguine about the capability of the Federal Assembly with respect to internationality relations:

The Chamber of Nationalities was established to act only when a conflict appeared, and if it didn't, the Chamber of Nationalities didn't operate. Constituted in this way, it is clear that the Chamber of Nationalities often didn't go into operation when such conflicts really existed. [Because] a fear automatically appeared that a conflict would reflect badly on a body such as the Chamber of Nationalities, the necessity arose for the discussions and direct negotiations among the interested parties, bypassing the Chamber of Nationalities. In the course of the last four years [1963–67] we have had several such cases. Upon consideration of these conflicts we decided that it would be better not to debate them at sessions of the Chamber of Nationalities, but to solve them by political means and internal discussions. [Dzinic, 1967: 334]

It is clear that by "political means and internal discussions" Kardelj was referring to the attempt by top-ranking party functionaries, characteristic of the entire period from 1945 on, to resolve disputes among ethnic regional groups outside the public view. By 1967 the role of the parliamentary system in the solution of these problems was seen in an entirely new light. It is in this period that one also finds increasing recognition in both Yugoslav official and scholarly discussions that economic and cultural conflict among the various nationality groups is a normal and expected feature of socialist political development in an industrializing society.

The immediate pretext for the reorganization of the Federal Assembly grew out of a dispute in late 1966 over the allocation of federal funds to underdeveloped areas. Dissatisfied with a decision by the federal administrative agency set up to assist the economic development of underdeveloped regions, representatives from the republic of Bosnia-Hercegovinia in the Federal Assembly demanded a special meeting of the Chamber of Nationalities to consider their objections.[12] The use of the Chamber of Nationalities for the airing of a regional dispute was unprecedented, although that was precisely one of the functions it was constitutionally empowered to perform.[13] It was the first time that the Chamber of Nationalities had been called into session since 1946, except for the purely symbolic performance of mandatory functions. The result of this initiative after two decades of parliamentary inactivity in the field of intergroup affairs was to trigger a movement in the Federal Assembly to amend the constitution in order to broaden the functions of the Chamber of Nationalities. In April 1967, after the hasty preparation of draft recommendations, the constitution was amended to improve the position of the Chamber of Nationalities within the Federal Assembly. Mandatory sessions of the Chamber of Nationalities now were required for a greater variety of issues coming before the legislature, and the number of members needed to initiate an optional meeting of the chamber was reduced from ten to five deputies. The legislative competence of the Chamber of Nationalities was also enlarged to encompass all aspects of federal policy touching upon the equality of Yugoslavia's national and minority groups. Moreover, the 1967 amendments recognized the Chamber of Nationalities as a semiautonomous house in the Assembly, which, although technically still part of the Federal Chamber, was to deal separately and on an equal basis with respect to all matters coming within the jurisdiction of that Chamber ("Constitutional change . . . 1969": 170–71).[14]

Despite the important nature of the 1967 changes, they represented essentially a halfway house on the road to the political institutionalization of the Chamber of Nationalities within the Federal Assembly. Considerable institutionalization finally was achieved in December 1968, when yet another round of constitutional amendments established the Chamber of Nationalities as the most important branch of the parliament. In addition to acquiring the status of a separate house in the Federal Assembly (as it had enjoyed before 1953), the size of the Chamber of Nationalities was enlarged from 70 to 140 deputies (20 delegates from each republic and 10 from each of the two autonomous republics), making it the largest chamber in the Assembly. More significantly, the new amendments broadened the functions of the Chamber of Nationalities to include all affairs falling within the jurisdiction of the Federal Assembly. In a departure from earlier Yugoslav practice, as well as that used by legislative bodies in most federal systems, the parliamentary chamber elected on the basis of territorial representation became the most powerful house in the federal legislature. The five-chamber Federal Assembly continued to operate on the basis of the bicameral principle, but after 1968 the Chamber of Nationalities, composed of "delegated" representatives from the Yugoslav republics and provinces, always was required to be one of the two chambers involved in the passage of legislation.[15] Moreover, on many important legislative matters, the Chamber of Nationalities enjoyed original or sole jurisdiction. After a long period of benign neglect and various ineffectual holding actions to contain nationality problems, the new position of the Chamber of Nationalities as the pivot of the federal legislative process fully legitimized the expression of regional and ethnic interests within the political system. (Figure 4.1 illustrates the formal position of territorial-ethnic representation in the Federal Assembly over the last three decades.) "We consider," wrote the president of the Chamber of Nationalities in *Borba* (Oct. 30, 1967: 2), "the existence of several peoples and nationalities in Yugoslavia as being an advantage for our socialist community, rather than a necessary evil which has to be disposed of as soon as possible by some kind of supra-national structures on the basis of Yugoslav unitarianism." Given the greatly diminished utility of other integrative factors (for example, the League of Communists, the federal administration, the military and ideological commitment), the Yugoslav leadership hoped that the newly invigorated parliamentary system would be capable of success-fully managing the national question. Before proceeding to examine the actual operation of the Chamber of Nationalities in the task of conflict management, however, it is important to consider the ethnic

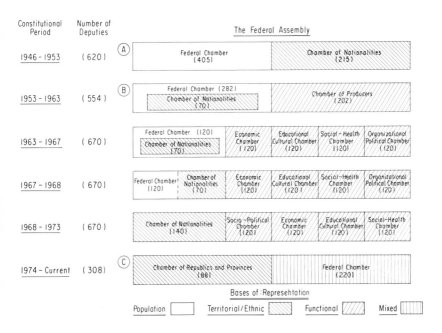

Figure 4.1 CHANGES IN THE FEDERAL PARLIAMENTARY STRUCTURE: 1946–74

    A. The figures are for the period 1950–53. The "People's Assembly" from 1946 to 1950 was originally elected in 1945 as a "Constituent Assembly." It consisted of 524 deputies: 349 elected to the Federal Chamber and 175 to the Chamber of Nationalities. The first election held under the provisions of the 1946 Constitution took place in 1950.

    B. The figures are for the period 1953 to 1958. The "Federal People's Assembly" elected in 1958 had 587 members: 301 in the Federal Chamber, 70 in the Chamber of Nationalities, and 216 in the Chamber of Producers.

    C. Constitution, Feb. 21, 1974.

composition of the Federal Assembly and the Yugoslav conception of legislative representation.

PARLIAMENTARY REPRESENTATION

The importance of the national question in Yugoslavia has made the distribution of high-ranking political positions among the country's ethnic groups a persistent source of attention and controversy. Evidence of discrimination against or favoritism toward particular nationality groups in the staffing of governmental posts has been seized upon by opponents of both the interwar and Communist regimes to illustrate the inequities of the prevailing system. Thus, the highly visible overrepresentation of Serbs in the interwar political leadership was one of the factors which undermined the ability of that regime to develop broad multinational support (see Tomasevich, 1955: 241–42; Cohen, 1973: 59–62).

The Yugoslav Communists were quick to grasp the political significance of this issue, and since their rise to power they have made a deliberate effort to consider ethnic backgrounds in the recruitment of elites. A comparison of the ethnic composition of successive Yugoslav legislatures before and after World War II suggests the important symbolic value which the Communist regime has sought to derive from this policy (Table 4.2). Despite the persistence of important internationality problems, the more equitable ethnic composition of the federal legislature in the Communist period relative to the size of various groups in the general population also reflects a genuine change in the distribution of political power among the nationalities compared to the unitary structure of the prewar period. The relatively minor influence of the parliamentary system during the early period of Yugoslav socialist development does not detract in any way from the political value which accrued to the regime from the more balanced composition of the legislature, however token the character of such representation may have been in practice.[16] The increased representation of the smaller nations and nationalities in the Communist period, most notable in recent years, is especially significant (e.g., the Macedonians, Montenegrins, Albanians, and Hungarians).

Interwar Yugoslavia (the Kingdom of the Serbs, Croats, and Slovenes until 1929) had devoted little recognition to the existence, let alone the interests, of the smaller ethnic groups and minorities (see Table 4.2). Despite the sizable contingent of Croatian and Slovene deputies in the interwar legislatures (in the case of the Croats even a larger percentage than their representation in the Communist period), however, it was clearly the Serbs who controlled political power in this period, not only by means of their majority in the national legislature but through their grip on all strategic positions in the country (in the cabinet, military, and the like). Moreover, throughout the interwar period those Croats and Slovenes who participated in the activity of the central political institutions in Belgrade often were regarded as virtual national traitors by the members of their respective ethnic groups. The ethnic composition of parliamentary bodies alone, therefore, tends to be a poor indicator of political realities in the Yugoslav case, obscuring the behavior of elected officials in representing their constituencies.

In addition to the problem noted above, the differential representation of ethnic groups in the Yugoslav Federal Assembly during the Communist period is misleading for another reason. Deputies in the Chamber of Nationalities are the representatives of the republics and provinces in the Assembly, that is, they are regional delegates, and are not chosen by ethnic groups or nationalities per se.[17] Since all of the Yugoslav republics and provinces are multiethnic (see Appendix A, page 164), a more accurate gauge of nationality representation would be the composition of the chamber of federal deputies from each territory in the federation taken separately. In fact, it is on precisely this level that the use of "ethnic arithmetic" has been most rigorously employed. Thus, the composition of each territorial delegation in the Chamber of Nationalities generally corresponds to the ethnic makeup of the republic or province from which it comes (see Pijade, 1950: 3–4). Moreover, official statements have stressed continuously that the equality of Yugoslavia's various nationality groups is expressed by the equal representation of republics and provinces in the Chamber of Nationalities and not by the overall ethnic composition of the deputies. In an effort to deter the formation of political alliances based on ethnic identity, the Yugoslav regime has encouraged representation on a territorial and functional basis in the parliamentary system. For example, Serbian deputies to the Chamber of Nationalities elected from Serbia, Croatia, and Bosnia-Hercegovinia are expected to represent, and be accountable to, their respective republican constituencies (or, in the case of deputies elected to the functionally specialized chambers, to their respective sectors of economic activity), not to their common ethnic group. Whether a deputy's nationality, territory, or occupation will have the most

TABLE 4.2
YUGOSLAV PARLIAMENTARY DEPUTIES BY NATIONALITY
(PERCENTAGES AND TOTAL NUMBER)

Nationality of Federal Deputies	Interwar Kingdom (Unitary)				Socialist Yugoslavia (Federal)				
	Total Population 1921[a]	National Assembly		Total Population 1953	Federal Assembly				Total Population 1971
		1923	1927		1953	1958	1969	1974	
Serbs	38.5	53.2	58.1	41.7	45.6	44.0	40.2	26.0	39.7
Montenegrins[b]	2.3	—	—	2.8	5.8	6.0	5.2	11.7	2.5
Macedonians[b]	4.8	—	—	5.3	7.4	7.0	8.1	11.4	5.8
Slovenes	9.8	7.4	8.6	8.8	10.7	10.0	9.8	13.6	8.2
Croats	23.2	30.1	26.0	23.5	20.0	22.0	20.0	15.3	22.1
Muslims[c]	—	—	—	—	—	—	6.1	6.8	8.4
"Yugoslavs undeclared"[c]	5.0	—	—	5.9	3.2	5.0	0.2	1.3	1.3
Albanians	3.5	3.9	1.3	4.5	3.2	3.0	4.7	8.4	6.4
Hungarians	3.8	—	1.0	3.0	1.6	2.0	1.8	1.6	2.3
Other nationalities	5.3	5.4	5.0	4.5	2.3	1.0	2.4	6.4	3.2
Unknown	—	—	—	—	—	—	1.5	0.3	—
Total	100.0	100.0	100.0	100.0	100.0	100.0	100.0	100.0	100.0
(number)	(12,473.0)	(312)	(315)	(16,936.5)	(554)	(587)	(620)	(308)	(20,522.9)

Sources: Nada Podgornik, Narodnosti u demokratskoj statistici (Belgrade, 1957); Statistika izbora narodnih poslanika Kraljevine Srba, Hrvata, i Slovenaca (Belgrade, 1924); Statistika izbora narodnih poslanika Kraljevine Srba, Hrvata, i Slvenaca (Belgrade, 1928); Savezna Narodna Skupština (Belgrade, 1955); Statistički Godišnjak FNRJ (Belgrade, 1958); Yugoslav Federal Assembly: Information and Documentary Bulletin 8 (Oct. 1969); Statistički bitten 888 (Belgrade, 1974).

a. The official census of 1921 did not treat groups such as Macedonians, Montenegrins, Muslims, "Yugoslavs," and so on as separate nationalities. The 1921 figures offered in this table for purposes of comparison were prepared by Yugoslav statisticians using a method fully described in the source cited above (Podgornik, 1957).

b. Montenegrins and Macedonians were classified as ethnic "Serbs" in the interwar period, and are therefore not treated as distinct nationalities in the parliamentary statistics. While it is possible to tell how many so-called "Serb" deputies elected to the National Assembly were from districts presently considered as part of Montenegro and Macedonia, there is no way of knowing the precise ethnic identity of these individuals.

c. "Muslim" was treated as a religious identification rather than as an ethnic designation in interwar statistics. Thus in 1923, 17 so-called ethnic "Croats" were elected to the National Assembly as members of the Jugoslav Muslim Organization (JMO). In the 1953 census, and in parliamentary statistics until 1969, Muslims who did not declare themselves to be members of other ethnic groups were classified as "Yugoslavs undeclared." In 1971 Muslims were treated as a separate ethnic group, and Yugoslavs as a supra/nonnational category. While the different methods of ethnic group classification in successive periods of Yugoslav development impair the comparability of the data in this table, the changes nevertheless do reflect the evolving configuration of ethnic identity and political influence in Yugoslavia (e.g., the decline of "Great Nation" hegemony).

influence on his attitudes and behavior regarding a certain issue depends on both the individual and the issue. In recent years, however, institutional procedures and political realities have contributed to the development of a strong sense of *regional* identification among Yugoslav federal legislators in the Chamber of Nationalities (and after 1974 in the Chamber of Republics and Provinces). The same tendency also has been apparent in other political institutions. Thus between 1969 and 1971 constitutional provisions and statutes formalized the requirement of *parity* (equal) republican and provincial representation (the so-called personnel key) in recruitment to all top-ranking governmental, party, and mass organization positions on the federal level (Appendix B, page 165). Considerations of *proportional* ethnic representation are handled by each republic or province in selecting their officials for federal positions (Trajkovski, 1970; Nin, Apr. 2, 1972: 16).

The question of parliamentary representation obviously involves more than simply the numerical distribution of various ethnic and regional groups in legislative bodies. A most important dimension of representation is the relationship between the territorial or ethnic representative and his constituency. To what extent does the deputy from a particular region or nationality regard himself as a spokesman for those groups he would appear to represent prima facie? What is the official or legal conception of a representative's role, and to what extent is this view shared by individual representatives or the members of the constituency he is elected to serve? To whom is the elected deputy primarily responsible, his own conscience or the interests of his district? How is the deputy to be held accountable for his actions? These are the types of questions which have historically bedeviled political activists and theorists in representative systems (Birch, 1971; Eulau, 1967; Pitkin, 1967; Riemer, 1967).

Marxist authors and official pronouncements in the majority of Communist party-ruled states have generally maintained that the elected parliamentary deputy be "imperatively mandated" to his constituency, with extremely little or no latitude for self-initiative. These arguments usually are based on Marx's favorable assessment of legislative practice by members of the Paris Commune in 1871. The legislative, executive, and judicial powers of the commune were merged in a single body of elected representatives bound to their constituents by formal instructions (*mandat imperatif*). "Since the time of the Paris Commune," one writer (Sobolewski, 1968: 99) observes, "the principle of responsibility of representatives to their electors, and the right to recall representatives have constituted the firm basis of the socialist theory of representation stated in every constitution of socialist countries today." The concept of imperative mandate is considered to be superior to the theory of representation in a bourgeois regime (independent or "free" determination), where, it is argued, the ability of each elected official to impose his own judgment, or that of his party, on the policy-making process corrupts the citizens' direct control of their political institutions.

As with most other aspects of their ideological and political development, Yugoslav thinking about the nature of legislative representation has deviated markedly from the path of other Communist party states. As early as 1946, when the influence of the Soviet model in Yugoslavia still was pervasive, a leading theoretician, Jovan Stefavovic, pointed out that the notion of imperatively mandated representatives mechanically carrying out the interests of their individual constituencies contradicted the Marxist principle of the "unity of power." If, he argued, Marxists contend that there is a need for a unified structure of governmental functions in a socialist state (legislative, executive, and judicial), which allegedly reflects the harmony of interests in society, then why should the individual representative be bound by the detailed instructions of separate groups of citizens in a multitude of electoral districts? (Hondius, 1968: 153) Reasoning along similar lines, Yugoslav constitutional specialists and political figures consistently have stressed the need for independent judgment and action on the part of parliamentary representatives in socialist regimes while still recognizing the deputy's ultimate accountability to his constituency. In the Yugoslav view, the latter obligation may be insured by the constituents' right to recall their representatives rather than by the formulation of binding instructions to guide the deputy's behavior.[18] Thus, the Rules of Procedure (1967: 23) adopted by the Federal Assembly in 1967 required that the federal deputy follow events in his district, inform his constituents, and carry requests from the local level to the Assembly, but that "in doing so he can also present his own opinions and take a stand on these matters accordingly."[19]

The emergence of the Chamber of Nationalities as an important center for republican and provincial participation in federal decision making, together with the intensification of ethnic and regional consciousness in Yugoslavia during the late 1960s, raised the question of representation from the realm of constitutional theory and design to a problem of vital political significance. The 1968 decision to give the Chamber of Nationalities primary responsibility for the passage of federal legislation touched off considerable discussion and controversy in Yugoslav political and academic circles about the concept of representation in a multinational socialist system. Some observers argued that the new parliamentary structure contained a built-in contradiction, giving the Chamber of Nationalities responsibility for both the expression of diverse regional and ethnic interests as well as for the coordination of these different interests. It was also feared that the "territorialization" of power in the Chamber of Nationalities among the various republican and provincial delegations would exacerbate regional conflicts and produce continual deadlocks in legislative policy making.

The heart of this debate centered around the degree and manner in which federal deputies in the newly constituted Chamber of Nationalities would be held accountable by their various republics and provinces. One particular source of anxiety in this respect concerned the procedure for electing federal deputies. Since 1953 the republican and provincial assemblies had "delegated" representatives to the Chamber of Nationalities from among their own membership. The 1968 amendments did not radically alter this method of election, but it doubled the size of the delegations and considerably increased their importance in political decision making. Many Yugoslav commentators felt that deputies from a particular republic or province elected in this manner to the Chamber of Nationalities would tend to act in concert, voting as a bloc of delegated agents on behalf of their regional constituencies and creating what was termed the "institutionalization of delegations." A central concern was, therefore, whether individual federal deputies delegated to the Chamber of Nationalities would be free to voice their own opinions or would be bound by an "imperative mandate" to carry out the instructions of their republics and provinces. It was felt that if federal deputies were obligated to serve simply as conveyor belts for the views of their territories or nationalities, it would seriously undermine the ability of the Chamber of Nationalities to achieve coordination of conflicting viewpoints and arrive at generally acceptable decisions. Critics also objected that disciplined bloc voting by the deputies as a regular practice in matters of disagreement between the republics would paralyze the operations of the federation, because it was anticipated that the adoption of certain types of legislation would require the agreement of *all* of the *delegations* in the Chamber, voting as separate units. As one apprehensive federal legislator remarked, the use of vetoes

> might become an instrument of specific political structures, often very narrow, specific teams in the republics and provinces . . . one can't exclude the possibility that the whole delegation in the Chamber of Nationalities might be in a position of complete dependence . . . the deputies of the Chamber of Nationalities would, at least partially, be deprived of their individuality in delivering their own judgment and initiatives, as well as in decision-making.[20]

The fact that the particular deputy voicing this fear was an independent and a vigorous critic of the government in the Federal Assembly who represented a new breed among Yugoslav legislators revealed the statement to be more than simply a procedural observation in some rubber-stamp parliament. In order to defuse these objections and weaken the potential ability of individual regions to obstruct the federal legislative process, official Yugoslav opinion rejected the principle of imperative mandate and the "institutionalization of delegations" in the operation of the Chamber of Nationalities, while at the same time recognizing the right of the republics and provinces to vigorously advance their interests through the parliamentary system.[21] The contradiction implicit in this view was to prove a major stumbling block for the parliamentary structure.

The above reservations concerning the threat of stalemate in the Federal Assembly were not shared unanimously throughout Yugoslavia. In Croatia, particularly, the idea that delegations to the Chamber of Nationalities would be required to implement the binding instructions of their republican and provincial assemblies carried considerable appeal as a device for challenging the control of the federal administration, which many Croats equated with the political hegemony of Serbia and the less developed regions of the country. From the Croatian perspective, the potential veto power of the republics in the Federal Assembly, so much feared by some segments of political opinion, was a legitimate and productive means by which to block unfavorable federal legislation. The dispute regarding the role of the federal deputy was only one aspect, undoubtedly to many participants a largely symbolic one, of a much broader debate over whether the republican or the federal party and state organs should be the locus of power in Yugoslavia. Thus, despite strong official opposition during 1967–68 to the principle of imperative mandate in parliamentary representation, the growth of Croatian nationalism over the next several years was accompanied by an effort of the leadership in that republic to use their deputies in the Chamber of Nationalities as agents for the protection and advocacy of vital Croatian "national" interests. As delegated representatives of their republics and provinces whose future political careers increasingly hinged on the goodwill of local and regional elites, the deputies in the Chamber of Nationalities were under considerable pressure to follow the directions of their regional constituencies in formulating federal legislation. Any deputy who failed to comply with such instructions faced personal ostracism in his native region and possible recall from office.

A striking illustration of this type of pressure on parliamentary deputies is the case of one Croatian representative in the Chamber of Nationalities, Milos Zanko, who was also a vice-president of the Federal Assembly. In a series of public statements Zanko had sharply criticized the Croatian political leaders for not adequately opposing the development of nationalism in their republic. Moreover, Zanko, an ethnic Croat, had assumed a "federal" perspective on several matters in dispute between his republic and the central authorities in Belgrade. In an interview several months before his removal, Zanko had urged federal deputies to take an independent position on issues affecting the "Yugoslav community": "Deputies in the Assembly make decisions according to their own convictions. . . . a deputy cannot be anybody's pawn. No deputy is answerable only to his own voters. Every deputy is answerable to all the peoples of our country. This is a body of the Federation entrusted with the task of pursuing the policy of the Federation, and promoting the prosperity and well being of all its peoples. The easiest thing to do would be to take refuge under the attitudes of official leading bodies and directives" (Politika, Sept. 13, 1969: 5).

The Croatian leadership responded to Zanko's independent position by labeling him an ally of "bureaucratic centralists" on the federal level who were opposed to economic decentralization and the equality of nationalities. In mid-January of 1970 at a meeting of Croatian political leaders, Zanko was removed from his position in the League of Communists and subsequently recalled from his seat in the Federal Assembly.[22] While the reasons for Zanko's removal involved much broader issues in the Yugoslav political process than simply the behavior of federal deputies, his case indicates, nevertheless, the atmosphere in which members of the Chamber of Nationalities labored and the pressures to which they were subjected. Zanko's case also illustrates the special built-in cross-pressures on representatives in all multinational political systems who must somehow reconcile demands (role expectations) from their "primordial" or regional electoral constituencies with the broader interests of the society. The outburst of regional and ethnic nationalism in Yugoslavia between 1969 and 1971 made it extremely difficult for the Yugoslav federal legislator to carry out this task effectively. As one observer of the Federal Assembly noted in May 1970, "As things now stand, it seems that it is in the nature of things that certain deputies in the Chamber of Nationalities will have to be more concerned with the stands of their republics than with the rights accorded them by the Assembly's Rules of Procedure" (Politika, May 24, 1970: 7).

DECISION MAKING IN THE FEDERAL ASSEMBLY: 1969–71

When one looks out from the gallery at the disposition of deputies' desks in the great hall of the Federal Assembly, one spontaneously gains the impression that the architect who had designed the Assembly building was in some way far-sighted, as if he knew that one day Yugoslavia would become a federal state of equal peoples and nationalities. One gains this impression at the sight of the deputies' benches arranged in amphitheater style in the hall of the Chamber of Nationalities, divided into sections as some large slices. Thus, when for instance, Mika Spiljak, the President of the Chamber of Nationalities, enters the hall to open a session, he always knows that the delegation of 20 deputies of Serbia is sitting at the left side of the President's desk. The Slovenian deputies in the same number are near them, and then come the members of the delegations of Bosnia-Hercegovina, Macedonia, and Montenegro, and on the right side, at the other end of the hall, are the members of the delegation of the Socialist Republic of Croatia. . . . No rules of procedure require them to take their seats in this order, according to their republics. They have simply become accustomed to doing so from the very beginning, primarily for practical reasons, in order to consult each other during discussions. [Politika, May 24, 1970: 7]

The description in the above quotation of deputies in the Chamber of Nationalities divided into neat republican "slices" aptly symbolizes the deep regional cleavages in Yugoslavia which were incorporated into the 1968 parliamentary structure. The important question, however, was whether the new institutional arrangements would prove capable of mitigating the conflicts generated by these cleavages, or if the airing of differences in the Assembly would inhibit their resolution. An examination of federal legislative activity between 1969 and 1971 reveals that much of the initial apprehension concerning the potential weakness of the parliamentary structure was well justified. It soon became apparent from the operation of the

Chamber of Nationalities that, instead of resolving conflicts, the new legislative process was reproducing faithfully the various features of the national question found outside the Federal Assembly. The representation of diverse regional and ethnic interests was being achieved in the parliamentary system, but without the reconciliation of attendant conflicts which affected the stability and survival of the Yugoslav state.[23]

The experience of the Chamber of Nationalities as a mechanism for conflict resolution is well illustrated by the difficulties encountered over the question of allocating federal funds to Yugoslavia's economically underdeveloped regions. It may be remembered that a controversy among the republics over precisely the same issue had provoked the first meeting of the long-dormant Chamber of Nationalities in 1967. The Yugoslav Communist regime had been committed to the economic and social development of Yugoslavia's less developed regions since its rise to power in 1945. This commitment, as one leading Yugoslav economist pointed out, derived from a combination of humanitarian, national, socialist, and economic motives (Bicanic, 1973: 182—84). The Constitution of 1963 (Article 27) formally recognized the obligation of the Yugoslav "community" to "ensure the underdeveloped republics and regions material and other conditions necessary for more rapid economic development, and for the creation of the material bases of social activities" (Constitution . . . , 1969: 38—39).

It was not until 1965, however, that a special federal fund was established on a permanent basis to promote economic projects in the underdeveloped areas. The creation of the fund, along with a series of other political economic reforms in the mid-1960s, greatly expanded the influence and concern of the republics and provinces over decisions affecting the allocation of aid to the underdeveloped regions. While all the Yugoslav republics and provinces contained areas which could be designated as underdeveloped, the question of allocating federal investment funds soon became a major bone of contention between the more advanced and the less developed regions of the country. Very briefly, the more economically advanced regions of the country felt that the huge outlay of federal investment funds for the growth of underdeveloped areas slowed down the development of their own regions. The use of such funds to subsidize economically unprofitable enterprises (the so-called political factories) and various grandiose projects in the underdeveloped areas was particularly offensive to the more advanced republics and provinces.[24]

The controversy over the use of federal funds for economic development was complicated by the fact that the geographical boundaries between the more advanced and less developed regions of the country coincide, albeit somewhat roughly with important historical and cultural divisions. Thus, the economically more advanced republics of Slovenia and Croatia, in the northwestern part of the country, had been under the control of the Austro-Hungarian monarchy and were traditionally Catholic areas, while the inhabitants of the economically less developed republics, in the southeastern part of the country (Serbia, Montenegro, and Macedonia), had been under Turkish control and were Eastern Orthodox by religious affiliation. Bosnia-Hercegovinia, the most ethnically heterogeneous Yugoslav republic and also an economically underdeveloped area, had been a crossroads of both Western and Eastern influence, as well as a continual subject of both Serbian and Croatian irredentist sentiments. Moreover, the fact that the Republic of Serbia is composed of two autonomous provinces—Voivodina, one of the most economically developed sections of the country, with a large (21.7%) Hungarian minority, and Kosovo, Yugoslavia's most underdeveloped area, with a predominantly (73.7%) Albanian population—increased the number of actors in dispute over the distribution of federal funds from six to eight. In addition to the problem of historical and cultural cleavages, the controversy during the 1960s between the economically more advanced and the less developed republics became intertwined closely with differences of opinion about how political power was to be divided and exercised in the Yugoslav system. Thus the proponents of more centralized political control and the use of more direct "administrative" measures were heavily concentrated in the less developed regions, while those groups favoring greater decentralization of authority and a reliance on more "liberal" forms of state control were more prevalent in the economically advanced regions (Rusinow, 1969).

The reappearance of the issue of economic investment in the underdeveloped areas on the agenda of the Federal Assembly in 1970 provides an interesting glimpse of the role of the parliamentary system as an instrument of conflict resolution. Confronted with the task of refunding the program of aid to the underdeveloped areas for the first time in 1970, the Chamber of Nationalities became bogged down in a continuous deadlock concerning the criteria by which funds for economic development would be collected and dispersed. Rather than attempting to reach a mutually acceptable solution, the federal deputies positively articulated the various demands and objections of their respective regional constituencies in an unyielding manner.

Describing a meeting of the Federal Assembly's Commission for Revision of the Laws on Underdeveloped Areas in April 1970, the parliamentary correspondent of one Yugoslav newspaper reported that

> a situation was created which gave the impression that the participants have divided themselves into the representatives of the developed and those of the under-developed areas. Anyway, one of them has frankly stated this.
>
> It could be concluded from this that every deputy, merely by voting for one or another status of the Fund, has had in mind a single idea—to appear personally as a consistent interpreter of interests for his republic. Thus, the deputies of the developed republics have voted for the financing mechanism which promises much less in respect to the future stability of policy, while those of the under-developed republics did quite the opposite. . . . it appeared that the deputies have pleaded the cause of their republics as financial experts of these republics, for which reason they failed as politicians. The Commission ended its sessions without having performed its task, with the promise that it will try once again to reach an agreement, but also with the statement that otherwise it will submit to the Assembly the opposing alternatives. [Borba, Apr. 12, 1970]

Another account of a meeting held by the Budget Committee of the Chamber of Nationalities in September 1970 concerning the same issue, still unresolved, reveals the uncompromising style in which republican interests were expressed in the Assembly. The specific issue in question was whether the social product (favored by the less developed regions) or the business funds of economic organizations (supported by the economically more advanced regions) should be the basis upon which to calculate contributions to the federal fund for the development of underdeveloped areas.

> Their views on the basis for determining the amount of the loan were divided almost in accordance with the republican key.
>
> Confronted with several possibilities, Mileva Planojevic (Serbia) made up her mind and suggested the social product as the most adequate criterion for determining the amount of the loan for the under-developed areas. . . . Anton Bubic (Croatia) considered that the volume of the business funds should be adopted as a basis precisely because of solidarity in Yugoslavia. Only such a solution will bring all economic subjects in the country into an equal position, without holding back any of them, said Bubic. Drago Lipic (Slovenia) agreed with Bubic, and stated that this solution would secure stability of the funds intended for the under-developed areas.
>
> Rejecting these explanations, Milija Kovacevic (Serbia) remarked that things should not be dimmed. It is necessary clearly to say everything, so that it could be seen what is behind every proposed alternative: the determining of obligations according to the volume of the business fund better suits the

development economies, and vice versa. Kovacevic suggested the social product as a basis, while Esad Ceric (Bosnia-Hercegovinia) explained that the representatives of the regions which are interested in accurately determining the volume of funds, and in securing their stability, are for the social product as a basis.

"But, what about incentives to the more productive and more effective?" asked Darinka Puskaric (Croatia). [Politika, Sept. 18, 1970: 6]

The outcome of the above parliamentary colloquy was to further postpone voting on the question of funds for the underdeveloped areas until an agreement among the republics and provinces might be worked out. It was not until March of the following year, after continued parliamentary inability to agree upon a solution, that a special Coordinating Commission of the Federal Executive Council decided temporarily to continue the earlier provisions for the collection and allocation of funds for underdeveloped areas. It was decided that a new law dealing with this matter from 1971 to 1975 would be submitted to the Federal Assembly by the Federal Executive Council only *after* agreement by the executive councils of the republics and provinces had been achieved. The fact that such a law was not finally adopted until November 1972, over two years later, and then only after the threatened use of a new procedure by the executive branch to bypass the Federal Assembly completely in cases of prolonged interrepublican disagreement on major issues, was testimony to the depth of regional controversy in Yugoslavia and the inability of the parliamentary system to resolve such differences independently.[25]

The above illustration of regional confrontation in the Federal Assembly during 1970 is only one example of numerous interrepublican conflicts which arose during this period, both within and outside of the parliamentary system. The purpose here is not to examine exhaustively the federal legislative process or the national question, but rather to show how the Federal Assembly, and particularly the Chamber of Nationalities dealt with regional and ethnic conflicts. In this respect the question of allocating investment funds to the underdeveloped areas indicates the difficulties faced by the parliamentary system. The unrestrained effort by the republics and provinces to advance their separate and usually conflicting interests continuously delayed the adoption of badly needed legislation and undermined the ability of the Federal Executive Council (the rough equivalent of a cabinet in other parliamentary systems) to effectively carry out its objectives. The inability of the federal deputies in the Chamber of Nationalities to do little more than register regional de-

mands and objections also meant that sooner or—as more frequently
proved to be the case—later the Federal Executive Council was able to
exercise its will in the adoption of legislation. A journalist commenting
on a February 1971 debate in the Chamber of Nationalities noted that
"all the deputies calmly delivered their critical remarks to the government, everyone expressed their demands, fleeing from any exchange
of views, and everyone in the end voted for the government's draft
proposals, the general formulation of which nobody disturbed"
(Popovic, 1971: 14). Instead of responsibly criticizing the proposals
of the Federal Executive Council or mobilizing a consensus behind
coherent alternatives and amendments to the legislation before them,
the deputies in the Chamber of Nationalities simply expressed a host
of conflicting regional demands. Thus, although the Chamber of
Nationalities succeeded in facilitating the raw articulation of republican and provincial interests, it did not serve to strengthen the vitality
or effectiveness of the Federal Assembly as a policy-making institution.[26]

It is important to note that although we have devoted most of our
attention to the lack of cooperation in the Chamber of Nationalities,
the major source of governmental paralysis in this period can be
attributed to interrepublican disagreements in the Federal Executive
Council. Constitutionally, the Federal Executive Council is the politi-
cal-executive body of the Federal Assembly and thus technically a
part of the Yugoslav parliamentary system. For purposes of evaluat-
ing alternative mechanisms for conflict management, however, it is
important to keep in mind the institutional distinction between the
executive branch and the legislative chambers. Thus, despite the
significant growth in parliamentary influence noted earlier in most
legislative matters, it was still the Federal Executive Council that
proposed, and the Federal Assembly that disposed.[27]

The composition of the Federal Executive Council on the basis of
parity representation from each republic and province and the operational requirement for the council to secure a "common platform"
before initiating legislative proposals made the executive branch an
excellent target for the obstructionist tactics of regional interest
groups. The ability of republican political leaders to delay the adoption of a crucial package of economic "stabilization" measures
throughout the winter and spring of 1970 and 1971 was probably
the most important example of this behavior.[28] Interestingly
enough, the much-publicized "republican veto" of federal legislation in this period derived primarily from the lack of consensus

among the republican representatives in the Federal Executive Council and not from the use of a formal veto during votes in the Chamber of Nationalities. In fact, the so-called special procedure envisioned by the 1968 amendments, by which a single dissenting republican or provincial delegation voting as a unit in the Chamber of Nationalities, might block the adoption of laws which it deemed to be harmful to its equality or constitutional rights, was not adopted until the fall of 1971, after the parliament had lost most of its jurisdiction for the resolution of such conflicts.[29] Thus, the major source of parliamentary inactivity in this period was a weak federal executive which could not obtain interrepublican unanimity on a legislative program, along with a federal legislature which either mirrored or endured such behavior.

Official disillusionment with the failure of the parliamentary system to help resolve a series of pressing issues throughout 1969 and 1971 was a major factor behind a decision to reorganize once again the structure of federal political institutions. As Edvard Kardelj (1970: 25–26), the chief architect of earlier parliamentary reform explained, the use of the "republican 'veto' " is "already infiltrating itself into our assembly life in an 'uncontrolled' manner through the force of pressure. History has shown that systems based on the right of 'veto' have been an historical failure." In July 1971, after barely two years of experience, the Yugoslav regime abandoned the use of the parliamentary system as a mechanism for the management of regional and ethnic problems. The formal structure of the Chamber of Nationalities was retained intact, but in an effort to forestall the probability of continued legislative paralysis, an entirely new framework of "interrepublican committees" was introduced within the federal executive branch and given the primary responsibility for working out agreements among the republics and provinces. Hoping to negotiate between the Scylla of minority veto and the Charybdis of majority rule as alternative methods for making decisions, the Yugoslav leadership established an elaborate procedure for the "coordination" of regional interests *prior* to the initiation of policy by the Federal Executive Council and its consideration by the Federal Assembly. The burden of the coordinating activity would be undertaken by members of the republican and provincial executive councils and their representatives in the various interrepublican committees at the federal level.[30]

As part of a calculated effort to mobilize consensus and help prepare for the anticipated difficulties which are likely to follow

President Tito's death or retirement, the new constitutional amendments adopted in 1971 also established a rather novel collective presidency having special powers to break interregional deadlocks in policy making. In addition to strengthening the executive agencies, the future "load" on federal decision-making institutions also was lessened substantially by the transfer of important federal functions to the republics and provinces. Indeed, the thrust of the 1971 amendments was aimed not so much at the framing of central political institutions as at the formal establishment of the Yugoslav system on a more "confederal" basis (see Kramer, 1971).[31]

One effect of the 1971 changes (which were subsequently incorporated into the new constitution of 1974 in modified form) was to considerably diminish the influence of the parliamentary system in federal policy making. It is the executive councils on both the federal and republican-provincial levels, rather than the legislative assemblies, which have been the major beneficiaries of the new approach to the management of conflict in the Yugoslav system. It is not surprising therefore that the 1971 constitutional amendments (and two years later the draft of the 1974 Constitution) were greeted with less than unanimous enthusiasm by the deputies of the Federal Assembly and other supporters of the "Assembly System." (See Socijalisticka Federativna, 1971: 18–20, 39–40; "Diskusija . . . ," 1973: passim.) Many legislators who had acquired considerable experience and identification with the parliamentary system at the local, republican, and federal levels now feared that many of their successful efforts to expand parliamentary control over legislative affairs would be swept aside. In addition to the greatly expanded power of the executive agencies, a particular source of concern was that the Federal Assembly might become a virtual rubber stamp for detailed agreements worked out in advance by the interrepublican committees. Since the deputies in the Assembly, particularly the Chamber of Nationalities, served the same regional constituencies as the representatives in the interrepublican committees, the possibility of the federal legislators rejecting, or even amending, such executive agreements was regarded as highly unlikely. The rather routine and extremely rapid adoption of complex legislative proposals in the Chamber of Nationalities (after 1974, the Chamber of Republics and Provinces) since 1971 appears to justify such fears. Indeed, some observers have wondered if a legislative chamber for regions and nationalities had even become somewhat of a redundant institution, given the new structure of interrepublican committees and other conflict-regulating agencies located in the executive branch.[32] After a long process in which policy-making activity gradually had been shifting toward Yugoslav legislative bodies, parliamentary stalemates and rampant nationalism have triggered a reaction back to forms of executive control, albeit of a more decentralized character. Whether or not this new approach can succeed without the dysfunctions and excesses of the earlier "administrative period" remains to be seen. The possibility that the formerly centralized executive apparatus simply may have been succeeded by a plurality of republican and provincial bureaucratic elites does not seem reassuring in this respect.

CONCLUSION

The Yugoslav effort to use parliamentary institutions for managing regional and ethnic conflicts did not prove to be successful. The representation of republican and provincial interests in the Chamber of Nationalities after 1968 did provide for a degree of political pluralism often found lacking in other one-party states. Issues were debated much more openly than had been the case formerly. After years in which the national question had been suppressed or ignored, the parliamentary system served as a safety valve though which to vent accumulated frustrations. These benefits, however, were achieved at considerable cost to the effectiveness of the policy-making process and the overall development of the parliamentary system. In the absence of additional mechanisms or motivating forces for the aggregation of interests on a cross-regional basis, the Federal Assembly could not perform its tasks successfully. The tendency of federal deputies in the Chamber of Nationalities to act exclusively as conduits for their regional and ethnic constituencies only amplified the conflicts already present in society and failed to resolve them. The character of sectional and ethnic representation in the Federal Assembly also weakened the capacity of the parliamentary deputies to responsibly monitor and delimit the activity of the executive branch and other political institutions in the legislative policy-making process (the Federal Executive Council, the federal administration, the president of the republic, the Executive Bureau of the League of Communists, and so on).

The brief examination of Yugoslav parliamentary activity offered above seems to suggest that while the formal structures and functions of legislative bodies may exert a certain influence on the pattern of sociopolitical cleavages in a society, the opposite relationship is more likely to be the case. The sharp divisions which appeared in the Chamber of Nationalities were only a symptom of the deep regional and ethnic cleavages which had developed outside of the parliamentary chamber. Given the intensity of these cleavages, it was not surprising that republican and provincial political elites seized upon the parliamentary institutions as another arena in which to advance the aspirations of their own regions, while blocking those of other sections of the country and the central authorities. No amount of institutional engineering could induce a congenial climate in which to resolve conflicts or substitute for its absence. In the case of Yugoslavia, from 1969 to 1971, the number and extent of these conflicts proved to be too great a load for an emergent parliamentary system at the critical first stages of institutional development and lacking a tradition of conflict management. Thus, the Yugoslav case also suggests that to put the weight and task of conflict resolution onto representative assemblies in countries with either weak or emerging governmental institutions may prove detrimental to both future legislative development and the overall stability of the political system.

While a systematic evaluation of Yugoslav federal institutions after 1971 is outside the scope of this article, evidence does suggest that they have had some success in resolving interregional conflicts (Tasic, 1973: 33–35; Kardelj, 1974: I 3; Zarkovic, 1977: I 18–I 19). It is difficult to determine, however, whether recent progress in arriving at decisions on the federal level is due more to the organizational elegance and effectiveness of the newly designed institutions (inter-republican committees, the "collective presidency," etc.) or to the regime's vigorous campaign against nationalism beginning with the purge of Croatian republican leaders in December 1971 and subsequently extended to the other republics and provinces. It certainly appears that the newly appointed regional leaders throughout Yugoslavia have been more disposed to arriving at mutually satisfactory solutions among the republics and nationalities than was the case earlier.[33] The renewed emphasis on the role of the League of Communists as a unifying "revolutionary" force (a throwback to the period before 1952) has also been an important impetus to the solution of problems.

It is also possible, of course, that the presence of republican and provincial representatives in small committees of the executive branch, shielded from the publicity of parliamentary debate and totally involved with the task of reaching interregional agreements has itself helped to resolve conflicts. Thus the new executive institutions composed of political spokesmen from the various ethnic and regional groups may act to facilitate the development of "overarching cooperation on the elite level" which many authors maintain is essential for effective policy making in "culturally segmented" or "divided" societies.[34] Cross-regional bargaining may help achieve the compromises and consensus which eluded legislative deputies in the Chamber of Nationalities from 1968 to 1971 during Yugoslavia's most "liberal" phase of political development. While we have suggested that institutions and procedures are more likely to reflect than to influence the character of political conflicts in a deeply fragmented society, the formal structure of government is certainly not without significance. As Robert Dahl (1973: 25) has recently observed, representative institutions may no longer be the most effective site for the resolution of antagonistic interests in a "segmented polity":

> The classic site of this process was the national parliament and its network of personal, bloc, and party activities. But parliaments have not been able to handle the job by themselves, and their inability to overcome fragmentation and immobilism doubtless has often contributed to dissatisfaction with parliamentary democracy itself. Hence in practically every polyarchy, other institutions have emerged to take over a share—usually a very large share—of the task. These institutions are typically more hierarchical than legislative bodies, their top leaders are endowed with more political resources, they have greater legitimacy, they usually have more technical skills, and they are better able to operate in secret.

It is not necessary to share an enthusiasm for hierarchy, technical expertise, or secrecy to understand the attraction of such factors as aids in the management of conflict. The perennial dilemma of institution building in Yugoslavia, as in all pluralistic societies, is how to satisfy a host of conflicting group demands—a lengthy process which often produces the total immobilism of governmental authority, while at the same time providing for the rapid and coherent execution of policy with the attendant dangers of excessive central control. The trade-off between the two extremes is man's classic search for a balance between freedom and order. In multinational societies with deep cleavages, this quest is usually played out in a maze of ethnic symbols, a deluge of nationalist rhetoric, and—much too often—in the blood of fraternal neighbors. The fact that the Yugoslav regime has demonstrated a rare willingness and imagination to experiment when confronting such problems gives us some basis for hope.

NOTES

1. In Yugoslav usage the term "national question" generally refers to the relationship between the various ethnic and regional groups in the country. As of 1977 official sources recognize six principal "nations" (Serbs, Croats, Slovenes, Macedonians, Montenegrins, and Muslims, the last group considered as an "ethnic affinity" since 1961) and eighteen "nationalities," formally designated as minorities (Albanians, Hungarians, Slovaks, and so on). There is also a small group of individuals who choose a supranational identity as "Yugoslavs" rather than any officially recognized nationality.

The territorial distribution of the above ethnic groups in Yugoslavia does not, however, coincide precisely with the administrative units of the federal system, that is, the six "socialist republics" and the two "socialist autonomous provinces." For example, to use the most extreme cases, the republic of Slovenia is virtually homogenous (94.0% ethnic Slovenes), while Bosnia-Hercegovinia is a mosaic of groups (39.6% Muslims, 37.2% Serbs, 20.6% Croats, and so on). Thus the problems which exist among the republics and provinces (which are generally referred to as "interregional" relations in this chapter) may or may not overlap with issues dividing the various ethnic groups (nations and nationalities). The importance of primarily interregional or interethnic problems to the "national question" in Yugoslavia depends on the specific issues, actors, and period of time being considered. (For a statistical breakdown of the Yugoslav population on the basis of nationality and region, see Appendix A.)

2. For a comprehensive historical treatment of the nationality issue in contemporary Yugoslav politics, see Shoup (1968). A more concise overview is Vucinich (1969). A useful survey of the interwar period is Clissold (1966: 154–207).

3. The constituent assembly elected in November 1945 to draft the new constitution also included an Assembly of Nationalities based on republican representation: 25 deputies from each of the six republics, 15 deputies from the autonomous province of Vojvodina, and 10 from the autonomous region of Kosovo-Methohija. Adoption of the constitution required a two-thirds majority vote in the Assembly of Nationalities and a second chamber, the Federal Assembly, elected on the basis of population. The Chamber of Nationalities, established in 1946, maintained this pattern with only a slight structural alteration; each republic elected 30 deputies, Vojvodina 20, and Kosovo 15. For an excellent description of constitutional development during this period, see Hondius (1968: 113–68).

4. Yugoslav authors generally give a quite candid assessment of the role of their legislative institutions in the postwar period. For example, a brochure on the parliamentary system intended primarily for a broad public audience states: "In principle, and viewed on the basis of the significance of the parliament given in constitutional texts, the parliament in our country after the war was a key and fundamental institution of political and state organization. Actually, however, the role of the parliament until recently was very small and by the constitution of 1946, and the Constitutional Law of 1953, the parliament was really a retarded institution. . . . Its role was expressed in voting approval for already specified policy rather than real decision-making. In these conditions it represented more of a parliamentary-decorative ornament for the real activity and power of the party-state apparatus" (Djordjevic, 1969: 910). The mechanics of party control over the parliamentary system in this period are carefully documented in Petranovic (1969: 256–79).

5. According to one Yugoslav author, the downgraded position of the Chamber of Nationalities after the 1953 constitutional reorganization reflects the feeling by the regime that "in general, a firm inter-nationality community had been established, in short that the national question was 'solved' and there was no danger of complications of inter-nationality relations. Such reasoning led easily to the conclusion that prevailing forms of constitutional-legal guarantees of national equality could be altered including a reduced role for the Chamber of Nationalities, and a change in its status and organization. . . . The Chamber of Nationalities was maintained, nevertheless, more as an instrument of prevention, as a "legal

consequence" of national equality and a declaration of the sincerity of the principle, rather than from a conviction that a mechanism for the defense of equality would be necessary to use in practice" (Mijanovic, 1970: 119–20).

6. The 1953 Constitutional Law obligated the republican deputies in the Federal Chamber to meet in separate session as a Chamber of Nationalities whenever a proposal for revision of the constitution or a draft of a federal social plan was on the agenda. They were also required to meet separately to discuss and give their opinion regarding "general laws," that is, those acts stating broad policy objectives but leaving the details of implementation to the republics. The Chamber of Nationalities had the optional prerogative of meeting to consider proposals which (in the opinion of at least six members of the chamber from one republic) affected the constitutional relationship between the republics and the federation. Rejection of such proposals and laws by the Chamber of Nationalities would lead to a complicated process for the adjustment of views with the Federal Chamber, and in some cases could prevent adoption of a law in the Assembly. In 1954 these procedures were changed so that sessions of the Chamber of Nationalities were no longer obligatory except when a proposal for revision of the constitution was before the Assembly. In other cases the meeting of the Chamber was optional and required a motion by six deputies from one republic or ten deputies from the Chamber. During 1953 and 1954 the Chamber had 19 sessions, each time mechanically fulfilling its mandatory functions by unanimous consent. After one more such meeting in 1955 the Chamber did not meet again, even for mandatory reasons, until 1963. For the 1953 Law and later changes, see Sluzbeni list (1953, 8 [3]: 25–26; and 1954, 10 [13]: 257). For the official argument behind the 1954 changes, see Pijade (1954: 4).

7. The Constitution of 1963 reorganized the Federal Assembly into a five-chamber body operating on a bicameral basis. In an attempt to underline the establishment of the workers' self-management system in different branches of economic activity, the single Chamber of Producers set up in 1953 was abolished and replaced by four functionally specialized "chambers of working communities," each having 120 delegates elected indirectly from economic and social institutions: the Economic Chamber, the Educational-Cultural Chamber, the Social-Health Chamber, and the Organizational-Political Chamber. (This last chamber was eliminated in 1969.) The Federal Chamber was preserved as the major branch of the Assembly, but after 1963 it was composed of 120 deputies "selected" by communal assemblies and then confirmed or technically elected by popular vote. (After 1965 the voters in many districts often had some choice between two or more candidates sharing the same party label.) The adoption of legislation involved passage by the Federal Chamber and any one of the other four houses into whose jurisdiction a particular matter might fall. Despite the overall significance of the 1963 constitution as a turning point in Yugoslav parliamentary development, the Chamber of Nationalities did not undergo any major changes in its structure or its operations. It remained a branch of the Federal Chamber having 70 deputies delegated by the republican and provincial assemblies. One leading Yugoslav constitutional specialist observed, however, that the rights of the deputies in the Chamber of Nationalities became "more institutionalized" after 1963 (Djordjevic, 1967: 347).

8. The most important Yugoslav contributions concerning parliamentary development include Nikolic (1969), Zecevic (1972), Blagojevic (1969), and Dzinic (1964).

9. One result of the change in the role of the party apparatus was a sharp reduction in the number of *professional* party and mass organization functionaries elected as deputies to the Federal Assembly: 1953–73%, 1958–68.5%, 1963–30.8%, 1969–29.4%. See Tozi and Petrovic (1969: 1594).

10. Recent statements by Yugoslav political figures attribute the intensity of internationality conflicts during the early 1970s to the pluralization of influence within the party structure. "The crisis came," writes a member of the League's Executive Bureau, "at a time when we were unable to separate federalism as an expression of equality from tendencies

toward federalism in the party, a federalism that led to separatism. The autonomy and independence of the republican parties and central committees developed to such an extent that it began to assume the nature of federal relations within the League of Communists. All of this led to the appearance of various political and other tendencies within the League of Communists, particularly to a weakening of the League's ideological unity. I believe that herein lies the reason why the party leadership could not be effective in recent years. . . . Democratic centralism was neglected, and all this unavoidably led to the creation of social forces that strive to break up Yugoslavia, forces which strived for separatism and national-ism" (Nin, Dec. 31, 1972: 14). For a more detailed discussion of the "tendencies of disintegration" in the League between 1969 and 1971 as seen by the Yugoslav leaders in retrospect, see "Tenth Congress. . ." (1974: passim.).

11. Some of the most useful studies on the intensification of internationality and regional problems in Yugoslavia during the period covered here include Lendvai (1969), Shoup (1972), Rusinow (1971), Burks (1971), Kramer (1972), and Stankovic (1971). For an account extremely critical of the Communist regime but containing useful information, see Popovic (1968).

12. For background on this issue, see Hondius (1968: 324–25) and Hoffman (1967: 649–59).

13. The unusual character of raising such an issue at a session of the Chamber of Nationalities was underlined by a deputy from Bosnia-Hercegovinia who felt compelled to inform his fellow legislators that his delegation "had carefully considered in which place and in which form to submit these problems which are, in our opinion, very significant, fundamental, and politically delicate. The delegation has decided to place the question before the Chamber, but only after long hesitation. That hesitation is not the expression of some fundamental attitudes about the Chamber of Nationalities. On the contrary we consider that the nature of our federation and parliamentary system is such that it would be necessary to create a Chamber of Nationalities if it didn't exist. But up to now meetings of the Chamber of Nationalities haven't been customary and just because of this a danger existed that problems which are submitted acquire the appearance of being extra-ordinary or super-dimensional among the public, and they are seen as different or greater than they are in reality something we did not wish. . . . At the same time we didn't want to minimize serious problems which are now current, but wished to put them in the place and in the forum which corresponds to our social system" (Socijalisticka Federativna, 1967: 128).

14. For an official view on the "experience, role and tasks" of the Chamber of Nationalities between 1967 and 1969 by its president, see Kommunist, May 8, 1969: 5.

15. The 1968 amendments eliminated the Federal Chamber but substituted another "popularly" elected house, the Socio-Political Chamber, in its place. For a useful description of the rather complicated changes in the structure and functions of the Federal Assembly, see "Constitutional change. . ." (1969).

16. An official publication aimed primarily at a foreign audience points out that "the election of deputies of all national groupings to the assembly of a social-political community is primarily ensured as a political question by the conscious action of such political subjects as the League of Communists of Yugoslavia, the Socialist Alliance of the Working People of Yugoslavia and other bodies. In view of the public nature and comprehensiveness of political activity, individuals primarily assert themselves in public activities and in the work while the nationality factor enters only as a corrective. To date no major difficulties have been experienced in ensuring a national composition of representative bodies which corresponds to the national composition of the population, or the employed, as the case may be" (Joncic, 1967: 46).

Despite the introduction of multicandidate single-party electoral contests for a portion of the seats in parliamentary assemblies, the Yugoslav regime has tried to avoid intergroup competition in voting, either by offering a single choice in multinational constituencies, by having multiple candidates all come from a single ethnic group, or by having candidates from different nationality groups in the same district stand for positions at different levels of authority (for example, a Serb for the Federal Assembly, a Croat for the republican assembly, a Muslim for the communal assembly). An empirical study in one Bosnian electoral district revealed that few people acknowledged voting for representatives on the basis of ethnicity or locality (neighborhood). In informal conversations, however, the question often arose, Why aren't our people also on the nomination list? (Mujacic, 1971: 1086–89)

17. This arrangement has prompted some Yugoslav scholars to question the designation "Chamber of Nationalities" for a legislative body composed and operating along the lines of territorial delegations (Nin, Nov. 17, 1968: 3). The regime appears to have accepted this criticism. In the new constitution adopted in 1974 the Chamber of Nationalities was renamed the "Chamber of Republics and Provinces."

18. Yugoslav authors emphasize that provisions for the recall of deputies should not be used as a general procedure in cases of disagreement between constituents and their parliamentary representatives, since this would inhibit the self-initiative and independence of elected officials to resolve problems (Caca, 1967: 216–19; Globenik, 1969: 59–70; Cemerlic, 1971: 9–15).

19. Empirical studies of the attitudes of Yugoslav legislators reveal considerable correspondence between the official conception of the representative's role and the views of those elected. In survey interviews with federal deputies in 1968, most respondents indicated that their most important duty was to "represent the interests of society as a whole" and "to inform their constituents about the most important policies, and to explain them." When given a list of choices, very few legislators interpreted their major role as the representation of their constituents' needs and interests or intervention on behalf of their constituents. It is interesting in this respect that surveys of voters' attitudes reveal a considerably more restrictive interpretation of the deputy's role, much closer to the concept of imperative mandate than the view supported by the Yugoslav regime. A complete analysis of such data and its implications will be found in Cohen (1977).

20. Zdenko Has, a deputy in the Socio-Political Chamber of the Federal assembly. (Izmene . . . 1969: 44–45).

21. "The deputies in the Chamber of Nationalities must express the attitudes of their republican assemblies in the Chamber of Nationalities, but neither to them nor to other deputies, does an imperative mandate apply. They will be independent political personalities," stated Vida Tomsic, the president of the Chamber of Nationalities, in Borba (Oct. 30, 1968: 2). The Rules adopted by the Federal Assembly in June 1970 emphasized the independent aspect of the representational role: "Members of the Chamber of Nationalities must, on the request of the republican or provincial assembly which has elected them, inform the Chamber of Nationalities of the said assembly's proposals and views regarding matters falling within the province of work of this Chamber. . . . In presenting the opinions of the commune assemblies or their chambers of work communities, or of the republican or provincial assemblies, deputies may also present their own opinions and take a stand on these matters accordingly" (Rules of Order of the Federal Assembly, Article 49, 1970: 26, see also Article 17:9).

22. See Stankovic (1970) and Rusinow (1972). Despite Zanko's humiliation at the Tenth Croation Party Plenum in January, he did not lose his post as a federal deputy until April when the Croatian Assembly (Sabor) formally adopted procedures for his recall from the Chamber of Nationalities. His continued presence at the Federal Assembly's rostrum as a vice-president in the interim period was regarded by Croatian officials as a symbolic affront to the interests of their republic (Borba, Feb. 27, 1970: 7).

23. Quite apart from the question of effectiveness in conflict resolution, the overall increase of parliamentary activity in this period is quite impressive. For example, from January 1 to July 15, 1970, the various branches of the Federal Assembly were in session

145 out of 199 days, holding a total of 670 meetings. The fact that only 47 of these meetings were held by the Chambers of the Assembly (separately or jointly) and that the remaining 573 sessions were held by various committees, commissions, and work groups, indicates the significant internal development and complexity of the federal legislative structure. Moreover, unlike earlier periods, the Chamber of Nationalities was the most active branch of the Federal Assembly in terms of meetings and legislative output (Borba, Aug. 4, 1970: 4). During the same period 323 questions were put by federal deputies to members of the Federal Executive Council and administrative agencies, an enormous increase over earlier periods (see Table 4.1).

24. On some of the problems connected with regional economic development, see Hoffman (1972: 159–74, 216–21) and Hamilton (1968: 131–56).

25. Under constitutional amendment 33, adopted in 1971, it was possible for the Federal Executive Council to request the enactment of "temporary measures" by the presidency of Yugoslavia on matters of vital importance to the federation, when no agreement can be reached among the republics and provinces. Such measures can be enforced for as long as two years without the agreement of the Chamber of Nationalities. The first such request occurred in October 1972, on the matter of funds for the underdeveloped areas. An agreement was reached among the republics and provinces, however, before the formal adoption of such measures. (Borba, Oct. 6, 1972: 6; Politika, Oct. 27, 1972: 7; Nov. 2, 1972: 5; and Nov. 3, 1972: 5.)

26. Not all the political cleavages in the Chamber of Nationalities were along straight republican and provincial lines. In July 1969, for example, on one of the first votes in the newly reorganized Chamber, there was a sharp division within the Croatian delegation concerning the appointment of federal administrative functionaries. On the final vote the majority of the members of the Croatian delegation voted contrary to the view expressed by the political leadership in their republic. Over the next few years, however, this kind of voting pattern was an exception and was used by the Republican leadership in Croatia to justify the assertion of greater control over representatives in federal bodies (Borba, July 26, 1969: 4).

27. Out of 1,015 laws proposed to the Federal Assembly from June 27, 1963, to December 4, 1968, 850 (83.7%) were initiated by the Federal Executive Council and the Federal Administration; 160 (15.8%) by bodies of the Federal Assembly (commissions and committees); and 5 (0.5%) by individual deputies. Although the chamber and deputies of the Assembly did make some significant progress in amending laws in this period, as well as in articulating criticisms of the government, the influence of the executive branch in the legislative process was still dominant. See Documentacija Savezne Skupstina, 1969; "The Federal Executive Council," 1970: 17–26.

28. Speaking in the fall of 1969, Mitja Ribicic, who was then president of the Federal Executive Council, referred to pressures exerted on him by his native republic of Slovenia: "Pressures are nothing new in our society, they were evident during the term of office of the former Federal Executive Council as well. I am not the first president of the Federal Executive Council who is under pressure from his material republic. Stambolic [a Serb, who was president from 1963 to 1967] was under the same pressure. Everyone knows how the situation was with Comrade Spiljak [a Croat who was president from 1967–69], under what difficult conditions he worked, and how from the beginning of my administration, problems arose between me and the political organization in my own republic" (Nin, Sept. 21, 1969: 3). In an effort to minimize the influence of regional/ethnic group pressures on members of the Federal Executive Council, the 1974 Constitution provides (Article 348) that only one portion of the Council membership be elected on a parity basis, that is, an equal number of members representing each of the republics and provinces. The various Federal secretaries and other higher administrative officials who comprise the majority of the Council are to be selected on the basis of their qualifications, although special account is to be taken of their "national composition."

29. Amendment 9 (1968) to the Yugoslav Constitution of 1963 provided that during the consideration of any legislation affecting the equality and rights of the Yugoslav republic and provinces, ten deputies in the Chamber of Nationalities might request the use of a "special procedure" for decision making in the Chamber of Nationalities. As finally elaborated by statute in November 1971, the "special procedure" involved the creation of a special commission of the Chamber to arbitrate the objections or questions raised by the sponsors of the procedure before the Assembly reconsiders the matter. If no agreement is reached in this commission, or the act is judged harmful to the interests of one of the republics or provinces, the issue is taken off the agenda. In fact, the first and only demand for such a procedure occurred in October 1971 at the request of the Macedonian delegation, when, because of the urgency of the matter, and in the absence of a statute regulating the procedure, the problem was handled informally—literally in the halls of the Federal Assembly during a pause in the work of the Chamber. The 1971 amendments allowing the presidency to circumvent a deadlock in the Chamber of Nationalities has made the question of voting procedure in the Assembly somewhat of a minor point. The special procedure remains, however, essentially a delaying tactic to draw attention to a republic's vital interests on sensitive issues. For the details of the "special procedure," see "Odluku o postpku . . ." (1971: 941–42). On the October 1971 Macedonian veto," see Nin (Oct. 10, 1971: 12–13) and Politika (Oct. 1, 1971: 5).

30. Interrepublican committees were established in 1971 for five areas of federal policy: (1) developmental policy, (2) the monetary system, (3) foreign trade and the foreign exchange system, (4) the market, and (5) finance. Each interrepublican committee has a chairman appointed by the Federal Executive Council from among its own members and eight delegated representatives, one from each republic and autonomous province. By statute, the members of the committees must "adopt attitudes in the committee in the name of the republic or autonomous province which delegated them to the committee, taking account of the interests of the republic or autonomous province and also the interests of the social community as a whole" ("Odluku o obrazovaniju . . . ," 1971: 689–90).

31. The Constitution of 1974 (Article 357) provides that "the Federal Executive Council and the competent republican and provincial agencies shall by mutual agreement set up interrepublican committees for particular matters" thereby further institutionalizing the practice begun by statute in 1971. The new Constitution also (Article 321) reduced the size of the state presidency from 23 members to 9 members (one member from each republic and province plus Tito), and the size of the Chamber of Nationalities (renamed the Chamber of Republics and Provinces) from 140 deputies to 88 "delegates" (12 members from each Republic and 8 from each Province). Given the fact that the draft Constitution of June 9, 1973, had provided that the Chamber of Republics and Provinces be composed of 55 delegates, even its reduced size of 88 may be a concession (whether to advocates of legislative development, or to the need for more political employment we do not know). One might speculate that a smaller sized Chamber can offer a more practical forum for the negotiation of conflicts, although the simultaneous decline of overall parliamentary influence would seem to make size a largely formal matter (Constitution, 1974: 276–77, 260).

32. One author referred in Politika (June 12, 1971: 5) to the new Coordinating Commission in the Federal Executive Council for the resolution of interrepublican and provincial conflicts as a "little Chamber of Nationalities." See also Nin (Nov. 7, 1971: 34–35). Various difficulties currently facing federal legislators such as lack of time and information for decision-making or for critical questioning of executive policy and also inadequate time for serious discussion of issues between assemblies on the republican/provincial level and their "delegates" in the federal legislature, were noted in a report on the first years' work of the Chamber of Republics and Provinces (Socijalisticka Federativna . . . Vijece Republika i Pokrajina, 1975: 51–54). It is worth noting that the new rules adopted by the Chamber of Republics and Provinces at the end of 1974 require (Article 18) "delegations" to "represent the views" of the republican and provincial assemblies which

elect them to the federal legislature. Delegates are free to state their views and vote as they wish, but the new conception of representation puts greater emphasis on their responsibility to regional constituencies, at least formally, than was the case earlier (see footnote 21), or as is the case in the Federal Chamber of the Assembly where the rules provide that delegates may "be independent in decision-making and voting (Article 10, Rules of Procedure . . . , 1974: 103, 231). The new rules in the Chamber of Republic and Provinces thus come closer to an "imperative mandate" conception of representation which ironically corresponds to the views espoused by regionally oriented political leaders in the "liberal" period of Yugoslav federalism (1967–71). Such rules have little effect on interrepublican relations or legislative behavior today, however, given the climate (1972–77) of party-directed "revolutionary unity," antinationalism, and recentralization.

33. For the 1971 events in Croatia and subsequent measures with respect to nationalism, see Rusinow (1972), Shoup (1972), Schopflin (1973), Lendvai (1972), Larrabee (1972), and Johnson (1974).

34. See, for example, Lijphart (1968), Nordlinger (1972), Presthus (1973: 3–19, 234–35, 347–53), and Steiner (1967). Jurg Steiner and Robert Lehnen (1974) have suggested that while restriction of the decision-making process to a few top leaders, who operate by amicable agreement, may be the best way to avert hostility in culturally segmented polities in the short-run, there are also good normative and long-range empirical arguments against such a solution.

REFERENCES

BICANIC, B. (1973) Economic Policy in Socialist Yugoslavia. London: Cambridge University Press.

BIRCH, A. H. (1971) Representation. New York: Praeger.

BLAGOJEVIC, B., ed. (1969) Mesto i uloga odbora i komisija predstanicka tela. Belgrade: Institut za Uporedno Administracija.

BURKS, R. V. (1971) The National Problem and the Future of Yugoslavia. RAND Corporation P-4761 (Oct.).

CACA, D. (1967) "Karakter mandata i efikasnost odgovornost clanova predstavnickik tela u nasem politickom sistemu." In Izborni Sistem u Uslovima samoupravljanje, ed. F. Dzinic. Belgrade: Institut Drustvenik Nauka. Pp. 216–19.

CEMERLIC, H. (1971) "Odnos predstavink prema Biracima." Godisnjak Pravnog Fakulteta 19 (Feb.): 9–15.

CLISSOLD, S., Ed. (1966) A Short History of Yugoslavia. London: Cambridge Univ. Press.

COHEN, L. (1973) "The social background and recruitment of Yugoslav political elites: 1918–1948." In Opinion-making Elites in Yugoslavia, ed. A. Barton, B. Denitch, and C. Kadushin. New York: Praeger. Pp. 25–68.

"Diskusija o nacrtu ustava." (1973) Anali praunog fakulteta u Beogradu (May–August).

_____ (1977) "Political institutionalization in a one-party system: the Yugoslav parliamentary system 1963–1973." Ph.D. dissertation, Columbia Univ., New York, N.Y.

"Constitutional change in Yugoslvia." (1969) Yugoslav Survey 10, 3 (Aug.): 1–22.

Constitution of the Socialist Federal Republic on Yugoslavia (1974) Belgrade: The Secretariat of the Federal Assembly Information Service.

Constitution of the Socialist Federal Republic of Yugoslavia: Constitutional Amendments (1969) Belgrade: The Secretariat of the Federal Assembly Information Service.

DAHL, R. (1973) Regimes and Oppositions. New Haven, Conn.: Yale Univ. Press.

DJORDJEVIC, J. (1967) Ustavno Pravo. Belgrade: Savremena Administracija.

DJORDJEVIC, Z. (1969) Skupstinski Sistem. Belgrade: Centar za drustveno-politicko obrazovanje radnickog univerziteta "Djuro Salaj."

Documentacija Savezne Skupstina (1969) Appendix 4 (Feb.). Belgrade: Savezna Skupstina.

DZINIC, F. (1964) "Porast i interesovanja za rad Savezna skupstine." In Jugoslovensko Javno Mnenje o Aktuelnim Politickim i Drustvenim Pitanjima, ed. F. Dzinic. Belgrade: Institut Drustevenih Nauka. Pp. 11–12.

_____ (1967) Izborni Sistem u Uslovima samoupravljanje. Belgrade: Institut Drustevenih Nauka, Universitet u Sarajeur.

EULAU, H. (1967) "Changing views of representation." In Contemporary Political Science: Toward Empirical Theory, ed. I. de Sola Pool. New York: McGraw-Hill. Pp. 53–85.

"The Federal Executive Council: its organization and method of work (1970)" Yugoslav Survey 12 (Aug.): 16–26.

GERSKOVIC, L. (1955) "The system of producers' Councils in Yugoslavia." International Labor Review 71 (Jan.): 34–59.

_____ (1967) "Problemi i perspective razvoja skupstinskog sistema Jugoslavije." In Rad Jugoslavenski Acadmije Znanosti i Umjetnosti. Belgrade: Knjiga 347. Pp. 1–66.

GLOBENIK, J. (1969) "Poslanicki mandat u sistemu samoupravljanje Socijalizam 1: 59–70.

HAMILTON, I. (1968). Yugoslavia: Patterns of Economic Activity. New York: Praeger.

HONDIUS, F. (1968) The Yugoslav Community of Nations. The Hague: Mouton.

HOFFMAN, G. (1967) "The problem of underdeveloped regions in Southeast Europe: a comparative analysis of Romania, Yugoslavia and Greece." Annals of the American Association of Geographers 57, 4 (Dec.): 649–59.

_____ (1972) Regional Development Strategy in Southeast Europe. New York: Praeger.

Izmene u saveznom ustava (1969) Beograd: Sekretarijat za informativnu sluzbu Savezne Skupstine: 41–45.

JONCIC, K. (1967) The Relations Between Nationalities in Yugoslavia. Belgrade: Medjunarodna Stampa, Interpress 24.

JOHNSON, A. (1974) Yugoslavia in the Twilight of Tito. Beverly Hills: Sage.

KARDELJ, E. (1965) "Organizacija i methodi rada savezne skupstine." Belgrade: Sekretarijatz informativnu sluzbu savezne skupstine.

_____ (1970) "Current problems of our political system." Socialist Thought and Practice 41 (Oct.–Dec.): 3–38.

_____ (1974) "Interview." Foreign Broadcast Information Service, Daily Report Eastern Europe 2, 73 (April): I 3.

KRAMER, H. (1971) "The nationalities question in Yugoslavia." International Journal of Yugoslavia." Yugoslav Survey 12, 4 (Nov.): 1–36.

_____, ed. (1972) "The nationalities question in Yugoslavia." International Journal of Politics, 2, 1 (special issue).

LARRABEE, F. (1972) "Yugoslavia at the crossroads." Orbis 16 (Summer): 377–96.

LENDVAI, P. (1965) Eagles in Cobwebs: Nationalism and Communism in the Balkans. Garden City, N.Y.: Anchor Books.

_____ (1972) "Yugoslavia in Crisis." Encounter 39, 2 (Aug.): 68–75.

LIJPHART, A. (1968) The Politics of Accommodation: Pluralism and Democracy in the Netherlands. Berkeley: Univ. of California Press.

MIJANOVIC, G. (1970) "Evolucija strukture predstavnickih tijela u SFRJ." Godisnjak Pravnog Fakluteta u Sarajevu 63 (March): 112–38.

MUJACIC, M. (1971) "Medju-nacionalni odnosi u jednom gradu: primjer dervente." Gledista 12 (Aug.): 7–8.

NIKOLIC, P. (1969) Savezna Skupstina u Ustavnom i Politickom Sistemu Jugoslavije. Belgrade: Savez Udruzenja Pravnika Jugoslavije.

NORDLINGER, E. (1972) Conflict Regulation in Divided Societies. Cambridge, Mass.: Center for International Affairs, Harvard University.

"Odluku o obrazovanju i radu medjurepublickih komiteta." (1971) Sluzbeni list 27, 37 (Aug. 28): 689–90.

"Odluku o postpku za sprovodjenje tacke 3. Amandmana ix." (1971) Sluzbeni list 26, 51 (Nov. 18): 941–42.

PETRANOVIC, B. (1969) Politicka i ekonomska osnova narodne Vlasti u jugoslaviji za vreme obnove. Belgrade: Institut za Savremenu Istoriju.

PIJADE, M. (1950) Balanced Representation in a Multi-National State. London.

―――― (1954) "Oko vece naroda, da li ne treba nesto ismeniti u njegvom nacinu radu?" Arhiv za pravne i drustvene nauke 1 (June): 4.

PITKIN, H. (1967) The Concept of Representation. Berkeley: Univ. of California Press.

POPOVIC, N. (1968) Yugoslavia: The New Class in Crisis. Syracuse, N.Y.: Syracuse Univ. Press.

POPOVIC, P. (1971) "Skupstinski lobi." Nedelje informative novine 1049 (Feb. 14): 14.

PRESTHUS, R. (1973) Elite Accomodation in Canadian Politics. London: Cambridge Univ. Press.

RIEMER, N. (1967) The Representative: Trustee? Delegate? Partisan? Politico? Boston: Heath.

Rules of Order of the Federal Assembly (1970) Belgrade: Secretariat of Information of the the Federal Assembly.

Rules of Procedure of the Assembly of the S.F.R. of Yugoslavia (1975) Belgrade: Secretariat of Information of the S.F.R. of Yugoslavia Assembly.

RUSINOW, D. (1969) "Yugoslavia: 1969." American University Field Staff Reports, Southeast Europe Series 16, 8 (Aug.).

―――― (1971) "The price of pluralism." American University Field Staff Reports, Southeast Europe Series 18, 1 (July).

―――― (1972) "Crisis in Croatia: part II: facilis decensus averno." American Universities Field Staff Reports, Southeast Europe Series 19, 5 (Sept.).

Savezna narodna skupstina (1955) Belgrade: Kultura.

SCHOPFLIN, G. (1973) "The Ideology of Croatian Nationalism " Survey 19, 10 (Winter): 123–46.

SHOUP, P. (1968) Communism and the Yugoslav National Question. New York: Columbia Univ. Press.

―――― (1972) "The national question and the political system of Eastern Europe." In Eastern Europe in the 1970s, ed. S. Sinanian, I. Deak, and P. Ludz. New York: Praeger. Pp. 121–70.

SOBOLEWSKI, M. (1968) "Electors and representatives: a contribution to the theory of representation." In Representation, ed. J. R. Pennock and J. W. Chapman. New York: Atherton. Pp. 95–107.

Socijalisticka Federativna Republika Jugoslavija, Savezna Skupstina, Stenografske Beleske veca naroda (1967) 3, 1 (Jan.): 128.

Socijalisticka Federativna Republika Jugoslavija, Skupstina SFRJ Stenografske Beleske Vijece Republika: Pokrajina (1975) 34, 15 (Oct.): 51–54.

Socijalisticka Federativna Republika Jugoslavija, Savezna Skupstina, Stenografske Beleske veca naroda (1971), 27 (June): 18–20, 39–40.

STANKOVIC, S. (1970) "The meaning of the Croatian Central Committee plenum." Radio Free Europe Research–Communist Area 0447 (Jan. 21).

―――― (1971) "Problems in contemporary Yugoslavia." Radio Free Europe Research–Communist Area 2 (July 15).

STEINER, J. (1967) "Nonviolent conflict resolution in democratic systems: Switzerland." Journal of Conflict Resolution 13, 3 (Sept.): 296–304.

―――― and ROBERT G. LEHNEN (1974) "Political Status and Norms of Decision-Making." Comparative Political Studies 7, 1: 84–105.

TASIC, S. (1973) "Kako se dogovaramo na vrhu." NIN (Apr. 1): 33–35.

"Tenth Congress of the League of Communists of Yugoslavia" (1974) Socialist Thought and Practice 14, 6–7.

TOMASEVICH, J. (1955) Peasants, Politics, and Economic Change in Yugoslavia. Palo Alto, Calif.: Stanford Univ. Press.

TOZI, D., and D. PETROVIC (1969) "Politicki odnosi i sastav skupstina drustveno politickih zajednica." Socijalizam 12 (Dec.): 1581–99.

TRAJKOVSKI, T. (1970) "Zastupljenost Republika i pokrajina u federacija." Socijalizam 13, 10 (Oct.): 1217–35.

VUCINICH, W. (1969) "Nationalism and Communism." In Contemporary Yugoslavia, ed. W. Vucinich. Berkeley: Univ. of California Press. Pp. 236–84.

ZARKOVIC, NIDOJE (1977) Foreign Broadcast Information Service, Daily Report Eastern Europe 2, I (Jan.): I 18–I 19.

ZECEVIC, M. (1972) Skupstina SR Srbije u periodu 1963–1969 Godine. Belgrade: Institut za politicke studije, Fakultet politickih nauka.

THE ETHNIC COMPOSITION OF THE YUGOSLAV POPULATION BY REPUBLICS AND PROVINCES (March 31, 1971)
(PERCENTAGES AND TOTAL NUMBER)

Ethnic Groups	Yugoslavia Total Population	Serbia Total Republic	Serbia "proper"	Vojvodina	Kosovo	Montenegro	Macedonia	Slovenia	Croatia	Bosnia-Hercegovina
Serbs	39.7	71.2	89.5	55.8	18.4	7.5	2.8	1.2	14.2	37.3
Montenegrins	2.5	1.5	1.1	1.9	2.5	67.2	0.2	0.1	0.2	0.3
Macedonians	5.8	0.5	1.1	0.8	0.1	0.1	69.3	0.1	0.1	–
Slovenes	8.2	0.2	0.2	0.2	–	0.1	0.1	94.0	0.7	0.1
Croats	22.1	2.2	0.7	7.1	0.7	1.7	0.2	2.5	79.4	20.6
Muslims[a]	8.4	1.8	2.4	0.2	2.1	13.3	0.1	0.2	0.4	39.6
"Yugoslavs"[b]	1.3	1.5	1.4	2.4	0.1	2.1	0.2	0.4	1.9	1.2
Albanians	6.4	11.7	1.2	0.2	73.7	6.7	17.0	0.1	0.1	0.1
Hungarians	2.3	5.1	0.1	21.7	–	0.1	–	0.5	0.8	–
Other Nationalities	2.7	3.7	1.7	9.0	2.3	0.3	8.9	0.3	1.3	0.3
Respondents who stated a regional designation[c]	0.1	0.1	0.1	0.3	–	0.2	–	0.2	–	0.1
Respondents who made no statement[d]	0.2	0.1	0.1	0.1	–	0.1	–	0.2	0.4	0.2
Unknown	0.3	0.4	0.4	0.3	0.1	0.6	0.2	0.2	0.4	0.3
Total	100.0	100.0	100.0	100.0	100.0	100.0	100.0	100.0	100.0	100.0
(number)	(20,522.9)	(8,446.5)	(5,250.3)	(1,952.5)	(1,242.6)	(529.6)	(1,647.3)	(1,727.1)	(4,426.2)	(3,746.1)

Sources: This table is based on data in Ruža Petrović, "National Structure of the Yugoslav Population," Yugoslav Survey 14 (Feb. 1970): 4.

a. Muslims have been considered as an ethnic group since 1961.

b. A supranationality designation discouraged by official policy.

c. For example, "Dalmatian," "Bosnian," and so on.

d. Article 41 of the 1963 Yugoslav Constitution allowed citizens to withhold declaration of their nationality.

REPUBLICAN AND PROVINCIAL REPRESENTATION IN FEDERAL POLITICAL INSTITUTIONS (1972)

Republics and Provinces	Percent of Total Population	Federal Executive and Administrative Organs						League of Yugoslav Communists					
		Members of the Federal Executive Council		Deputy Federal Secretaries and Under-Secretaries		Administrative Advisors and Dept. Chiefs		Executive Bureau		Presidium[a]		Standing Members of the Conference[b]	
		(N)	%	(N)	%	(N)	%	(N)	%	(N)	%	(N)	%
Bosnia-Hercegovinia	18.3	(4)	14.3	(12)	17.7	(13)	14.0	(1)	12.5	(7)	14.6	(10)	14.3
Montenegro	2.6	(4)	14.3	(6)	8.8	(15)	16.1	(1)	12.5	(7)	14.6	(10)	14.3
Croatia	21.6	(4)	14.3	(9)	13.2	(16)	17.2	(1)	12.5	(7)	14.6	(10)	14.3
Macedonia	8.0	(4)	14.3	(10)	14.7	(12)	12.9	(1)	12.5	(7)	14.6	(10)	14.3
Slovenia	8.4	(4)	14.3	(10)	14.7	(13)	14.0	(1)	12.5	(7)	14.6	(10)	14.3
Serbia:													
Serbia "proper"	25.6	(4)	14.3	(11)	16.2	(12)	12.9	(1)	12.5	(7)	14.6	(10)	14.3
Kossovo	6.1	(2)	7.1	(5)	7.4	(5)	5.4	(1)	12.5	(3)	6.2	(5)	7.1
Vojvodina	9.5	(2)	7.1	(5)	7.4	(7)	7.5	(1)	12.5	(3)	6.2	(5)	7.1
Total	100.0	(28)	100.0	(68)	100.0	(93)	100.0	(8)	100.0	(48)	100.0	(70)	100.0

Sources: Nedelje Informativne Novina (July 9, 1972): 12–13; Politički i Poslovni Imenvik SFR Jugoslavije: 1972 (Belgrade: Novinska Agencija Tanjug, 1972).

a. In addition to republican and provincial delegations, the Presidium is also composed of 3 representatives of the Yugoslav armed forces, as well as Tito, who is president of the League of Communists, for a total of 52 members.

b. The conference created in 1969 consists of 280 delegates: 70 standing members elected at each congress of the League of Communists for a term of five years, and 210 delegates elected each year by local organizations. By statute the Executive Bureau and the Presidium are responsible to the conference during the period between the quinquennial congresses.

Chapter 5

PERMANENT SUPREMACY AND PERPETUAL OPPOSITION:
THE PARLIAMENT IN NORTHERN IRELAND, 1921–72

IAN BUDGE
CORNELIUS O'LEARY

INTRODUCTION

Most Western European and English-speaking countries have successfully bridged the single or multiple cleavages dividing their populations. Northern Ireland stands with Spain, Portugal, Greece, and Cyprus in the minority whose cohesion has been maintained by force. As in the Iberian countries, the use of force sprang from a conflict between Catholics and their opponents. It is unique, however, in that the anti-Catholics won. Northern Ireland also finds no parallels in Europe in its combination, from 1921 to 1972, of coercion with reasonably free elections and a regularly elected parliament. The closest comparison is perhaps with the southern American states after Reconstruction, whose legislatures also discriminated successfully against a minority in their midst while maintaining fairly democratic practices among the majority. With or without analogies, the role of the Northern Ireland Parliament in this ambiguous situation is of general interest as a case study in the management of conflict and as an example of how far a democratic parliament can go in the way of reconciliation without periling its own existence.

By world and, indeed, by Western European standards Northern Ireland is a small country. Its area is 5,237 square miles and its present population approximately 1,500,000. Nevertheless, the intensity and permanence of its central politico-religious division are hard to parallel even in the largest countries—a division dominating social and economic life to an even greater extent because of the confined provincial bounds. In seeking to examine the role of the Stormont Parliament[1] within its torn society it is essential to begin with the development of the religious cleavage and its wider social and political manifestations. Only thus can one appreciate the causes of the political *immobilisme* and administrative activism which characterized parliamentary institutions. Therefore we shall summarize the historical events leading to the emergence of Northern Ireland in 1922 as a semiautonomous province within the United Kingdom and describe the history of that province from 1922 to 1972; we shall then assess the marks that history has left upon the population in the form of basic cleavages and attitudes towards regimes; and subsequently we shall examine the role of the major interest groups before going on to discuss the formal constitution and institutions of the executive and legislature. The analysis of relations between the parliamentary parties takes us beyond the formal level to the actual work of the legislature, its divisions on important issues, and so to a final assessment of its management of popular divisions.

DEVELOPMENTS IN THE FOUNDATION OF NORTHERN IRELAND

Had the Northeast experienced the same historical evolution as the rest of Ireland, there would have been no partition and no Northern Parliament in 1922. Most of the island went through processes of colonization similar to those of Africa and Asia, albeit they antedated developments in these continents by 300 years. From the mid-sixteenth century on, the encroaching English appropriated the land of the native aristocracy and gentry,[2] and in so doing reduced the native peasantry to a position of great dependence. Like most colonists, the new English gentry were different in culture and religion from the natives: they were Protestant, and the peasants Catholic. They succeeded by the end of the seventeenth century in establishing military supremacy over the whole island and in retaining almost complete local and central executive power (backed by the mother country) until the end of the nineteenth century. The absolute supremacy of foreign rulers sparked off a few badly organized and abortive revolts, succeeded, as in India and the British African colonies, by mobilization of the peasants and creation of a mass nationalist movement. By finally resorting to guerrilla warfare and terrorism this movement secured dominion status for 26 counties as the Irish Free State in 1922.

The process of colonization in the Northeast, however, resembled the North American rather than the African or Asian models. That is, instead of retaining the natives for exploitation, the colonizers killed or expelled them and replaced them with a working and middle class of an ethnic and religious composition similar to that of the new rulers. These humbler colonists came from England and Scotland. The latter tended to Presbyterianism rather than Episcopacy, a cause of future internal division. But as Protestants, they made common cause with Episcopalians whenever threatened by the dispossessed Irish Catholics.

By the end of the seventeenth century a Protestant community at all levels of society was firmly established in the counties of Antrim and Down, around the growing commercial port of Belfast. Protestants spread more thinly out from this area to the south (County Armagh) and to the west, where the city of Londonderry founded by London merchants stood as a bastion against largely Catholic Donegal and the half-Catholic counties of Derry, Fermanagh, and Tyrone.

The relative peace and prosperity of the eighteenth century were secured by a ferocious assertion of the Protestant ascendancy, through legislation passed in the subordinate Irish Parliament in Dublin—never challenged, and hence tacitly approved, by the British executive and Parliament at Westminster, which had a veto over Irish laws and policy. The laws penalized all non-Episcopalians; hence, the Presbyterian bourgeoisie of the North were affected along with Catholic peasants. The resentment of these groups was utilized by the Episcopalian gentry when, in turn, they began to feel their own prosperity threatened by executive management of the Irish economy in British interests. Taking advantage of the withdrawal of British troops during the American War of Independence and the mobilization of volunteers to resist possible invasion, Episcopalian aristocrats successfully pressured Britain into granting legislative independence to the Irish Parliament in 1782. The fact that Protestants felt able to reduce their dependence on Britain testified to their sense of security after 90 years of internal peace. Some now wanted to go further and remove civil disabilities from all non-Episcopalians. Even though the restricted property franchise would have limited the effects of the measure, the possibility of a Catholic majority in Parliament was introduced, and many of the volunteer leaders balked. The Society of United Irishmen, which pressed for this proposal along with an assertion of complete Irish independence, was particularly strong in the Belfast region. The British-dominated executive tried to intimidate its supporters, and the situation gradually drifted into the unsuccessful rebellion of 1798. The rebellion gained mass support among the Catholic peasants of County Wexford, in the Southeast, and among the Presbyterians of Antrim.[3] In order to safeguard future security, the British government now pressed for union of the British and Irish parliaments, and the shaken Protestant gentry acceded in 1800.

During the nineteenth century the Catholic population of Belfast, the Protestant capital, grew to between 25% and 33% of the total population, and anti-Catholic rioting became a recurrent phenomenon. At times it approached the dimensions of war; the street riots of 1886 against the first Irish Home Rule Bill lasted four months, resulted in 32 killed, 371 injured, and £90,000 worth of damage. The first religious riot, resulting in two deaths, occurred in 1813, only 15 years after Ulster joined Ireland. (For dates and statistics of riots, see Budge and O'Leary, 1973: Table 3.1.) The growth of sectarian tension derived partly from the replacement of Moderates by Evangelicals in the leadership of the Presbyterian Church, but primarily from the growth of the Orange Order.

Encouraged by the British executive, a militant and classless Protestant secret society had emerged in 1795 which named itself after William of Orange—the king who finally crushed the Irish Catholics in 1690—and included among its goals the defense of the constitution and the Protestant religion. With official blessing the movement established itself all over Ireland in the first third of the nineteenth century; indeed, its success in penetrating the army and Britain itself led to an ineffective official ban in the middle years of the century. Whether banned or not, the origins of most nineteenth-century riots in Belfast can be traced to Orangemen. Each riot in turn led to increased segregation of the religious groups, as the "wrong sort"— the minority in each area—were burned out or evicted.

Meanwhile the Northeast, profiting by its closeness to Britain and the existence of native flax crops, industrialized on the basis of linen manufacture while the rest of Ireland remained agrarian. Its dependence on Britain for supplies of coal and iron and its commercial prosperity based on the British market gave the Northeastern population economic as well as cultural incentives for maintaining the Union unchanged.

When in the late nineteenth century mass peasant-based support for home rule grew in Catholic areas, rioting in the North was supplemented by a mass Unionist alliance, linking manufacturers and the middle class with the populist Orange Order. The Nationalists gained support in this area only in the Catholic enclaves—which were, of course, far from insignificant but still a minority.

The existence of a popular Unionist movement, solidly concentrated geographically, explains in part why Britain had such difficulty in making concessions to the powerful Nationalist movement over the 40 years from 1880 to 1922. The situation is comparable to that created by the French colonists in Algeria or the British in Rhodesia, but compounded by the geographical concentration and deep Irish roots of the Northern Protestant community.

Faced with unending guerrilla warfare in the south and west, and a breakdown of authority in the Northeast,[4] the British attempted a compromise. By the Government of Ireland Act of 1920 they set up two bicameral parliaments, one for the six heavily Protestant counties of the Northeast and one for the rest of the island. These bodies had identical powers, greater in substance than earlier home rule acts had conferred, and were linked through a mainly consultative body, the Council of Ireland, to which both were to send 20 representatives. The Council of Ireland (as the Explanatory Memorandum to the Government of Ireland Bill asserts) was to initiate proposals for united action if and when the two parliaments should merge into a parliament for all Ireland.

However, Irish Nationalist aspirations could no longer be satisfied with such qualified autonomy. The Parliament of Northern Ireland came into existence in May 1921; the Parliament of Southern Ireland was stillborn. The treaty of July 1921 was followed by the Anglo-Irish Treaty of December 1921, which conferred dominion status on the whole of Ireland, but allowed the Northern Ireland Parliament to opt out within one month of April 1922—a right which was duly exercised. Northern Ireland now emerged as a distinct political entity with a unique status within the United Kingdom.

NORTHERN IRELAND 1922-72

The new Parliament in Belfast was completely Unionist in composition. In the elections for the Northern House of Commons in May 1921, for which a system of proportional representation had been adopted in the hope that it would moderate straight sectarian voting, Unionists secured 40 seats, and the remaining 12 were divided between old Nationalists and new Republicans. This system (the Hare, or British, system) differs from the continental systems in that it maximizes the freedom of the voter. He may cast a preference for every candidate on the ballot paper, irrespective of party, in the order he pleases. This system was also prescribed for elections to the stillborn Southern Irish Parliament and subsequently for the Parliament (Dail) of the Irish Free State, later the Irish Republic. Although the opposition parties disagreed violently on political objectives, they agreed on taking no part in the proceedings of the new subordinate Parliament. Republicans have never done so; two Nationalists took seats after the elections of 1925, but the full Nationalist contingent was not represented until 1928. Since the Senate was elected by members of the House of Commons, its composition in the 1920s was also entirely Unionist.

The new government, unhampered by opposition, proceeded energetically with its task of setting up a viable political system. It speedily established control over the peace-preserving forces—apart from the British army—and the local authorities. The former aim was secured by setting up two new forces—a regular police force (the Royal Ulster Constabulary) and a special constabulary for use in riot control. Furthermore, a draconian law, the Special Powers Act, enabled the Minster for Home Affairs to arrest and detain persons without trial. The latter was achieved by abolishing proportional representation, which the British had introduced all over Ireland in 1920 to secure adequate minority representation, and by reverting to the simple majority system in single-seat constituencies with its built-in bias towards the largest party.

This last measure was a breach of the spirit, if not the letter, of the Government of Ireland Act and was the only act passed by the Northern Parliament from which royal (that is, British) assent was withheld between July and September 1922. However, assent was eventually given, since from the Unionist point of view the only way to secure the viability of the province was by regaining control of the local authorities of West Ulster. The Catholic-Nationalist majority in Londonderry, Tyrone, and Fermanagh had already opted to join the Irish Free State. These draconian measures succeeded in repressing both Nationalist dissidents and rioting loyalists. After 1923, when the government showed itself strong enough to repel attacks from beyond the border, and still more so after 1925 when the governments in London, Dublin, and Belfast agreed to recognize the status quo, it became clear that the new polity would last. The new functionaries—governor, judges, cabinet ministers—whether elected or appointed, were all politically homogeneous. The governor was a leading Unionist peer, the judges were also Unionists, the civil servants were either Ulster born and of Unionist leanings or new arrivals from Whitehall, ready to accept and work the system as best they could. Two of the very senior new arrivals—from the old Irish administration in Dublin—who helped set up the Ministries of Education and Agriculture were Catholic Unionists, but they were exceptional. Normally Unionism was synonymous with Protestantism. The possession of a loyal and efficient Civil Service, trained to British standards, was of major importance in securing the enduring stability of the new regime.

Political consolidation was completed in 1929 by changing the Stormont electoral system from proportional representation, as established by the Government of Ireland Act, to single-member, simple-majority constituencies on the Westminster model. Unionist pronouncements at the time indicated that the change was made in order to extinguish smaller parties, such as the class-based Northern Ireland Labour party (NILP), in favor of a straight confrontation between Unionists and Nationalists. This was intended to turn every election into an implied plebiscite on the border, with all the advantages on the Unionist side.

As this brief historical sketch has emphasized, Northern Ireland was the creation of Unionism, and Unionism was the political expression of Northern Protestantism. This fact was accepted and indeed welcomed by Unionist leaders, who well understood that in emphasizing the religious question they consolidated a permanent majority. Sir James Craig (later Lord Craigavon), the first prime minister, spoke of "a Protestant government" and "a Protestant Government for a Protestant people." Sir Basil Brooke (later Lord Brookeborough and third prime minister) spoke thus while a cabinet minister in 1933: "Many in the audience employ Catholics, but I have not one about my place. Catholics are out to destroy Ulster[5] with all their might and power. They want to nullify the Protestant vote, take all they can out of Ulster and then see it go to hell" (Mansergh, 1936: 240). Nationalist politicians were no less belligerent and uncompromising, but of course they had no power to commit the state to any course of action.

The political usefulness of religious confrontation was underlined for Unionist politicians by the severe impact of the depression on the population during the 1920s and 1930s. Underemployment in the rural areas produced abysmal living conditions but concealed the true extent of unemployment. In the industrialized city of Belfast, however, where the two basic industries of linen and shipbuilding were among the worst affected by the slow decline, culminating in the depression of the 1930s, unemployment rose to 25% of the insured population in 1925, 1931, and 1938. Even in 1940 provincial unemployment was estimated at a fifth of the population. In 1932 there was an unprecedented nonsectarian riot of unemployed workers in Belfast. Although this was succeeded by normal sectarian street battles in 1934, it was a danger sign for the Unionist coalition.

Two responses of the Unionists have already been noted: the first was to change the electoral system so as to disadvantage particularly the Labour party, which sought to attract both Catholic and Protestant support on a working-class basis, and the second was to urge job discrimination in favor of Protestant workers. Both tactics might have been unsuccessful had they not been supplemented by intense efforts on the part of the Unionist government and Parliament to bring social services and conditions in Northern Ireland up to British standards and to put industry and agriculture on a competitive footing. Such domestic policies were entirely within the spirit of Unionism, since they reduced differences with Britain, while at the same time they bestowed material benefits on the Protestant working class.

In putting such policies into effect, the government was faced with major difficulties. It inherited from the previous Irish regime a deplorable housing stock, inadequate and badly managed schools plagued with sectarian demarcation disputes, poor health services run by local authorities on principles of financial economy rather than adequate care, and minimal social security based on the nineteenth-century Poor Law. The economic depression reduced direct government revenues, which at best comprised only one-fifth of taxes levied in the province. Under the Government of Ireland Act, the major taxes—income, custom, and excise—were levied and raised by the British government, and the province got a share for domestic expenditure only after deductions for services "reserved" to Westminster (such as the Post Office) and an "Imperial contribution" to cover overall national needs, defense, and foreign affairs.

These problems constituted the major focus of the government's and Parliament's attention, after the ever-present necessity of maintaining Unionist supremacy. Essentially during the interwar period, policy consisted in insuring parity of social services, particularly unemployment assistance, with the rest of the United Kingdom, in spite of a much lower per-capita yield of personal taxation—£3.40 as against £7.50 in Britain in 1924. Acceptance of this principle by Britain, after long and tortuous negotiations in 1929 and 1936, meant that the imperial contribution was converted into a residual charge on Northern Irish revenues, if indeed there was not a net subsidy from Britain. This concession was secured only by acceding to British demands for levies on local authorities for specific services (for example, education) and by raising the rate of income tax to increase domestic contributions to the cost of social services. The mobilization of all available revenue for this object, together with the subsidizing of industry and agriculture to improve their competitive position, meant that little money was left for housing, education, and similar needs. What could be done was done, but "the volume of new building . . . fell far short of what was needed," and the standard of school equipment and amenities was "a generation or more behind most of England and Wales" (Lawrence, 1965: 114 and passim). And Poor Law workhouses, indiscriminately housing orphans and the physically and mentally disabled, were not replaced until after World War II.

In areas where finance was not a constraint the Unionist authorities were remarkably active in administrative initiatives, particularly in updating previous British legislation passed under the Union to fit special Ulster conditions. These tasks were undertaken both through public acts and statutory orders authorizing ministers to act in detail (Mansergh, 1936: 18).

The administrative activism of the government and Parliament contrasted strongly with their uncompromising *immobilisme* towards the Catholic-Nationalist minority—a third of the population. This combination of strategies paid off politically, however. Excluded from any say within the Northern state and impotent to effect its overthrow, the Nationalists were reduced to gestures such as refusing to accept the status of official (and hence loyal) opposition, making often justified charges of gerrymandering and discrimination which consumed interminable hours of parliamentary time, and sporadically boycotting parliamentary proceedings. These "boycotts" were of two kinds: some Nationalists would stand with the avowed intention of *not* taking their seats; others (as in the Parliament of 1933—38) would absent themselves for long periods. This general political apathy, which guaranteed Unionist predominance, was evidenced by the high percentage of uncontested returns in the Stormont elections of 1929 and 1933.

As in other areas of the world, the war of 1939–45 sped up many developments. A further wedge between Nationalists and Unionists was driven by the South's neutrality and Northern Ireland's active commitment on the Allied side. The division was furthered by the Southern withdrawal from the British Commonwealth in 1949 and the proclamation of a republic—adroitly exploited by the Unionists in calling an election as an expression of Northern loyalty, and forcing the Northern Ireland Labour party to split between pro- and anti-Partitionists.

The North's participation was a material advantage to Britain in the middle years of war by providing bases from which to protect the Northwest sea approaches. In partial recognition of this fact, the British government committed itself in 1942 to the principle of parity in all Northern Irish social services. The conditions brought to light by wartime bombing also stressed the need for extensive social reconstruction. After the death of Lord Craigavon in office in 1940, his successor, J. M. Andrews, had to face internal Unionist discontent over these conditions, as a result of which he was overthrown in favor of Lord Brookeborough in 1943. The new administration pressed ahead with numerous commissions of inquiry, whose detailed plans were much influenced by parallel British inquiries. Aided by British subventions, these were put into vigorous effect in the postwar years; an estimate of British payments in the 1960s put them at £100,000,000—about one-third of the annual provincial budget (O'Leary, 1969: 123–24).

Besides its detailed work on the construction of the welfare state in Northern Ireland, Parliament and the government pressed on vigorously with legislation for housing construction and a successful program of industrial diversification and development. Its obvious success in ameliorating living conditions and in repelling cross-border attacks by the illegal "Irish Republican Army" during the years 1956–62[6] put the Unionist government in a strong position by the time of the retirement of Lord Brookeborough from the premiership and the succession of Captain Terence O'Neill (April 1963). The opposition then was tiny, fragmented, and disillusioned. Nationalist MPs acted merely as Catholic spokesmen and had little interest in the legislative process. The same was true of Catholic members with socialist leanings (Republican Labour, Irish Labour, Socialist Republican). The NILP, though the official opposition, was too small to be effective.

Viewed from this position of strength it seemed a logical step for the new prime minister to consolidate the regime further through better relations with the alienated Catholic minority—35% of the whole population but nearly 50% of the schoolchildren. In contrast to Lord Brookeborough's uncompromising pronouncements of the 1930s, O'Neill visited Catholic schools and hospitals and talked with Catholic priests. These gestures were crowned by an invitation to the prime minister of the Irish Republic to discuss matters of common interest at Stormont—the first meeting of the two Irish premiers since 1927. In 1965 O'Neill held a general election in which his party gained two of the four Labour seats in Belfast.

There is considerable survey evidence to show that O'Neill's policy of studied moderation enjoyed majority support among the population at large, Unionist voters, and even Unionist politicians (Budge and O'Leary, 1973: 204). However, from the moment his opening to the Catholics became visible, it was attacked by Protestant extremists. In 1966 the Protestants provoked riots and summer-long disturbances in Belfast in which three people were killed. In 1966 and 1967 there were two revolts within the Unionist Parliamentary party which O'Neill put down by the expedient of broadcasting to the people and challenging his opponents to state the reason for their opposition. This they were not willing to do, and both revolts ended in votes of confidence of specious unanimity within the various party bodies.

O'Neill was safe as long as he seemed to keep the support of middle-of-the-road Protestants and Catholics. On the Catholic side, the Nationalists had reciprocated by accepting the status of official opposition in 1965. Possibly because of the threat from his own extremists, in subsequent years O'Neill did not promote any practical measures to relieve Catholic grievances—mainly the economic disparities between East and West Ulster, where the bulk of Catholics lived; the restricted franchise in local government elections; and the system of allocating public housing through local authorities. The last two points were linked, because occupancy of a house conferred a title to vote in local elections. In western areas, where Catholic and Protestant proportions were equal, housing allocations were managed for political purposes. Thus, in Londonderry in 1922 a Nationalist council had opted to join the South. It was disbanded, and wards were twice rearranged so that the two wards with a slight Protestant majority returned more councillors than a third with an enormous Catholic majority. The balance was maintained by refusing Catholics permission to build in the Protestant wards and by allowing them municipal housing only in the south ward. Had the system been reformed, the Unionists might have lost up to 15 out of the 55 local authorities they controlled in the late 1960s (out of a total of 66).[7]

The failure of the official Nationalists to gain real concessions, together with the rising expectations engendered by O'Neill, promoted the rapid growth of a largely Catholic civil rights movement from the middle of 1968. The civil rights marches were met by counter-marches by extreme Protestants, coupled with ineffectual prohibitions by the minister for home affairs. Under pressure from the British prime minister, who threatened to activate Section 75 of the Government of Ireland Act, which reserves to the British Parliament ultimate authority over Northern Ireland, O'Neill publicly promised five specific reforms to meet Catholic grievances. The civil rights marchers refused to be won over, since universal franchise had not been conceded; street affrays became more violent and O'Neill's position inside the Unionist party became insecure. The prime minister played the only card open to him by calling an election in February 1969, in which he encouraged unofficial candidates to stand against those official Unionists who opposed him. In the Belfast area a few of the "independent pro-O'Neill Unionists" won seats, but not enough to make an impact. Generally, on the Unionist side the electors returned official nominees, whether pro- or anti-O'Neill. The main result of the election was to unseat official Nationalists in favor of civil rights activists and to strengthen the smaller opposition parties, such as Republican Labour, which could claim some affiliation with that cause.

Faced by Unionist dissidence, continuing clashes between police and marchers, and widespread popular unrest, O'Neill resigned in April 1969, in favor of Major James Chichester-Clark, who made further concessions in the form of the universal franchise and a restructuring of local government. The situation had got out of control, however, and the traditional Orange processions in the summer provoked further affrays. In mid-August the Catholic population of the Bogside, a suburb of Londonderry, barricaded the area against threats of a Protestant incursion and subsequently resisted attempts of the police to penetrate the suburb—amidst announcements of a "Free Derry" and the flying of Republican flags. Protestants in Belfast reacted to this Republican uprising by mob attacks

on the Catholic population in which the uniformed special constabulary (a part-time auxiliary police force) played a prominant part.
After 48 hours of anarchy, 7 persons were killed and 1,300 families,
mostly Catholic, were rendered homeless through fire or threats.
British troops thereupon occupied Belfast and Derry in order to
interpose themselves between the belligerents.

Two developments followed from the Belfast and Derry riots. On
the one hand, the Unionist governments under Chichester-Clark and
Brian Faulkner (who succeeded to the premiership in 1971) engaged
in far-reaching plans of political reform. The Macrory Report recommended the transfer of most local functions to the less partial central
administration. The special constabulary was abolished. A parliamentary commissioner for complaints (ombudsman on the British model)
was appointed. This program culminated in Faulkner's proposal in
the summer of 1971 to set up four powerful parliamentary committees, with far-reaching powers of oversight and inquiry into the
administration, at least two of which would be chaired by members
of the Opposition.

By this time, however, the Nationalist parties were again boycotting Parliament as a result of the other development which followed
from the riots. Taking advantage of Catholic tension and insecurity
and the disruption of the police force, the two factions of the IRA
(provisionals and officials) established themselves in Catholic areas
on the grounds that armed self-defense was the only security against
Protestant incursions. From the summer of 1970 both factions
encouraged street riots and sniping at British troops, thus gradually
changing their image among Catholics from defenders to enemies.
When two young men were shot by British troops during a riot in
Londonderry in July 1971, and an inquiry was refused, all Nationalist groups withdrew from Stormont.

The authorities wielded the carrot of reform but were also faced
with a determined effort by the IRA to overthrow the regime and
the possibility of counter-reaction by Protestant extremists. In August 1971 Faulkner coupled a ban on traditional Protestant parades
with the reactivation of internment on suspicion under the Special
Powers Act. Upwards of 600 men, almost all Catholic, were imprisoned. The IRA reaction was to intensify its campaign with
indiscriminate bombing and assassination, which by April 1972
brought the casualties of disorder to 400 killed, double that number
wounded, and massive destruction of property. The escalation of
costs for the British government eventually moved it in the spring

of 1972 to activate its latent constitutional power to rule the province directly and to suspend the Stormont Parliament and government for a year.

POPULATION CLEAVAGES AND POLITICAL ATTITUDES

The bare facts of history themselves demonstrate the intensity and salience of the religious cleavage. Table 5.1 displays the relative proportions of the religious groups over the different areas of the province in 1961. These have remained fairly constant from far back in the nineteenth century: proportions in 1900 were at the extreme only five percentage points removed from those in the table.

Among Protestants, in the census of 1961, the Presbyterian Church accounted for 47% of the total, the (Episcopal) Church of Ireland for 38%, Methodists for 8%, and minor denominations for 5%. The most direct indicator of strong involvement with the churches is attendance: 66% of a provincial sample attended church at least once a week. This figure represents only 46% of Protestants and 95% of Catholics; but the Protestant figure is still more than double the comparable proportion for England and Wales (Rose, 1971: chap. 8; Budge and Urwin, 1966: 101–05). Attendance in the industrial city of Belfast is lower than in the province as a whole, but 54% of the population still attends church at least once a month (Budge and O'Leary, 1973: 243).

Table 5.1 shows very clearly the different religious composition of the east, where three quarters of the population is Protestant, and of the west, where slightly more than half are Catholic. Religious

TABLE 5.1

PERCENTAGE DISTRIBUTION OF CATHOLICS AND PROTESTANTS IN NORTHERN IRELAND IN 1961[a]

		Protestant %	Catholic %	Total Number
East Ulster	Antrim	76	24	273,000
	Belfast	72	28	415,000
	Down	71	29	266,000
	Armagh	53	47	117,000
	Londonderry	49	51	165,000
West Ulster	Tyrone	45	55	133,000
	Fermanagh	48	52	51,000
	Northern Ireland	65	35	1,420,000

a. This was the last census to provide religious statistics.

differences are exacerbated by economic disparities. During the year 1968, for instance, the average unemployment in Northern Ireland as a whole was 7.2%, in the west 12.6%, and in the predominantly Catholic towns of Londonderry and Strabane, 13.4% and 18.2% respectively. Some of these disparities can be attributed to the natural economic advantages enjoyed by the east, but some were due to government policy in the west, which managed to secure only 8 out of 58 new factories.

Besides the general contrast between east and west, disparities also open up between the heavily industrialized city of Belfast and its immediate environs and the rest of the province. The activities of Belfast center around shipyards, engineering, and textiles, although policies of diversification have resulted in a variety of large and small factories concerned with a wide range of manufacture. Within Greater Belfast is concentrated about 40% of the population. The remainder are scattered in numerous small towns and across the countryside. Only 30 towns have a population of more than 2,500. Only one of these (Londonderry, with more than 50,000 inhabitants) compares at all with Belfast. There is a large agricultural sector consisting of 54,300 farms, the overwhelming majority medium or small, and most worked only by the farmer and his family. Half are devoted to near-subsistence farming with cash incomes of below £500 (1963 value). Other occupations fall into the three main categories of textiles, engineering, and food-processing, in all of which large firms predominate (Lawrence, 1965: 30–32).

The large, conservative-minded agricultural and small-town element helps to account for the muted state of class feeling in Northern Ireland. Forty-seven % of a provincial sample identified themselves as middle class in 1968, and among the Protestants in the sample the proportion was 52% (Rose, 1971: Table 9.5). Even in industrial Belfast, middle-class identifiers comprised 35% of the population and working-class identifiers 53%; spontaneous class identification was also low (Budge and O'Leary, 1973: 236). The general absence of class feeling must also derive from the centrality of the politico-religious cleavage and the predominance this has given to the conservative Unionist party. Northern Ireland clearly demonstrates the primacy of religion and politics over class.

This is demonstrably evident in voting behavior. A calculation made for the local and Stormont elections of 1964 and 1965 in Belfast attributed to religion six times the effect of class (Budge and O'Leary, 1973: 224). Catholics vote for all the non-Unionist parties—

Northern Ireland Labour as well as the Nationalist and Nationalist-oriented Labour parties which are principally centered in Belfast. More than three-quarters of Protestants vote Unionist, 11% for Northern Ireland Labour (proportions are lower for Unionists and higher for Northern Ireland Labour in Belfast) and less than 1% for any other party (Budge and O'Leary, 1973: Tables 7.3, 7.10; Rose, 1971: Table 7.9). In contrast, the class composition of Unionists and Nationalists is quite mixed. Only Northern Ireland Labour, whose electoral appeal is explicitly to class interests, is heavily based on one class—the urban manual working class (Budge and O'Leary, 1973: 207—15).

Party competition throughout the history of the province has been linked closely with questions of the retention of the regime. In 1966 in Belfast positive comments about the parties centered around strong and benevolent leadership but extended to their welfare and development policies. Negative comments, on the other hand, stressed the rigid position of Unionists on the border and their intolerance and discrimination in favor of their own supporters. The Nationalists attracted largely negative comments, related to their maintenance of the old divisions (Budge and O'Leary, 1973: 199—206). In the province as a whole in 1968 Unionists were seen by half the electorate as a one-issue party stressing the Union with Britain, and Nationalists by almost the same proportion as standing solely for a United Ireland (Rose, 1971: Tables 7.4, 7.5). No other party policy was stressed in either case by more than 15%.

It is not surprising, therefore, that attitudes towards the constitution and regime vary strongly with party and associated religion. In 1968, 54% of the total population indicated, on balance, approval of the regime. Sixty-eight % of Protestants affirmed support and 22% were uncertain. Thirty-three % of Catholics approved on balance, compared to 34% who disapproved and 32% who were uncertain. Overwhelmingly, Catholics opposed the use of violence to change the political regime in the North, although more than half thought it might be right in certain circumstances to hold illegal demonstrations. On the other hand, 52% of Protestants approved "any measures" to retain the regime, although two-thirds disapproved of illegal assemblies (Rose, 1971: Tables 5.7—9).

These responses demonstrate the fairly narrow margin of support within which the parliamentary institutions of Northern Ireland had to operate. Most people, at some stage or other, were prepared to contemplate illegal action in pursuit of their constitutional objectives. Even supporters of the regime could not be relied upon to give consistent compliance. Indeed, it is obvious, both from the historical and the survey evidence, that one of the major problems for Stormont was to restrain the readiness of its own supporters to resort to violence of a type which could—and in 1969 did—topple the regime. In interpreting the unyielding pronouncements of Unionist politicians in their "Protestant Government for a Protestant People," one must remember the extent to which they were prisoners of their own supporters. The success of the Unionists in maintaining their own cohesion for 50 years in face of challenges from "Protestant Unionists" and other ultraloyalists was a considerable political achievement, bought at the price of "no surrender" to the Catholics. There was, in fact, a widespread consciousness of the extent to which constitutional change of any kind could unleash passions which might engulf the whole of society (Budge and O'Leary, 1973: 358).

INTEREST GROUPS UNDER THE STORMONT REGIME

The pervasive influence of religion over Northern Irish politics immediately focuses attention on churches as interest groups. Although all the Ulster churches are organized on an all-Ireland basis, the Protestant churches have their major concentration of adherents in Ulster, while the major strength of the Catholic Church is in the Republic. Catholic bishops (including the Cardinal Primate of All Ireland at Armagh) have consistently favored a United Ireland, but have been quietist politically, seeking in their public pronouncements to gain redress for Catholic grievances rather than to inflame opposition to the regime. This stance has also characterized the parish clergy. Inevitably, the Church had to negotiate with the regime about the position of Catholic schools. It defeated proposals made in 1946 that grants could only be made to voluntary schools with state nominees on the boards of management: Stormont capitulated and gave grants unconditionally. The Church, however, was unable to obtain state support for the chief Catholic hospital in Belfast until 1971 at the very end of the Stormont regime. By negotiating about such matters, the Church maintained it had "recognized" the regime, but could not give any more positive sign of approval in view of the regime's bias against Catholics. The Protestant churches have been involved in similar controversies about education which, however, were carried on without mutual animosity. All Protestant churches accepted the regime de jure as well as de facto. While individual clergymen might criticize aspects of discrimination, they have all been prisoners of their own community's distaste for a United Ireland in which a conservative Catholicism could predominate.

In politics the chief Protestant bulwark has been less the churches themselves than the Orange Order, whose origins were described earlier. Membership was estimated in 1968 at about 43% of Protestant men in the province, that is, about 110,000. The order's main aims are maintenance of the constitution and the Protestant religion; it is militantly anti-Catholic. Its halls and lodges are found in every part of the province. Annual processions throughout the summer commemorate the main events in the establishment of Protestant Ascendancy, and have frequently touched off riots and affrays between Protestants and Catholics, most recently the crisis of the summer of 1969. Orange lodges are affiliated with the Unionist party at both the constituency and provincial levels. One-fifth of the members of the Ulster Unionist Council, the governing body of the mass Unionist party, are nominees of the order and all male Unionist MPs up to the mid-1960s were members. These close connections make the party closely responsive to the order and reciprocally bind the order closely to the party. Although it obviously could not have approved of the course of events in the late 1960s, the official Orange leadership never directly attacked the prime minister but contented itself with general statements expressing anxiety at the course of events. The order's main influence probably lies in the opportunities its meetings and processions offer Protestant extremists to provoke violence whenever they feel their community is endangered.

As compared to the Orange Order, business appears to exert little direct influence on the Unionist party. Conservative in general ideology, the party has adopted a highly pragmatic policy on development and welfare: incentives of all kinds have been offered to industry and agriculture to stimulate economic development and relieve unemployment. Yet many nationalized bodies have been set up—the Northern Irish Housing and Transport Authorities, for example—and Unionist ministers have devoted major efforts to extending health and welfare services and public housing.

Trade unions equally lack the direct political influence associated with the Orange Order, partly because their loyalty to the regime was suspect through their association with the NILP, which gave unambiguous recognition to partition only in 1949. Although more than 90% of the 191,000-odd members belonged in the mid-1960s to unions with headquarters in Britain, most of these were represented in a Northern Ireland committee of the Dublin-based Congress of Irish Trade Unions. Only in 1964 did the government recognize the committee and establish an economic council on which unions and businesses were represented.

More formidable interest groups in many ways were the local authorities, particularly since most were dominated by Unionist cliques which might be at odds with the provincial government. Belfast Corporation, the largest of the authorities and accountable to almost a third of the total population, supported a city Unionist party which is not officially recognized by the central party and which on occasion ran its own candidates against official nominees. In the 1930s, the corporation raised one of the few legal actions against the government, based on the claim that it had exceeded its constitutional powers. The government in turn initiated several inquiries into corruption in the corporation and replaced it with nominated commissioners from 1942–45—as it did with Londonderry in 1968. Like the Orange Order, the Unionist authorities have probably raised the most difficulties for the government when pushing official policies to extremes and provoking reactions which may be hard to control.

The same is true for the police forces, the main coercive arm of the Unionist regime. The regular police force, the Royal Ulster Constabulary, was directly recruited and organized by the central authorities. Of its 8,000 members at the end of the 1960s less than 10% were Catholic. The part-time special constabulary (the B-specials) were wholly Protestant and devoted almost entirely to tasks of countering Republican subversion and helping the regular police with demonstrations, riots, and such. Loosely organized in local companies, they were highly effective in countering IRA raids. The function of the organization was also to keep Unionist extremists in the localities under some sort of central control; conversely, their official standing when they did get out of control—as in the Belfast riots of 1969—proved a grave embarrassment to the government.

The most powerful groups were thus those with an interest in perpetuating the politico-religious division, rather than any associated with the potential cross-cutting cleavage of class. (On general cross-cutting, see Budge and O'Leary, 1971 and 1972.) In each case, Unionist leaders were able to exercise some influence through institutional links, but equally these links made the leaders accountable to extreme groups and strengthened the general impression of the

Stormont regime as a "Protestant Parliament for a Protestant People."

FORMAL LEGISLATIVE INSTITUTIONS

Both constitutionally, through the constituent act, and by majority inclination, the Northern Ireland Parliament was modeled on the British Parliament at Westminster. Two chambers—Senate and House of Commons—and a governor appointed by the crown had formally to consent to legislation and support a government. Actually the governor's consent was given automatically, and the Senate and the Commons never came into conflict as a result of their common dominance by the Unionist party. Senators were elected by MPs on the basis of proportional representation so their party composition mirrored that of the Commons (McGill, 1965). The government consisted of the leader of the majority party as prime minister and senior colleagues nominated by him to lead individual ministries and form the cabinet. All had to be members of the legislature. Although government functions continually expanded during 1922—72, the number of ministries did not change much—there were seven in 1922 and eight by 1964, six of which were the same. There were seven ministers in the cabinet in 1922 and nine by 1964, with three noncabinet appointments (Lawrence, 1965: 22—23).

Together with three officials of the House itself, official positions were held by 15 of 52 members of the House of Commons; these 15 were selected from the 35 to 40 members belonging to the official Unionist party. By getting the support of five backbench Unionists, in addition to members of the government bound by the doctrine of collective responsibility, the prime minister could gain a majority at private meetings of the parliamentary Unionist party. Members were then under party discipline to vote in accordance with its resolutions. The prime minister's tight grip on party and thus legislative proceedings accounts for the extraordinary stability of governments. Lord Craigavon was prime minister with very much the same cabinet from 1921 until his death in 1940. His successor, J. M. Andrews, was toppled in 1943 by a party revolt under the stress of war conditions. Lord Brookeborough, however, held the premiership from 1943 until his voluntary retirement in 1963. The internal Unionist opposition to O'Neill took six years—from 1963 to 1969—to dislodge him. Chichester-Clark's and Faulkner's short terms of office are attributable to British intervention rather than to purely domestic developments. All prime ministers had had long continuous terms in office before acceding to the premiership, so the degree of continuity in office is underestimated by these figures.

Cabinet stability is only one illustration of the extent to which Unionist dominance altered the workings of the Westminster system. Where in the British Parliament procedural devices for the shortening of debate—for example, the "guillotine" or the "kangaroo"—were accepted by both sides as necessary to implement the program of the government of the day, in Stormont they simply enabled the permanent majority to ignore minority wishes. This contrasted with the situation before 1920 when the strong Nationalist group in the British House of Commons was able to hold up legislation until the wishes of the Northern minority were consulted (Budge and O'Leary, 1973: chaps. 3 and 4). The absence of any permanent committee system with a seniority system meant that Opposition MPs could not establish strategic positions in the legislative process independent of the government. Faulkner's offer of such a system, with chairmanships reserved for the Opposition, came too late in the day ever to be put into effect. The experience of the Belfast Corporation—a Unionist-dominated body with permanent committees—suggests that even had there been strong parliamentary committees, the Unionists would have monopolized chairmanships (Budge and O'Leary, 1973: 159). Only three cabinet ministers in the whole history of Stormont were non-Unionists and only one—appointed in 1971—was a Catholic.

ELECTIONS AND PARTIES

The basis of Unionist dominance is documented in Table 5.2, which shows seats gained for all elections from 1921 to 1969 inclusive. After 1929, when proportional representation was abolished, returns were made on the basis of plurality voting in 48 single-member constituencies: four MPs, until the abolition of university seats in 1969, continued to be elected by proportional representation from British graduates of Queen's University, Belfast. A noticeable feature of elections after 1929 was the high proportion of uncontested seats. Unionists and Nationalists were so firmly entrenched in many constituencies that it was not worthwhile for rival parties to contest them. The fluctuating nature of other parties' representation is also noticeable: Liberals gain an occasional seat; the same is true of various Nationalist Labour parties based in Belfast;

and at high points, Northern Ireland Labour gained as many as four seats (all from Belfast), but the constants in the situation were the majority Unionists and minority Nationalists. While the Opposition might be fragmented, official Unionists were subject to frequent challenge by Independents and Protestants of various types, reinforcing the intransigence of some popular elements and of the pressure groups noted earlier.

Pressures on Unionist MPs derived not only from external electoral challenges but also from their constituency associations. The small size of the province and the personal nature of political relationships made for close contacts between the MP and members of his constituency association, who had the ultimate right of nomination. Whereas in the British Conservative party the incumbent MP generally has a presumptive right to renomination, Unionist constituency associations held a selection committee before each election which might deny the sitting MP the nomination. Under these circumstances the MP had a strong interest in maintaining established lines of policy acceptable to local activists.

Pressures of this kind are peculiar to the Unionists who, with Northern Ireland Labour, are the only groups to have regular committees and paid organizers. The Nationalist organization consisted

TABLE 5.2
DISTRIBUTION OF SEATS IN GENERAL ELECTIONS
FOR THE NORTHERN IRELAND PARLIAMENT,
1921–69 INCLUSIVE

	Unionist	Ind. Unionist	LIB.	IND.	NILP	NAT. LAB.	NAT.	Republican Sinn Fein
1921	40	0	0	0	0	0	6	6
1925	32	4	0	1	3	0	10	2
1929	37	3	0	0	1	0	11	0
1933	36	3	0	0	2	0	9	2
1938	39	3	0	0	1	1	8	0
1945	33	2	0	3	2	2	10	0
1949	37	2	0	2	0	2	9	0
1953	38	1	0	1	0	3	7	2
1958	37	0	0	1	4	2	8	0
1962	34	0	1	1	4	3	9	0
1965	36	0	1	2	2	2	9	0
1969	36	3	0	3	2	2	6	0

Key: LIB. = (British) Liberal party; IND = no party affiliation; NILP = Northern Ireland Labour party and precursors. NAT. LAB. = Independent Labour, Republican and Irish Labour, Socialist Republican; NAT. = Nationalist party.

of preelection conventions of priests and people; in effect, they constituted a loose "party of notables" which did not even have a formal provincial convention until 1966. The postwar Nationalist Labour parties were basically held together around one personality. These organizational features contributed to the extreme fragmentation which has been a feature of Opposition weakness in Northern Ireland. However, the Social Democratic and Labour party, formed in 1970 through a merger of some Nationalist and Nationalist Labour MPs and eventually the second largest party, provided itself with the machinery of a modern party—a party headquarters, official constituency associations, and an annual conference. But they participated in the legislature for little more than a year.

In contrast, the official Unionists have a well-articulated organization reaching down from the Parliamentary party to the grass-roots constituency association, taking in the parallel organization of the Orange Order on the way. The Parliamentary party, grouping MPs and Senators, met regularly to discuss detailed political policies and legislative tactics. Although the prime minister designated by the governor automatically became leader of the Unionist party, he had, of course, to retain the support of the Parliamentary group in order to survive politically. More than that, he had to retain the support of the 100-member Standing Committee of the Ulster Unionist Council, which met annually or more often. The council itself represents the mass party, being elected directly from constituency associations and containing nominees of affiliated organizations, such as the Orange Order and similar Protestant organizations, and of the Unionist Labour Association. Normally it meets annually to receive reports and debate resolutions advanced by the constituent associations.

PARLIAMENTARY PARTIES AND THE WORK OF THE LEGISLATURE

We have already noted that the bulk of parliamentary business consisted in the detailed extension and amendment of British legislation for Northern Ireland. This concern followed partly from the fact that Parliament was not a fully independent legislature and had to keep pace with the rest of the United Kingdom in various spheres. A more serious constraint was the financial dependence of the Northern Ireland government on the British government: administrative and legislative action requiring additional expenditure had to be cleared in advance with the British treasury and, to obtain this approval, had to conform to British practice (Lawrence, 1965: 90–93). Ultimately, of course, it was the Unionists' determination to bring standards in the province up to those of Britain that entailed financial dependence. The British example was willingly accepted and followed, with impressive results in terms of improved living standards and economic development (Lawrence, 1965: 178–87; Mansergh, 1936: 322–23).

As far as these activities went, legislation was uncontentious. All parties agreed on increasing the size of the total cake: in 1936 the Nationalist leader, Campbell, congratulated the minister of finance upon securing an additional half million pounds from Britain for the Northern Ireland Unemployment Fund with the remark: "There is no Irishman, North or South, but desires to get as much British revenue as possible" (Mansergh, 1936: 319). Better social services, aid to education, and hospitals were uncontentious in themselves.

Party disputes did arise over the distribution of these benefits when Nationalists criticized discrimination against Catholics. Thus in the area of health services the Northern Ireland Act of 1947 followed the British acts, but with a significant difference concerning the voluntary hospitals: whereas the English and Scottish acts provided that "where the Character and Associations of any hospital transferred . . . are such as to link it with a particular religious denomination, regard shall be had in the making of appointments to the Board of Management to the preservation of the character and associations of the hospital," the Northern Ireland Act omitted this clause. This meant that Catholic-run hospitals could come into the scheme only by becoming totally secularized. Among others, the main Catholic teaching hospital, the Mater in Belfast, felt itself unable to enter the scheme on these terms. There was some sympathy for Opposition protests on this point from Belfast Unionists, since the Mater provided general services to North Belfast. But the minister of health refused reimbursement even for outpatient services, which the committee was willing to provide freely as if it were a state hospital. General Unionist solidarity left the hospital out of the Health Service until the demise of Stormont (Budge and O'Leary, 1973: 159–61).

Discrimination in the much expanded provision of public housing was a perennial source of ineffective Opposition protests, as we have noted. The postwar educational reforms provided an occasion on which the Opposition might have found common ground with fundamentalist Unionists, since both groups objected to the secularizing tendency of the bill. Unionist opponents objected to the change whereby teachers could no longer be compelled to give (undenominational) Bible instruction in state schools, on the ground that compulsion was constitutional. The Nationalists objected to the provision whereby voluntary schools could not qualify for increased aid unless they came under a management committee designated by the government. In this case, representatives of the Catholic Church had the power to block state action, since they simply refused to come under the type of management favored by the government, the so-called "four and two" committees, in which the Church nominees would have only half the voting power of the state nominees. Faced with a boycott, the minister yielded to the extent of increasing the state subsidy without demanding secular control, only to be faced with intensified internal opposition on this point from the very same Unionists who were opposing the absence of compulsory Bible teaching in state schools. The Nationalists, on the other hand, continued to demand complete state subsidies for their schools without state control. The critical division "was carried by a majority of 19 to 8–27 votes in a House, excluding the Speaker, of 51" (Lawrence, 1965: 119–21). The adverse votes, like the abstentions, were cast by a mixture of Nationalists and Unionists. Cross-voting in this case— which, with additional Orange pressure, eventually forced the minister out—should not be confused with policy agreement between Nationalists and Unionists, since part of the reason for the Unionists' opposition was the concession to Catholics.

Some genuine voting alliances did occur on matters of local interest. Some Unionists and Nationalists joined in opposing the bill for the suspension of the Belfast Corporation in 1943 (carried by 23 votes to 10, of which 4 were Unionist). And in the matter of locating the New University of Ulster at Coleraine rather than Londonderry, local Nationalists and Unionists joined in public protests from 1965 to 1967. Such temporary alliances were unimportant, however, beside the continuing Unionist indifference to Catholic complaints about the regional imbalance and political and social discrimination, which was as evident under O'Neill as in earlier periods.

Systematic analysis of all occasions during the period 1921–69 when any Unionist MPs voted against the government (Whyte, 1972a) confirms the conclusion that there was no support among Unionists for Nationalist demands. Leaving aside the all-Unionist Parliament of 1921–25, the number of divisions on which at least one Unionist opposed the government could be as high as one-third (1938–45), and was 30% for the parliaments elected in 1949, 1953, and 1962. Recurring themes in the dissident votes were (1) disquiet about excessive delegated powers or unnecessary expenditure, (2) opposition to government regulation of the economy, (3) promotion of rural and farm interests, (4) teetotalism, and (5) the war effort. Two additional themes were (6) extended social welfare provisions which obviously would benefit Catholics as well as Protestants, but which was not argued in these terms, and (7) "liberalism"–objection to restrictions on court reporting and to capital punishment. Only one theme in this last group implied any support at all for Catholics: Phelim O'Neill's campaign in 1968 for more generous treatment of voluntary schools. But this was late and confined largely to one individual. It was balanced by a Protestant lobby who thought the government was being too kind to Catholics, an issue prominent in the 1920s and again in the 1940s.

As Whyte points out, some issues which caused great dissatisfaction left no trace on the division lists–the two major examples being the fall of the Andrews government in 1943 and of the O'Neill government in 1969. But on these questions and others like them–all fought out at Unionist party meetings–there is certainly no sign of pro-Catholic sentiment, and quite the reverse in the case of O'Neill.

Party divisions were thus extremely rigid even in the social and economic field, where postwar increases in total expenditure provided many opportunities to trade off benefits from which both politico-religious groups could have gained. Although legislation in this area occupied the bulk of parliamentary time, it was not in anyone's eyes the most important function of parliament, which in a state threatened both by internal dissaffection and external irredentism was inevitably the maintenance of the regime. Here the Northern Ireland Parliament was fully autonomous, de facto since 1922 and de jure since 1949–in the Ireland Act of 1949 the British government and parliament declared that no cession of territory could be made without Stormont's consent. The very existence and functioning of the Parliament at Stormont was thus in a sense its most important act and guaranteed the continuance of the province as a separate entity. The Nationalists were entirely consistent in seeking to withhold legitimacy from parliament and province by their boycott from 1921 to 1928. (The minority of Republican Sinn Fein MPs have always boycotted Stormont.) The attitude of Nationalists for the period 1928 to 1965 was summed up in the words of one MP: "We will not allow ourselves to become an official Opposition in this House. We will only intervene when we feel that we can expose injustice. But we reserve the right to come in or stay outside as and when our people may decide" (Mansergh, 1936: 248). These words were put into practice by sporadic withdrawals during the 1930s. During the years 1928 to 1965 the Nationalists and their allies could not be said to have participated fully in parliamentary proceedings, nor to have given their general consent to Stormont's existence, whatever action they took on individual pieces of legislation. Their acceptance of the status of Loyal Opposition in 1965 might have consolidated the status of Parliament and province had it cleared the way to resolution of everyday Catholic grievances. But it did not; thus, 1969 saw the replacement of Nationalists by a more extreme Opposition which renewed its objections to the existence of the regime and once more employed the tactic of the boycott. This time, in conjunction with other pressures on the regime, it was successful in securing the final suspension of Parliament.

While ultimately successful, the boycott's initial effect in the 1920s was to enable the Unionists to assert their authority over the Six Counties without opposition or debate, through the reorganization of the police forces, the abolition of proportional representation in local government elections, and the Special Powers Act of 1922. Later invocations of the act to meet IRA incursions (as from 1956–62 and in 1971) were always strongly opposed by Nationalists and their sympathizers and strongly endorsed by Unionists. Another step in the consolidation of the Unionist majority, and thus of the regime, was the abolition of proportional representation for Stormont elections in 1929. This was opposed by the nine Nationalist MPs, three Labor MPs, an Independent, and an Independent Unionist, but unanimously supported by the official Unionists (Mansergh, 1936: 134–35).

In no sphere of parliamentary activity did there appear up to 1964 any signs of significant cooperation between the Unionists, on the one hand, and the Nationalists, on the other. The period initiated by O'Neill's gestures towards Catholics constitutes not only a partial exception to this general tendency but a prelude to the demise of the Parliament itself, and thus deserves separate examination. Meanwhile, it is worth asking what the role of individual MPs was under the Stormont system, and what scope existed for activity on behalf of constituents or interest groups. Weinbaum has noted in his study of the Afghan *shura* (Chap. 3 in this volume) that, even though representatives are confronted by a relatively autocratic and autonomous government, they may still perform constituency services which contribute to some extent to general integration.

MPs at Stormont fell into three fairly stable, numerically equivalent, and rather divergent groups: the Opposition, the backbench Unionists, and members of the Unionist government. The latter were bound to act as a strongly cohesive body concerned with the province as a whole rather than individual constituencies. The other two groups were constrained by the tradition of ministerial and collective government responsibility and Unionist party discipline. Ministerial responsibility meant that civil servants could not be approached directly on behalf of constituents, but only through the minister or parliamentary secretary. Collective governmental responsibility usually meant (except in the controversial cases noted above) that the cabinet as a whole upheld the individual minister's decision on any constituency matter and was thus able to appeal to the party solidarity of the Unionists to uphold the decision. The backbench Unionist MP was unable, as a result, to put strong pressure on an individual minister; in cases where strong local interests were involved, he could, as we have seen, abstain or vote against the government, but the government generally carried its policy in the end. Such clashes were, however, the exception rather than the rule. The Unionist MP was, after all, voted in to support a Protestant government, and that government's policy was to favor the Protestant areas. This made for a general harmony of interests within which the dialogue between MP and minister generally had fruitful results.

The same factors, of course, militated against any influence which Nationalist-inclined MPs might try to exert. The minister would be supported by government and party in resisting Nationalist pressures, which were, in any case, going against general government policy. The individual MP could expect as little change as was given to his party as a whole.

Representation of a locality was not a factor which crosscut the religious or party affiliations of an MP. Because of the rigidity of basic cleavages, it was usually quite apparent whether Catholics or Protestants had secured his election. The MP could not hope to win over his political opponents by performing services for them, while such actions would at the same time alienate his majority and prevent reelection. Thus MPs conceived of their role as service to the local majority. Constituency relationships thus reinforced the religious cleavage evident in the province as a whole.

ATTEMPTED RECONCILIATION AND THE DEMISE OF THE NORTHERN IRELAND PARLIAMENT

O'Neill's conciliatory gestures towards Catholics after his entry to the premiership were pursued mainly outside Parliament through visits and meetings, and appeared inside as a moderation of tone and stress on economic and social rather than religious problems. The initiative paid off in parliamentary terms, however, in the acceptance by Nationalists of the status and obligations of the loyal Opposition. Within five years of these reciprocal gestures, the province was plunged into violence of a severity not experienced since the 1920s.

Attempts to explain this paradoxical progression affect our view of Parliament and its associated institutions as a cohesive factor in the community. A plausible explanation is, in fact, that the Stormont Parliament could work only as a perpetual confrontation between majority Unionists and minority Nationalists. Any attempt to break from the mold of sectarian politics also broke the mold in which Parliament was cast.

The plausibility of the thesis can be examined in relation to events. Viewed retrospectively, O'Neill's policy towards Catholics was one of greater tolerance rather than partnership: in the middle of his term of office only 9 Catholics were to be found among 102 members of statutory bodies, such as the Housing Trust and Milk Marketing Board (Rose, 1971: chap. 3, note 59). Nevertheless, the Unionist alliance of moderate and extreme Protestants had flourished under an elitist leadership which combined verbal intolerance with a disregard for extreme Protestant shibboleths in practice. Such a combination had been nicely calculated to unite both moderate and extreme Protestants behind the Unionist government. O'Neill's gestures increasingly alienated the extreme Protestants—who after all were used to taking the symbol for the reality—without winning over the Catholics, apart from the small Catholic middle class. For O'Neill's tactic was still to secure Unionist predominance, even though on economic rather than religious grounds, and this offered nothing to the Nationalists. Catholic acceptance might have been secured by timely reforms in the allocation of housing or the distribution of economic development, given from a position of Unionist strength any time from 1963 to 1968. Resulting Catholic quiescence would have discredited the extremists' cry of "Ulster in danger."

But this is hypothetical. Even in the absence of Catholic reaction (1964–68), O'Neill's reforms drove a wedge between the two factions in the Unionist party, and it is by no means clear that the split would not have provoked rioting and Catholic reactions, and ultimately would have led to conditions similar to those which produced the demise of Stormont. It is difficult to say conclusively that any conciliatory policy would have led to that result. But if we accept, from the historical record and the figures quoted earlier, that moderate Protestants did not have the numerical strength to govern the province on their own and that Catholics were unlikely to be reliable allies, there was little alternative to the existing Unionist alliance if stability was to be preserved. And since extremists demanded confrontation and intolerance as the price of their support, there is an important sense in which the very existence of Parliament depended on exacerbating the religious conflict.

FUNCTIONS OF THE NORTHERN IRELAND PARLIAMENT: CONCLUSIONS AND SUMMARY

The main conclusion of our analysis must be that Parliament in Northern Ireland, far from facilitating the integration of the two religious communities, managed for most of its existence to intensify bitterness between them. For most people, throughout most of its existence, Parliament was the Unionist party at work, and other parties were there on sufferance or not there at all. When this role was abandoned, when the Opposition took a fully legitimate part in parliamentary proceedings, the Unionists split, and in the ensuing turmoil Parliament itself disappeared.

Since its legitimacy was impugned, Parliament could hardly serve any internal integrating function. Catholic interests were, as far as possible, reconciled and protected by the Church and local notables, including politicians—but not through Parliament. Within the Protestant community, the various interests ranged wider and were more likely to conflict. The main brokerage institution here was the Unionist party, particularly its Central Council and Standing Committee and its elected government. The Parliamentary party also discussed and settled controversial issues, but we have seen that, even at the height of controversy under O'Neill, the government could usually dominate its meetings sufficiently to get support for its policies. The government, rather than the Parliamentary party, stands out as the dominating body.

All the institutions of the Unionist party predated the establishment of Parliament, even the government, for there had been a provisional Unionist government in Ulster in 1912. Since these bodies by themselves were quite capable of ruling the province and reconciling Protestant interests, what, then, was the function of Parliament? Was it there only because it was one feature of the compromise hammered out with Britain during 1920–22? Without British influence, would Northern Ireland have come under a semi-authoritarian regime like that of Spain or Portugal?

Even if the Government of Ireland Act had given this particular form to provincial institutions, it is likely that the Unionists would have chosen to handle their affairs through a democratic Parliament that they could dominate, for no other reason than that this was the way they were accustomed to handling political affairs. But, in fact, Parliament had other uses for the Unionists. It continually demonstrated that they possessed a popular majority. Since periodic elections also posed the threat of a Catholic takeover—should Protestants lose their unity—Parliament provided a powerful motive for compromising internal disputes. Finally, the dependence of the prime minister upon a formal choice by the governor, masking a real choice by the outgoing cabinet and endorsement by the Unionist majority in Parliament, removed the selection of leaders from the mass Unionist organizations with their extreme elements—which were only asked to endorse a choice already made—and left actual nomination in the hands of the moderate group preponderant in Parliament.

EPILOGUE

As mentioned above, in March 1972 the powers of the Northern Ireland cabinet and Parliament were entrusted by decision of the British cabinet to a new functionary, a secretary of state for Northern Ireland, with a seat in the cabinet, aided by several junior ministers.

The first holder of this office, William Whitelaw, made it clear that he regarded his duty as twofold—to deliver the Northern Ireland people from violence by a larger military establishment *and* to provide a new constitutional structure. To that end he engaged in extensive discussions throughout the summer with all shades of religious and political opinion in the province.

In October the secretary of state issued a Green Paper (the traditional civil service term for a discussion paper) called *The Future of Northern Ireland.* This document provided a fair historical account of the Northern Ireland political system and the constitutional proposals advanced by the various parties, ranging from a condominium ruled by Britain and the Irish Republic, as advocated by the (Catholic) Social Democratic and Labour party (SDLP), to complete integration with Britain as envisaged by the Rev. Ian Paisley. Also, in a concluding chapter, it set forth some criteria which the British government felt any new constitutional scheme should meet. Some of these were familiar. Northern Ireland must remain part of the United Kingdom for as long as the majority of the people should desire, and arrangements for security must remain in the hands of the British government. But others showed a marked departure from the principles of 1920: any new institutions must have a clear and unambiguous relationship to the central (British) authorities, appropriate to the role of a regional authority; they must take account of the fact that Northern Ireland has many common interests, apart from a land frontier, with the Republic of Ireland; and, above all, they must provide for a much wider consensus than had hitherto existed within Northern Ireland and be capable of assuring minority groups of an effective voice and, indeed, a share in the exercise of power.

The Green Paper was intensively discussed all during the winter of 1972, while the violence continued unabated. (A counterpart to the IRA, the Ulster Defence Association had emerged in the Protestant sectors of Belfast in the early summer of 1972. Unlike the IRA, it specialized in individual assassinations rather than destruction of property.) Predictably, the paper was given a qualified welcome by the Catholic parties and met with varying degrees of hostility along the Unionist spectrum, with William Craig urging total rejection. Eventually, on March 25, 1973, the British government issued its White Paper (firm proposals). Since, at the time of writing, these are being given legislative effect, the cause of brevity will be best served by giving the substance of the legislation now being enacted. The governor, cabinet, and Parliament of Northern Ireland are to be abolished. In their place, the secretary of state for Northern Ireland will act in the name of the crown and will administer certain services reserved to the United Kingdom government (the police, the appointment of magistrates and judges, and the criminal law). Other services formerly administered by Stormont will be transferred to a new

Assembly of 78 members. The constituencies from which these assemblymen will be elected are to be identical with the 12 existing Westminster constituencies but they are to return 6 to 8 members apiece by the single transferable vote method of proportional representation—as laid down in the Government of Ireland Act.

The Assembly will be a legislative body. There will also be an executive, the members of which will be the political heads of the existing ministerial departments under a chief executive. The chief executive will not be elected by the Assembly but nominated by the secretary of state after consultation with the parties; it will be his responsibility to insure that the executive is broadly based. The bill incorporates a charter of human rights—safeguards against discriminatory religious or political legislation—and, in addition, the secretary of state is empowered to veto any piece of legislation that he considers to be discriminatory.

The Northern Ireland Constitution Bill and Emergency Provisions Bill effectively bury the Government of Ireland Act and the institutions it created. They represent an admission by the British government that a British-type parliamentary system based on majority rule is unsuited to a segmental society such as that of Northern Ireland, and that the price of restoring stability will be the active involvement of the minority community in the political system. Pessimists may say that it is now too late for such a solution, since the two communities are more polarized than ever. But it is difficult to envisage any other solution with the remotest chance of success. Were the elections to the Assembly, scheduled for June 28, 1973, to result in a majority of extremists and a perpetual deadlock, it is extremely unlikely that the British government would produce any fresh proposals.[8] On the other hand, pressure may build up in Britain for a gradual withdrawal of the troops with predictably catastrophic consequences. At the time of writing it looks as if the moderate parties, particularly the Alliance party,[9] will benefit from the well-known partiality of the proportional representation system to such groups.

The Parliament of Northern Ireland, therefore, is sent to join other defunct legislative bodies like the dominion Parliament of Newfoundland and the Senate of New Zealand. Given the divisive nature of the society in which it was embedded, it could hardly have been expected to perform miracles of integration. But the salient fact is that (apart from the last years) no attempt was made by the perpetually governing party to achieve this integration. Other segmented societies from inauspicious beginnings have developed stable and fully legitimate regimes—Switzerland is the outstanding example. Had the Unionist governments attempted to conciliate the Catholics, they might well have generated in Northern Ireland a sense of community. During 1966 to 1967 there was evidence both from the Belfast survey and the Northern Ireland survey that Catholics were beginning to appreciate that the solution to their grievances had to be sought in a Northern Ireland context.

One-third of Rose's (1971) Catholic respondents accepted the Constitution, and most of them expected fair play from officials. It cannot now be proved that that proportion would not have grown bigger had different decisions been taken by the ruling party, but neither can it be disproved. This remains one of the might-have-beens of history.

The main role of the Parliament of Northern Ireland was to sustain a regime which exacted compliance by force. Even within the majority, the real work of integration was done through the Unionist party, which accommodated Orangemen and non-Orangemen, working and middle classes, and the different Protestant denominations. Apart from registering support and selecting leaders, Parliament's main work lay in the detailed legislative and administrative enactments required to raise provincial standards, especially in the area of social legislation, to those of Great Britain. It is in its relative success in this area, which the coerced settlement of 1922 to 1972 at least rendered possible, that its main achievement lies.

NOTES

1. The Northern Irish Parliament was popularly called "Stormont" after the suburb of Belfast where its buildings were situated, in order to distinguish it from "Westminster," the United Kingdom Parliament (also described from the Northern Irish perspective as the "Imperial" Parliament).

2. The "native" aristocracy and gentry of the sixteenth century were descendents either of the Celtic aristocracy of preconquest Ireland, or of Norman invaders of the twelfth century. By the sixteenth century the two lines were fairly indistinguishable and they were all Catholic.

3. It was estimated that out of 183 Presbyterian ministers in the Northeast, 18 actively sympathized with the rebellion and 10 were imprisoned or executed. (For a fuller account, see Budge and O'Leary, 1973: 10–13.)

4. An intermittent campaign of arson and terrorism of Belfast Catholics lasted from 1920 to 1922. The number of violent deaths in the city during those years was 544, with nearly 232 in 1922 (Budge and O'Leary, 1973: 142–43).

5. The six counties of Northern Ireland, with three which joined the republic, constitute the historic Province of Ulster. The name is often applied, though in strict usage inaccurately, to the six counties only.

6. Nineteen persons were killed in the raids during 1956–61. The IRA is illegal both in

the South and the North and disapproves of present republican institutions and regimes only slightly less than those of the Unionist North.

7. It is only fair to add that in Belfast, the largest city, the franchise was not unduly biased (Budge and O'Leary, 1973: chap. 6) and this is probably true of East Ulster as a whole. Areas with a high proportion of Catholics, and particularly those areas which were Nationalist controlled, did considerably worse than more strongly Protestant areas, indicating some political management by the provincial administration as well as by local authorities.

8. Editor's note: The results of the June 28 Assembly election were as follows: Twenty-three seats were won by former Prime Minister Brian Faulkner's Union party; the Catholic SDLP captured 19 seats; the Northern Ireland Labour party 1 seat; and the nonsectarian Alliance party 8 seats. Nearly two-thirds of the 78-seat Assembly are now held by members who agree, with certain reservations, that the Protestant majority must share power with the Catholic minority. Those opposed to the kind of compromise outlined in the British White Paper of March 1973 are now clearly in the minority in the Assembly.

9. A middle-class, overtly nonsectarian, party (resembling the old Liberal party) formed in 1970 by some professionals and businessmen, both Catholic and Protestant. At the time of this writing four MPs—three formerly Unionist and one Nationalist—have joined its ranks.

REFERENCES

BUDGE, I., and C. O'LEARY (1971) "Cross-cutting cleavages, agreement and compromise: a test of three leading hypotheses against Scottish and Northern Irish Survey Data." Midwest Journal of Political Science 15, 1 (Jan.): 1–30.

_____ (1972) "Attitudinal and background cross-cutting: further evidence from Glasgow and Belfast." Midwest Journal of Political Science 16, 4 (Nov.): 712–22.

_____ (1973) Belfast: Approach to Crisis. London: Macmillan.

BUDGE, I., and D. W. URWIN (1966) Scottish Political Behaviour. London: Longman.

H.M.S.O. (1972) "The Future of Northern Ireland." A paper for discussion. London.

H.M.S.O. (1973) "Northern Ireland Constitutional Proposals." Cmnd. 5259. London.

LAWRENCE, R. J. (1965) The Government of Northern Ireland. Oxford: Oxford Univ. Press.

McGILL, P. F. (1965) "The Senate of Northern Ireland." Ph.D. dissertation, Queen's Univ., Belfast.

MANSERGH, N. (1936) The Government of Northern Ireland. London: Allen & Unwin.

O'LEARY, C. (1969) "The Northern Ireland General Election, 1969." In Verfassung und Verfassungwerklichkeit, ed. F. A. Hermens. Cologne and Opladen: Westdeutscher Verlag.

ROSE, R. (1971) Governing Without Consensus. Boston: Beacon Press.

WHYTE, J. H. (1972) "Intra-Unionist disputes in the Northern Ireland House of Commons." Belfast: Department of Political Science, Queen's University. Mimeographed.

Chapter 6

PARLIAMENT'S ROLE IN THE INTEGRATION–
MODERNIZATION OF CANADIAN SOCIETY, 1865–76

ALLAN KORNBERG
SAMUEL M. HINES

> That there should be a country called Canada distinct from the United States is a mere accident of history, in fact, a political paradox. Nature has not conferred upon Canada any particular personality of her own. There is no geographical difference to separate her from her great neighbor to the South. It is a problem to determine wherein lies Canada's centre of gravity: politically it is in England, and geographically it is in the United States—in either case outside her own boundaries. Her very existence is connected with this problem; for a purely British Canada could never be anything but a colony, and an American Canada could only be a group of states in the Union. [Siegfried, 1947: 23]

> Perhaps the unity of the past 100 years has been illusory. Perhaps Canada will disintegrate tomorrow. Lacking folk heroes, national symbols, and other unifying national myths, Canada continues to plod along, perhaps always on the brink of Balkanization, and certainly ever preoccupied with the search for a "national identity." Indeed, paradoxically, this perennial quest for a national identity may be the single most characteristic feature of the identity we seek. [Van Loon and Whittington, 1971: 174–75]

INTRODUCTION

Cicero once said that there is "nothing in which human excellence can more nearly approximate the divine than in the foundation of

AUTHOR'S NOTE: The research, of which this book chapter is a part, is funded by a grant to the Comparative Legislative Studies Program of Duke University from the Agency for International Development. Although we are grateful for the agency's support, we naturally absolve them of any responsibility for the viewpoints expressed in this paper. Any errors in fact or interpretation also are our own.

new states or in the preservation of states already founded." For students of comparative politics in the last half of the twentieth century, this statement may seem paradoxical at best, given the proliferation of new states and the continued revision of territorial boundaries since 1947—revisions that have occurred, for the most part, in a context of violence and political disorder. Regardless of whether the formation of new states is a divine task, their maintenance throughout history certainly has been the principal concern of those who lead them. In particular has this been the case in countries in which sharp cleavages based upon ethnic, racial, religious, or economic particularism divide the population. Canada is one such country. The ethnic-religious cleavage between French-Catholic Canadians (over 80% of whom reside in the province of Quebec) and other-than-French Canadians, of course, has been the most important historically and continues to this day to attract the most attention. The threat that French-Canadian nationalism currently poses to Canada's national integrity and the intensity of feelings that this nationalism evokes in French-Canadians is well illustrated in a recent comment by René Levesque (1968: 10), the leader of the nationalist Parti Quebecois, currently the governing party in the Quebec National Assembly: "Inevitably, the social development of Quebec is related to the development of the Quebec nation to the point of being indistinguishable from it. As they grow more free, more democratic, better educated, and richer, Quebechois necessarily are more clearly conscious of their identity as a group, and have a better understanding of sovereignty as the essential condition for improving their collective life. Social progress nourishes nationalism, until nationalism appears as the indispensable key to social progress."

Although the economic cleavages between Canada's urban-industrial heartland of Ontario and the "have-not" provinces in the west and the Atlantic provinces have not attracted as much international attention, they have been as enduring as the aforementioned cultural cleavages. Indeed, one could reasonably argue that economic regionalism has had as great an effect on the conduct of domestic politics—for example, the splintering of the party system Meisel, 1963)—as has the ethnic-religious conflict between Quebec and English-speaking Canada. Small wonder, then, that social scientists (Porter, 1965; Hargrove, 1967, 1970; Schwartz, 1967) have remarked on the seeming obsession of Canadian political leaders with the problems of national unity and national identity,[1] or that Canada should have been considered an appropriate case study for inclusion in a volume on the problems of national integration and the legislative role therein. Accordingly, in this chapter we will examine the part played by the provincial parliament of United Canada (Ontario and Quebec) in facilitating and/or retarding the integration of Canadian society in the two years preceding the passage of the British North America Act of 1867 and by the newly created Dominion Parliament (that is, Canadian House of Commons) in the decade following the historic event that established Canada as a nation-state. We shall employ the content analytic method and use as our data base the reports of debates on the proposed "confederation" in the Parliament of United Canada as well as "scrapbook" reports of debates in the House of Commons in the years 1867-70 and 1873-76. Our effort, we feel, is in accord with the recent tendency to apply to Western contexts the developmental perspective and the concepts and approaches that were used initially to study the development of non-Western political systems. By so doing we hope that we ultimately may enhance our knowledge of the several processes involved in the modernization-development of Western and non-Western societies alike (Almond, 1966: 869-79).

INTEGRATION AND MODERNIZATION PROCESSES

The literature dealing with the concepts of integration, modernization, growth, development, and nation building is voluminous, and the use of these concepts in the literature is characteristically ambiguous. In another paper we have discussed the relationship between the concept of "modernization" and its equivalents (i.e., development, growth, nation building) and concluded that modernization was more historically meaningful, operationalizable, and empirically verifiable than the other concepts. Modernization, for us, refers to the "enhanced capacity of a social system to accommodate itself to simulataneous rapid change within its sectors and to events in the total outside environment" (Kornberg, Hines, and Smith, 1973: 475). Integration (more specifically, national integration) refers to the process through which loyalty toward, and deference to, a society's central institutional arrangements are generated among the several strata of its population. This loyalty and deference are intended to *transcend* more particularistic loyalties in the population, but, as Jean Grossholtz (1970: 93-113) has noted, the latter need not be destroyed in the process. Successful national integration ought to facilitate balance and order within a society. By "balance" we mean the widely shared belief that a state and its central arrangements will give approximately equal weight to interests of the several major social, economic, and political groups and regions within a society so that the interests of a particular group or region are not overtly and continuously sacrificed, or even made secondary, to the interests of other groups or regions. By "order" we mean the condition of societal stability that in part is a consequence of a widely shared perception that particularistic interests are being more or less equitably balanced by the central institutional arrangements of a state. Without such order a society finds it difficult to modernize itself, since its capacity to accommodate simultaneous rapid internal and external change within several sectors is seriously impaired. Thus, it is useful in our view to think of the several processes involved in national integration and modernization as two analytically distinct but empirically overlapping aspects of the larger process of societal development. The former reflects the problem involved in achieving social order within a society, the latter the problem of change.

In Chapter 1 in this volume, Malcolm E. Jewell has listed a number of ways in which national legislatures can serve as vehicles of national integration. He points out, for example, that in a political system in which social, economic, or political minorities can be a source of disintegration, the legislature can provide an arena in which representatives of these minorities can meet with representatives of the dominant group or groups to compromise (in our parlance, "balance") their differences. Accordingly, a parliament can provide minorities with both symbolic and tangible benefits that can serve to strengthen their support of a regime. He goes on to observe, however, that there is nothing inherent in the legislative process to guarantee integration or disintegration in a divided society. The problem of the scholar, then, is to determine the process by which, and the conditions under which, legislatures either facilitate or impede national integration.

As will be indicated in our analyses, we share Jewell's latter assumption; our content analyses are intended to delineate the ways in which the deliberations of the members of the provincial parliaments of United Canada and the newly established national parliament contributed to or impeded the integration of the new state. We reasoned that the members of these legislatures could have facilitated Canadian integration in three ways. First, they could have begun the process of fostering loyalty and gratitude to a new central government by taking measures that would help provide security against external aggression. Second, they could have laid the groundwork for the balanced economic development of each of the several regions. Finally, they could have facilitated the development of a distinctly Canadian identity by frankly and openly discussing the ethnic-religious and other cleavages that divided the public they represented. They then might have considered substantive or symbolic measures that could have helped dampen particularistic cleavages and at the same time encouraged the development of an identification with a new and larger national entity called Canada that would transcend ethnic-religious and regional loyalties. Another way in which they could have helped foster a national identity and consciousness would have been to take action to link the several provinces in a way that encouraged a variety of social interactions among their populations. Such increased social interactions not only might have increased the awareness and sensitivity of people in the several provinces of one another's needs and concerns and helped reduce intergroup suspicions and animosity, but they also might have helped to develop a feeling of oneness among people, a feeling that each of them was a part of the newly established nation, Canada.

On the other hand, we also reasoned that the deliberations of Parliament during these critical formative years might have had the opposite effects to those suggested above. For example, they could have contributed to the disintegration of the new Canadian nation by encouraging the belief that the economic interests of one region or one group were being favored; or they could have exacerbated ethnic-religious divisions; or they simply could have been inept and thus encouraged a feeling that there was little if any use in looking to the new national government to help solve new or even old problems. But, before describing the findings and inferring from them the extent to which they are consonant with our theoretical speculations, we should like (albeit briefly) to familiarize the reader with the content analytic technique and the data base on which our analyses were generated.

METHODS AND MEASURES: CONTENT ANALYSIS OF PARLIAMENTARY DEBATES

In recent years a growing concern over the roles and functions of communication in society has led to the application and refinement of techniques and research methods designed to measure, both quantitatively and qualitatively, the effects of communication and the content of messages. Simply stated, "content analysis is a multi-purpose research method developed specifically for investigating any problem in which the content of communication serves as the basis of inference" (Holsti, 1969: 2). More succinctly, "content analysis is the application of scientific methods to documentary evidence" (Holsti, 1969: 4).

We initially intended to examine parliamentary debates during the ten-year period prior to the passage of the British North America Act (1867) and to compare this period with debates during the decade after Confederation. Consequently, we conducted a preliminary inspection of the available source material and found to our dismay that materials for the period prior to 1867 had not been collected in a format suitable for our purposes. Indeed, the debates of the Legislative Assembly of United Canada are only now being "reconstructed" and published as a series—beginning with the first session after the union of Ontario and Quebec in 1841—through the efforts of the Centre d'Etude du Quebec and the Centre de Recherche en Historie Economique du Canada Français. As the editor of the first volume in that series has noted: "The chief characteristic and purpose of the Canadian Parliament is to decide the country's policies through debate. Yet the words of its talkers in their talking place were not systematically recorded . . . and our historians are helplessly grounded in this documentary lacuna from which they must produce their studies" (Nish, n.d.). We also found that the verbatim recording of debates in the Canadian House of Commons in Hansard did not begin until 1880. However, we did find that the debates in the Parliament of United Canada on the subject of confederation had been carefully preserved and detailed.[2] Consequently, we have used the reports of these debates in the analyses that follow. We also found that there were "scrapbooks" containing newspaper accounts of the major issues that were debated in the newly established Canadian House of Commons during the decade following confederation. Of the ones in our possession, the most complete and detailed are for the periods 1867–70 and 1873–76.

Although the lack of systematically collected and complete verbatim reports of parliamentary debates makes the use of content analytic techniques both very difficult and methodologically questionable, we have tried to use this technique to quantitatively analyze, insofar as possible, the major themes that dominated parliamentary debates for the period under investigation. We made no attempt to use computerized content analysis. Rather, we relied upon a team of four interacting graduate student coders. We followed the procedure suggested by Richard Merritt in his book *Symbols of American Community* (1966), while at the same time trying to avoid the shortcomings in his analysis noted by Holsti (1969: 89, 96, 142). Holsti criticized Merritt for his failure to clarify certain links between the concept of "national awareness" and its operational definition (i.e., the relative frequency of occurrence of American place names in colonial newspapers). Holsti suggested that the use of coding *themes* expressing a sense of community would have permitted more valid inferences to be drawn from the data, although it probably would have resulted in lower coder reliability scores. Mindful of Holsti's stricture, and consonant with our reasoning noted above, we have tried to identify four types of themes in the reports of debates: "strategic," "political," "sociocultural," and "economic."

The coders were told to record all statements in debate reports that were concerned with these thematic areas. They then classified the remarks of the several speakers in each area as either "integrative" (i.e., nationalistic, holistic) or as "divisive" (i.e., particularistic). To further refine our analysis of the data on the Confederation Debates, we have classified each of the four general issue areas into specific issue categories.[3] But, since the material from the "scrapbook" reports (1867–70 and 1873–76) was more limited, we have used only the four general categories noted above in our analyses of postconfederation debates.

Once the data were collected, the thematic statements were broken into reconstructed sentences in order to better delineate the speaker's position vis-à-vis integration. For example, J. B. E. Dorion was reported to have said the following in a speech delivered on Thursday, February 16, 1865: "It is said that this Confederation is necessary for the purpose of providing a better mode of defense for this country. I am not of that opinion." Our reconstructed form of this statement was: I / am not of the opinion / that Confederation is necessary for defense. This thematic statement would then properly be coded under the "strategic" category as general responsibility for security/defense: particularistic. To help insure against coder error, we used standard intercoder reliability checks (Budd, Thorp, and Donahew, 1967: 66–68), with results of .82 on the first check and .85 on the second.

PARLIAMENT AND THE INTEGRATION–MODERNIZATION
OF CANADIAN SOCIETY, 1865–66: AN OVERVIEW

Modernization, according to Marion Levy, is a "universal social solvent" inasmuch as "the patterns of the relatively modernized societies, once developed, have shown a universal tendency to penetrate any social context whose participants have come in contact with them" (Levy, 1972: 29). Inherent in Levy's comment is the notion that the modernization of a society is (contrary to mechanistic and closed organismic theories of development) in large part the result of exogenous or external factors which decisively influence the otherwise indigenous pattern of social change. Some countries, primarily the earliest modernizers (e.g., England, France, the United States), have been far less subject to external pressures than others (e.g., the "late modernizers" of the Third World).

The Canadian case, when viewed in this way, becomes particularly interesting because Canadian modernization began early in comparison to the Third World, but was and still is significantly shaped by certain external factors, namely the foreign policies and international economic practices of Great Britain and the United States. More importantly for the period of Canadian history under consideration, changes in trade relations with the United States and the political environment of the American Civil War and changes in British colonial defense policy strongly influenced the passage of the British North America Act of 1867 which formally established Canadian independence (Bourne, 1967; Keenleyside, 1971; Burt, 1971; Creighton, 1967; Stacey, 1967).

The significance of these two factors is readily apparent in a reading of the Confederation Debates. We find that the issues of future relations with the United States after the expiration of the Reciprocal Trade Treaty and Britain's future role in the defense of British North America against an anticipated American attempt at annexation are salient. Because these issues were so important, the formative years of Canadian modernization seem not altogether unlike those of Third World countries. In the latter, sensitivity to great power politics and a potentially hostile international environment combine to create great concern for domestic security, and the goal of modernization translates first and foremost into the goal of survival.

In the next section we shall look at the movement to confederate, focusing upon the content of the debates themselves. We then will turn to the activities of Parliament after 1867.

CONFEDERATION

According to one eminent Canadian scholar, academic historians have not engaged in "acrimonious disputes" over the subject of Canadian Confederation, although several interpretations have been offered through the years (Cook, Brown, and Berger, 1967: vii). Of those writing in the nineteenth century about the event, most perceived Confederation as simply a "prelude to a larger federation—that of the British empire—not the first giant step in the establishment of an independent Canada" (Cook, Brown, and Berger, 1967: vii). This ideal of imperial federation not having been realized, subsequent interpretations in the twentieth century have focused upon Confederation as the natural culmination of a movement towards independence, leading to the establishment of a fully autonomous Canada within the British Commonwealth. Since we are seeking to describe Parliament's role in the integration of Canadian society during the first ten years of Canada's independence, we would do well to keep in mind that most of the members of Parliament were probably uncertain, at best, what the future held for Canada's relationship with Britain, but they assumed at a minimum that the ties between the two countries would remain strong.

Canada's political development has been characterized by historians as resulting from the extremely tendentious adjustment of men and institutions, involving not only the English-French Canadian conflict, but other significant regional-ethnic conflicts coupled with changing stimuli from and responses to the United States and Great Britain. The political unification of Canada, it has been said, was more a product of the hard work of John A. MacDonald and the Conservatives than a result of a common appreciation of the benefits to be derived from Confederation, and the persistence of the union during the first six years was even more indebted to the forceful efforts of MacDonald and his party (Creighton, 1958, 1967; Wise, 1970; Beck, 1968: 1−12).

In 1865, at the time a proposal for Confederation was being considered by the United Parliament of Canada, the options available to Canada were reasonably clear in the minds of the members of Parliament. Walter Shanly of South Grenville summarized the problem thus:

> It appears to me that there are just three stages of political existence possible for us here, when we emerge from the chrysalis-form in which we have hitherto existed. First, there is the attempt to stand alone as a separate

nationality on this continent—that is one alternative. Secondly, there is the prospect held out to us in the resolutions—namely, a union of all the British North American Colonies, under the flag of England, becoming more and more every year a homogeneous British people, and building up a consolidated British power on this continent. The last and inevitable alternative, if we reject the other two . . . is absorption into the United States. [PD, 1865: 922]

Others, like the Honorable John A. MacDonald, presented the situation in a somewhat exhortative fashion:

It seems to me that if we wish to be a great people; a great nationality commanding the respect of the world, able to hold our own against all opponents, and to defend those institutions we prize: if we wish to have one system of government, and to establish a commercial union, with unrestricted free trade, between peoples of the five provinces, belonging to the same nation, obeying the same sovereign, owing the same allegiance: if we wish to be able to afford to each other the means of mutual defense and support against aggression and attack—this can only be obtained by a union of some kind between the scattered and weak boundaries composing the British North American Provinces. [PD, 1865: 27]

For French Canadians, the principal reason for accepting the Confederation scheme appears to have been a desire to terminate their uneasy legislative union with English-Canada (Ontario) and replace it with a plan they felt would give them more autonomy. This view is clearly in evidence in an excerpt from a speech by Joseph Dufresne of Montcalm:

I accept the union for many reasons, but chiefly as a means of obtaining the repeal of the present legislative union of Canada, and securing a peaceable settlement of our sectional difficulties. I accept it, secondly, as a means of obtaining for Lower Canada (Quebec) the absolute and exclusive control of her own affairs; thirdly, as a means of perpetuating French Canadian nationality in this country; fourthly, as a more effective means of cementing our connection with the Mother Country, and avoiding annexation to the United States. [PD, 1865: 922]

It is worth observing, although some identification with Britain is suggested, that no mention is made of *any* Canadian identity other than French-Canadian. Thus the French-Canadian position, as illustrated above, is clearly particularistic—a reflection of French Canada's consistent (to this day) desire to maintain a separate identity while admitting to a certain inevitability of cooperation with English-speaking Canada (Hargrove, 1970).

The participation of the maritime provinces in the scheme was predicated upon the assumed economic benefits to be derived from the establishment of an Intercolonial Railway. Much of the opposition to the idea of Confederation came from those who also were motivated by economic concerns, but who were disturbed over the disproportionately high financial contributions (burdens) they would be asked to assume. The latter objections were voiced primarily by MPs from Upper Canada (Ontario). In their attempts to explain Confederation, Canadian historians consistently have emphasized (a) defense against a possible invasion by the militarily formidable United States and (b) the serious economic problems in Ontario, Quebec, and the maritimes that were caused partly by internal factors and partly by the provinces' dependence upon the United States and Great Britain. They also have noted, however, that these issues were not new. Indeed, defense and economic problems had largely precipitated the calling of the Charlottetown Conference to consider the economic union of the maritimes in 1864. The 72 resolutions that were passed by the Quebec Conference of that same year provided the legal-structural format of union and were the subject of the parliamentary debates on which we now focus. Why, then, if economic and strategic problems were "old hat" in 1864, were the political elites of the several provinces ready to consider seriously a political union of all of the British colonial possessions in North America in that same year? According to Donald G. Creighton (1958: 293–304), the distinguished Canadian historian, the reason was political—at least in the united province of Canada. Specifically, it was the seeming inability of the major parliamentary groups to maintain the legislative support required to stay in office that eventually led opponents of a larger union to relent. In particular, the willingness of the politically powerful George Brown, the legislative leader of the reformist "Clear Grits," to accept the concept of broader union of provinces to achieve parliamentary stability in Canada was especially critical. Creighton (1958: 295) notes that

> the long-awaited crisis had at last arrived in the affairs of the distracted Province of Canada. On March 21 [1864], after less than a year of office, the new Reform administration resigned; and on June 14 the Conservative government which followed it was defeated in the House by two votes. It was obvious that what the province needed was not so much a new ministry which would repeat the short, uneasy career of its predecessors, as a new constitution which would give at least the hope of some governmental stability for the future. For ten days the representatives of the different parliamentary groups negotiated. On June 22, George Brown, with two other members representing the Reformers of Canada West, agreed to join with the Conservatives in a coalition government pledged to end the impasse in Canada through fundamental constitutional change.

S. F. Wise supports Creighton's interpretation of the sequence of events that culminated in political union. He notes (1970: 243), for example, that the impulse for Confederation derived "from the irrational pressure cooker of Upper Canadian (legislative) politics" and that

> in significant aspects, Confederation was a triumph of Upper Canadian "imperialism"; its slogan, "peace, order and good government," came directly out of the conservative lexicon; and the manner of its attainment, through negotiation and legislation rather than popular ratification, was entirely characteristic of the undemocratic and elitist Canadian political style."

If Wise is correct in asserting the Confederation was "forced" on British North America by the English-speaking Protestant legislative elite of Ontario, we should find in our inspection of the Confederation debates that there was considerable resistance to the scheme by legislators from Quebec. In fact this appears to be the case. We found that the reactions of legislators in the Parliament of United Canada to the concept of a Confederation, in its most general sense, was overwhelmingly favorable. Indeed, of the 71 very general reactions that we were able to find, fully 56 were favorable. However, a closer inspection revealed that 11 of the 15 unfavorable comments (73.3%) were made by legislators from Quebec, whereas 56 of the favorable reactions (80.3%) were from Ontario representatives. We shall present a detailed analysis of the thematic statements contained in the Confederation debates shortly. For the present we would like to observe once again, since this book is concerned with the varying roles played by legislatures in the integration of societies, that internal processes within a legislative body—in this instance, the inability of legislative leaders to build coalitions that were capable of governing—apparently served as the catalyst for a series of events that were to culminate in the establishment of a new nation.

THE CONFEDERATION DEBATES IN THE PARLIAMENT OF UNITED CANADA, 1865

An analysis of the thematic statements made by members of the Parliament of United Canada in their debate over Confederation indicates that 57.4% of their remarks were, what we have termed, "integrative-holistic" (i.e., favored Confederation) whereas 42.6% were "divisive-particularistic" (i.e., critical of and opposed to various aspects of Confederation). However, support for or opposition to

Confederation by MPs varied fairly sharply with their ethnic background. Thus, of the 127 statements made by English-Canadian legislators 64.5% were integrative-holistic and 35.5% were divisive-particularistic. Of the 54 statements made by French-Canadian MPs 40.7% were integrative and 59.3% were divisive (see Table 6.1).

Since our data were the most complete for these debates, we were able to classify general "political," "economic," "sociocultural," and "strategic" statements made by MPs into a number of specific subject-matter categories. The distributions of the statements made by English- and French-Canadian MPs in each of the four categories are displayed in Table 6.1. With regard to integrative-holistic comments, we may note that the major differences between French- and English-Canadian MPs were that the former were somewhat more concerned than the latter with the federal character of the proposed new nation and with the positive contribution that a larger political union of the several provinces would make to collective security and defense. Interestingly, however, English-Canadian MPs tended to dwell more on the positive contribution Confederation could make to the narrowing of ethnic-religious differences in Canada.

TABLE 6.1

ARTICLES OF CONFEDERATION DEBATES (1865)—A THEMATIC ANALYSIS (IN PERCENTAGES)

Category	Integrative		Divisive	
	French	English	French	English
Political				
a. Federal principle	18.2	11.0	21.9	17.8
b. Representation in Parliament	0	7.3	6.2	2.2
c. Political parties	0	0	0	2.2
d. Federal court jurisdiction	0	0	9.3	0
Economic				
e. Transportation-commerce	13.6	17.1	3.1	15.5
f. Economic nationalism	27.2	21.9	12.5	31.0
Sociocultural				
g. Ethnicity-identity	0	8.5	25.0	11.3
h. Religion	0	0	18.7	0
Strategic				
i. General security and defense	27.2	19.5	0	4.4
j. Defense against the U.S.	13.6	11.0	3.1	15.5
k. Strengthen the British Empire	0	3.6	0	0
	(N=22)	(N=82)	(N=32)	(N=45)

Ethnic-related differences between MPs were somewhat sharper insofar as their divisive comments were concerned. Not unexpectedly, almost half of the divisive-particularistic comments made by French-Canadian MPs dealt with the deleterious consequences Confederation might have for the maintenance of a specific French and Catholic identity by Quebechois. French-Canadian MPs tended to fear that in such a union the French language and culture would be submerged by a larger and more dominant English culture and eventually would disappear. In some of their minds, the destruction of French-Canadian culture had motivated the passage of the legislation that created the current United Province of Canada. A Mr. Paquet opined that:

> I did not take long to convince myself, as any Lower Canadian member may do on reading his celebrated report, that everything he [Lord Durham] had in view was calculated to secure our annihilation as French-Canadians, and that he desired neither more nor less than to subject us to a ruling power exclusively English.
>
> Instead of preserving the Constitution, they change it and indeed destroy it, by granting to Upper Canada preponderance in representation. I affirm that the proposed Confederation of the provinces is only a legislative union in disguise. [PD, 1865: 789]

In contrast, almost half of the divisive comments made by English-speaking members were structured in economic terms. Understandably, since their ethnic groups constituted a majority, English-speaking members also were less concerned than their French colleagues with adequate representation in the proposed new parliament and judiciary (see Table 6.1). However, the long-standing demand by the Reformists for representation by population and (as of 1864) the support of their demand by both the French and English wings of the Conservative party of Canada East (Quebec) helped insure that the subject of representation in the political institutions that were to be established by the proposed union was adequately aired.

Nonetheless, it is apparent from the data in Table 6.1 that the principal issues arising in the debates over Confederation were economic and strategic. From a strategic point of view, little emphasis was placed on the overall strengthening of the British Empire. However, concern over possible hostilities with a large, well-armed United States prompted numerous comments about the need to prepare for such eventualities. Members of Parliament believed the national economic and security-defense benefits that would result from Confederation were highly desirable. Despite their desirability, they still voiced considerable concern that sectional or particular economic interest would suffer under the proposed Confederation. In summary, the impasse in the Canadian provincial legislature, the very real concern with the military threat posed by the United States, the uncertainty with regard to the mother country's future economic policies toward them—as well as MacDonald's and other leading Conservatives' sensitivity to French-Canadian fears and aspirations—all combined to insure that the legislative response to Confederation would be an overwhelmingly favorable one. Because of this broad support, and because the opponents of Confederation were a heterogeneous and rather disorganized lot, the question of approval of the planned union was never really in doubt. According to Waite (1963: vii),

> the Opposition's difficulty was that it was heterogeneous. Its core was the Liberals of Canada East, French and English, held together by common experience and Liberal principles rather than by common interests. To the Liberals were joined some dissentient Conservatives from Canada East—English-speaking—who feared a separate province of Quebec; a few French Conservatives who disliked the idea of Confederation; some Conservatives from Canada West who hated Reformers; and a group of Reformers who hated Conservatives, and who rallied behind a little group led by Sandfield MacDonald. Such a motley Opposition did not have much of a chance, and they probably knew they had not.

MODERNIZATION THEMES AND LEGISLATIVE ATTITUDES IN THE CANADIAN PARLIAMENT, 1867–77

In order to gain the support of many of the delegates to the Quebec Conference who presumably would be responsible for heading the ratification movement in their respective provinces, the leaders of the Confederation movement in Canada had agreed to make a number of economic concessions to the maritime provinces in the proposed new union. For example,

> the bankers of Prince Edward Island were extremely anxious to unload the burden of their railroad bonds on the new Dominion government; the provincial government wanted to avoid unpopular increases in taxation for these internal improvements. In the past the maritime provinces had depended entirely on taxation levied by the provincial governments, for even the support of clearly municipal enterprises.
>
> In exchange for the customs duties, which the provinces now surrendered, it was agreed in the Quebec convention that the dominion treasury should grant annually to each province a sum equal to eighty cents per capita of

population, as determined by the census of 1861, and that these federal subsidies should be paid six months in advance. In addition, the debts of the provinces, up to a specified amount, were to be assumed by the new federal government, and each province was to receive a specific contribution for the support of its provincial government. [Wittke, 1942: 184–85]

As our findings will indicate, much of the debate in Parliament throughout the first ten years of Canadian history was taken up with discussion of these economic issues, not the least important of which were the commitment to build an intercontinental railway and the westward expansion of the Dominion to the Pacific coast.

Throughout much of this period, then, opposition to and criticism of the newly established central government was economic in character and primarily was voiced by MPs from the maritimes and the west (see Table 6.2). The prevailing attitude at the first session of the Canadian Parliament in 1867 was one of acceptance of Confederation, but with certain reservations and ample skepticism, largely on the part of MPs from the maritimes. For example, at least one MP from New Brunswick, a Mr. Anglin, stated that although the "scheme of Union was the offspring of corruption, injustice, and fraud," he would "give the Government a fair trial, so as to work the Constitution successfully" (PD, 1865: 18). Representatives from Nova Scotia were especially vocal in their criticism. The following comment by E. M. MacDonald exemplifies the nature of their disappointment:

The representatives of Nova Scotia must be excused if they decline to join in congratulating His Excellency on the success of the Confederation scheme. Congratulations and rejoicings are for the victors and not for the vanquished. Canada may rejoice at the success of her strategy; but it is too much to expect of Nova Scotia that she will rejoice at the loss of her political institutions and her political liberties. Nova Scotia is in this Dominion as a conquered country, deprived by most foul and unfair means of her long enjoyed privilege of self-government. [PD, 1865: 21]

As Table 6.2 indicates, the most divisive issues in 1867 were those threatening political autonomy and economic autarky. The specific issues most frequently cited by MPs from the maritimes were duties, tariffs, and currency reform. In particular, New Brunswick MPs feared "increased taxes, higher tariffs, Canadian (Ontario and Quebec) competition in the provincial market, and loss of local monopolies" (Bailey, 1967: 91).

By 1868 both the concept and the reality of the new union had become more acceptable, although representatives from New Brunswick and Nova Scotia continued to be critical of the government.

TABLE 6.2

MPS' PERCEPTIONS OF MODERNIZATION MEASURES IN TERMS OF THE INTEGRATION OF CANADIAN SOCIETY: PARLIAMENTARY DEBATES (IN PERCENTAGES)

Year	Integrative Speeches					Divisive Speeches					Total
	Political	Economic	Sociocultural	Strategic	(N)	Political	Economic	Sociocultural	Strategic	(N)	(N =)
1867	33.3	44.4	–	22.2	(18)	25.0	67.5	12.5	–	(32)	(50)
1868	–	36.4	13.6	50.0	(22)	–	30.7	–	69.2	(13)	(35)
1869	9.0	36.3	9.0	45.4	(22)	17.6	35.3	–	47.1	(17)	(39)
1870	–	100.0	–	–	(20)	23.0	61.5	15.4	–	(13)	(33)
1873	21.0	79.0	–	–	(38)	5.0	95.0	–	–	(19)	(57)
1874	13.6	77.3	–	9.1	(22)	22.2	77.8	–	–	(27)	(49)
1875	21.4	60.7	17.9	–	(28)	15.8	42.1	42.1	–	(19)	(47)
1876	–	86.4	13.4	–	(30)	17.2	58.6	24.2	–	(29)	(59)

MPs from the latter province were especially concerned. They felt the MacDonald government's emphasis on defensive preparations against a possible United States attack might irritate that country precisely at the time that delicate cross-national negotiations were being conducted to link New Brunswick with the New England railway system in order to significantly increase the volume of trade between Nova Scotia and the northeastern United States. The goodwill of the United States government was considered vital for the success of this scheme, and it was not likely to be enhanced by military preparations directed against that country. Thus, rather than eliciting the support and loyalty of the supposedly grateful citizenry of Nova Scotia, the new national government's consideration of measures to protect the territorial integrity of Canada instead inspired considerable irritation and anger in these same citizens. Nor were their feelings likely to be assuaged by lectures such as that delivered by a Mr. McGhee, an MP from the eastern townships of Quebec:

> A portion of Nova Scotian complaints may be within the power of this House to remedy . . . but Nova Scotia must only ask us to consider these subjects [tariff, stamp tax, etc.] from a broad point of view, and to deal with herself, not with exceptional partiality, but in the same spirit of evenhanded fairness which we extended equally to Quebec, Ontario, or New Brunswick.
> The Union is not to be consolidated by any temporary conciliating concession to evanescent popular prejudice, not by any momentary humoring of some particular local or sectional phase of public opinion, but by our constant, earnest and unremitting care of the commercial welfare and progress of the Province.
> And besides this attention and practical consideration, we need, above all, the healing influence of time. . . . Time will show us the Constitution of this Dominion as much cherished in the hearts of the people of all its Provinces, not excepting Nova Scotia. [PD, 1865: 162]

Despite Nova Scotian unhappiness, strategic matters occupied much of the time of Parliament in 1868. Controversy centered on the issue of the conscription of manpower. Those favoring conscription generally argued that the practice would provide the basis of a military force that would enhance Canada's national importance and deter "hawkish" elements in the United States from considering any military adventure in Canada. Those opposed to the measure argued that it would deter immigrants from coming to Canada, that they would instead go to the United States, and that new immigrants were required as settlers and homesteaders if the government really was serious about expanding westward.

The dominant issues considered by Parliament in 1869 remained strategic and economic, both of which were linked to westward expansion, given the impending transfer of Manitoba to the Canadian government. Expansion in itself was considered by many as a defense against possible United States encroachment. The assumption was that if the newly established Dominion government did not lay formal claim to the "Northwest" (i.e., Manitoba, the territories now comprising the provinces of Saskatchewan, Alberta, and British Columbia) they would go by default to the Americans, thousands of whom were aggressively seeking new land. The fear was that American settlers would establish squatter's rights to the millions of acres of unoccupied land in the Northwest, that incidents would be staged that would bring the settlers into conflict with the authority of the Dominion, and that the United States then would seize upon these incidents to lay claim to the western half of the continent under the guise of protecting the rights of its citizens. Also considered was the extension of Canada eastward. Indeed, much of the political discussion in 1869 centered on the question of whether the federal government would grant $150,000 to Newfoundland for certain crown lands in the event that that province joined Canada. The sociocultural and, to some extent, political discussion focused on the natives of Manitoba, particularly those of mixed French and Indian descent (Metis) and what the rights of these people were to be when Manitoba became Canadian. Most of the divisive comments were made by MPs who argued that the intended expansion of the Dominion would have deleterious consequences for the provinces that already comprised Canada. Too rapid expansion, of necessity, would result in the dilution of energies and resources required for the development of Canada as it was currently constituted, or so it was claimed.

There was no discussion of strategic matters in 1870 and almost no discussion of sociocultural and political issues. Almost all of the debate on the latter two issues centered on the problems generated by the inclusion in the Dominion of Manitoba with its large Metis population. Instead, the great bulk of debate was concerned with economic matters, specifically, with the establishment of protective tarrifs, currency reforms, and the necessity for raising additional revenues through higher taxes.

Those favoring a protective tariff argued that it was the best, if not the only, means of insuring the development and survival of infant Canadian manufacturing interests. And, although MPs arguing in support of protective tariffs at times acknowledged that such measures might initially benefit particular provinces such as Ontario, eventually the whole country would surely prosper. Not unnaturally, those arguing against these measures emphasized their inequity and the adverse effects they would have on agriculture. Notwithstanding these arguments, support for a protective tariff broadened to include the formidable Joseph Howe, long a critic of Confederation and protection. Howe acknowledged that "the Maritimes had for the last twenty years been in favor of the principle of Free Trade. The proposed protectionist policy was popular, not because they were now less in favor of Free Trade, but because the United States was using a high protective tariff as a method of political coercion. They were still in favor of the principle of Free Trade; but they would even depart from sound principles of political policy rather than injure the country" (PD, 1865: 37).

Unfortunately, as we noted above, there are no Scrapbook Debates for the years 1871–72. However, on the basis of secondary sources, we can safely assume that a major issue for much of that time was the Treaty of Washington signed between the United States and Great Britain. MacDonald, who had argued the Canadian case in Washington as vigorously as possible, was unhappy with the treaty, but felt he must support it on the ground that the conditions were the most favorable Canada could expect. His opponents claimed Canadian interests had been sacrificed to patch up Anglo-American relations that had deteriorated because of England's covert and not-so-covert sympathy and support for the Confederacy. MacDonald had acquiesced to these arrangements. Moreover, Canada would not be compensated for the Fenian raids launched from American territory, although, according to the critics, she should have received compensation. Canada, they claimed, also should not have given the United States access and navigational rights to the Saint Lawrence for a pittance, and MacDonald should have extracted far more for the commercial fishing privileges that the Americans would enjoy in Canadian waters. Indeed, Alexander MacKenzie tried to make MacDonald's support for the Washington Treaty the principal issue of the 1872 election.

During the 1871–72 period MacDonald and his Conservative government also continued to push their policies of westward expansion and railway development. Both programs were experiencing considerable difficulty; a contract for the building of a transcontinental railroad had not even been let. The newly admitted representatives from British Columbia were particularly incensed by this and argued, not unjustifiably, that the government's failure to begin the construction of a rail link with British Columbia was a betrayal of the agreement under which that province had entered Confederation. To these problems MacDonald added a "third ingredient of developmental policy." During the 1872 election campaign he unveiled his "national policy," a policy structured in terms of national benefits that were to accrue from a system of protective tariffs (Beck, 1968: 15).

Although successful in 1872, he did not quiet opposition objections to the as yet nonexistent railway. However, he did press his advantage as the leader of a newly returned government and proposed in 1873 to standardize, through national legislation, the provincial laws respecting weights and measures, and wrecks and salvage, and also to promote his national policy. Again, strategic and sociocultural matters received short shrift from Parliament. Attention focused instead on economic affairs and on the "Pacific scandal." The scandal arose from the revelation that Sir Hugh Allan, president of the Canadian Pacific Railway Company, to whom a charter and a contract to build the new transcontinental railway recently had been awarded, seemingly had paid for the privilege by contributing some $350,000 of corporate funds to Conservative party coffers in the election of the previous year. The affair, according to Creighton, "broke the Conservative government; and for a time it seemed as if it would break Sir John MacDonald as well" (1958: 334).

The 1874 election that the Pacific scandal made necessary brought to power the first Liberal administration since Confederation. MacKenzie, the Liberal prime minister, had vigorously opposed MacDonald's national policy when in opposition and was not inclined to support it now that he was head of the government. Nor was he as committed to the building of a transcontinental railroad as MacDonald had been. He proposed instead that a water route extending westward from Lake Superior be used to link the Northwest with Canada. It is true that his government tried to enlist private companies to begin the building of a railroad, offering them what the government regarded as liberal subsidies. However, the efforts were to no avail. As Table 6.2 indicates, MacKenzie's unwillingness to adopt protective measures and the temporary shelving of the railroad project generated intense opposition, particularly among Conservative MPs from British Columbia. Some even threatened that British Columbia would secede from the Confederation, since it was obvious that the proposed transcontinental railroad to the Pacific would not be completed by 1881.[4] Nor were the luckless Liberals helped by the economic panic of 1873 and the resulting depression that did not really abate until 1879. The Conservative opposition, quite naturally, blamed the depression on the government. The stagnation of the economy, they claimed, was a consequence of the government's unwillingness to push ahead with the building of the Pacific railroad; the unemployment and depressed wages they blamed on the government's failure to adopt the national policy on protective tariffs.

The transcontinental railroad and westward expansion dominated the parliamentary debates in 1875 as well. The opening of the Prince Edward Island railroad in that year provided the opportunity for Conservatives to reintroduce the whole question of federal funding of transportation projects, both rail and canal. Again, debate focused on the nonexistent Pacific railroad. Indeed, the latter now was being invested with symbolic as well as substantive importance as the following excerpt from a speech by Mr. Colin McDougall illustrates:

> The binding together of this great Confederation by that iron band would not only have the effect of bringing us together more closely as far as distance was concerned, but it would have the effect of bringing us together socially . . .
> This great enterprise would be the means of still better opening up of the Northwest country that is going to make us a great nation. . . .
> [The Canadian Pacific Railway] was a national enterprise calculated to bind the people of the whole Dominion together, and make them feel that they were one people. [PD, 1865: 10]

By 1875 security and defense issues were no longer crucial, since the American threat to Canada apparently had dissipated. Political and sociocultural issues, however, continued to occupy some of the attention of members. Much of the debate on the latter issues centered around Louis Riel, the leader of the aborted Metis' attempt to establish an independent government in Manitoba rather than see that province join the Dominion. After Manitoba entered the Confederation, Riel actually had won election to Parliament but was prevented from taking a seat in the Commons because of his supposed criminal and traitorous acts. There was vigorous debate, for example, over whether Riel, who had been implicated in the murder of one Thomas Scott, should receive amnesty. Given Riel's French-Catholic background, the issue soon became a surrogate for the ethnic-religious conflict that had been relatively subdued until then.

In 1876 economic policies such as free trade, protection, canal building, and so forth, again dominated debate. The free trade versus protection debate generated a number of acrimonious exchanges between MPs representing the more populated and urbanized areas and those representing primarily agricultural constituencies. Some MPs, as the excerpt below indicates, tried to bridge the gap and to argue that manufacturing and agricultural interests were not necessarily incompatible.

> Those [interests] of the manufacturer are not necessarily adverse to those of the farmer, nor vice versa; they are coadjutors, working for the common benefit, and an appeal to the farmers as a class, as against the manufacturers as a class, is the purest demogoguerism. [PD, 1865: 475]

However, the number of speeches on economic matters that we have classified as divisive (see Table 6.2) indicates quite clearly that protective tariffs were regarded by many MPs outside of Ontario as benefiting primarily Ontario. British Columbian MPs also continued to press their demands for the promised Pacific railroad and to make veiled threats that secession would be the inevitable consequence of the failure to complete a rail link to the coast. A Mr. Thompson, for one,

> hoped he should never see the day when British Columbia would be under a foreign flag; . . . if the people were deliberately insulted and the Government refused to carry out their plighted faith, the people of Canada, much as he would grieve over such an occurrence, need not be surprised to see another flag than that of the Dominion flying over that territory. [PD, 1865: 1133]

As the depression continued, the concept of protection became more attractive both within Parliament and (assuming MPs were reflecting popular opinion) outside of the House. Indeed, Conservatives increasingly claimed the imposition of tariffs would provide the panacea needed to end the nation's problems. MacDonald, their leader, called for major federal investment in railways and canals. He promised that if a Conservative government was returned in the next election, it would certainly give such projects the highest priority. In the interim, he seemed to offer the pious hope that the members of the government at least would examine some of the many policy pearls he had so magnanimously and frequently cast before them.

> While the people of the Great West would be seriously disappointed at the information that the Pacific Railway was not to be prosecuted immediately, . . . other parts of the country would learn with equal regret and equal

disappointment that the completion of the canal system was to be post-poned; ... he hoped and believed that before the session closed sufficient arguments would be used to honorable gentlemen opposite to induce them to reconsider the position they had apparently taken with respect to these great works. [PD, 1865: 14]

A SUMMARY AND A BEGINNING

In Table 6.3 we have summarized the data derived from our content analyses of the reports available to us of the Canadian Parliament's debates during the years 1867–70 and 1873–76. Two of our findings indicate the decidedly integrative leanings of MPs during those years.

First, we find that a majority (54.2%) of the speeches made by members of Parliament were integrative rather than divisive, and that the proportion of integrative speeches increased over time (1873–76). Further, we may safely assume that a fairly substantial number of speeches that have been classified as "divisive" reflected govern-

TABLE 6.3

SUMMARY OF THEMES ARTICULATED BY MPS IN PARLIAMENTARY DEBATES, 1867–70 AND 1873–76 (IN PERCENTAGES)

Category	Integrative		Divisive		Total	
Political Theme						
1867–70	32.0	[36.3] [a]	48.3	[63.7]	[100.0]	(N=22)
1873–76	68.0	[53.1]	51.7	[46.9]	[100.0]	(N=32)
Total	100	(N=25)	100	(N=29)	14.6%	(N=54)
Economic Theme						
1867–70	33.1	[53.6]	37.2	[46.4]	100.0	(N=118)
1873–76	66.9	[58.4]	62.8	[41.6]	100.0	(N=117)
Total	100	(N=133)	100	(N=102)	63.9%	(N=235)
Sociocultural Theme						
1867–70	35.7	[45.4]	28.6	[54.6]	100.0	(N=11)
1873–76	64.3	[37.5]	71.4	[62.5]	100.0	(N=24)
Total	100	(N=14)	100	(N=21)	9.5%	(N=35)
Strategic Theme						
1867–70	92.6	[59.5]	100	[40.5]	100.0	(N=42)
1873–76	7.4	[100.0]	0	[0]	100.0	(N= 2)
Total	100	(N=27)	100	(N=17)	11.9%	(N=44)

a. Percentages in brackets represent row figures; those unbracketed are column figures.

ment-opposition relationships characteristic of British-model parliamentary systems (i.e., the government proposes and defends its policies, the opposition attacks them and suggests alternatives) at least as much as they reflected disintegrative or particularistic sentiments. It also should be remembered that in Western societies the expression and defense of local and particularistic interests by legislative representatives is an integral and time-honored concept in the theory of popular representation. It is a concept to which Western political theorists have ascribed great value even while recognizing that local-particularistic interests and a "general" or "public" interest are not always congruent. Therefore, it should not be assumed (at least in our view) either that every divisive speech by a MP was intrinsically "bad," or that the instrumental effect of every divisive speech was to seriously impede national integration during this period—although, undoubtedly, some of the speeches and actions of MPs probably did not actually facilitate the process!

Second, we also find that all but two of the speeches on strategy and defense were made before 1873, a fact that tends to support the view of development scholars who have argued that in a potentially hostile international environment the first goal of modernization is simply to survive as a national entity. Also, since the majority of these speeches were very positive (i.e., integrative) with regard to the need for defense, we may assume that Parliament's concern for the defense of Canada during the first years of existence may have contributed psychologically if not materially to national integration.

We are less sanguine with respect to Parliament's contribution to national integration as reflected by discussion of issues that we have labeled sociocultural. First, there were relatively few such speeches, particularly during the period 1867—70. Second, the majority of these were divisive. A reasonable speculation, based on these findings, is that most MPs felt that a frank and open discussion of ethnic-religious and other cultural cleavages at that time probably would exacerbate rather than ameliorate them. Accordingly, discussion (or, rather, public discussion) of these issues in Parliament, which Malcolm E. Jewell and others have suggested is an appropriate forum, was avoided.

In addition, we cannot assume that Parliament's discussion of political issues having a bearing on national integration facilitated that process. It is true that some of the issues involved (e.g., the representation of groups and provinces in the political institutions that were to be established) had been rather thoroughly discussed at the Quebec Conference and in the subsequent debates on Confederation in the several provincial legislatures. Nonetheless, in comparison to the amount of attention that economic issues received during the eight-year period for which we have data, Parliament spent surprisingly little time on political matters with a bearing on either integration or modernization.

The issues on which Parliament very obviously did spend time were economic—principally the possible construction of a transportation-communication network and a tariff system. The fact that fully 43% of the speeches made by MPs on economic issues were classified as divisive—even granted the two caveats concerning divisive issues registered above—certainly indicates there was a far from unanimous feeling among MPs that these policies were in the national interest or that they would contribute to national development and integration. However, despite their differences, MPs ultimately did embark on an ambitious program of internal development: canals were dug; factories were built; a tariff policy was generated; a transcontinental railroad was completed in 1885; and the country did make an auspicious start on modernization. In retrospect, one could argue that in laying the foundation for the construction of a national railroad, Parliament made possible the single most important event in Canada's history. For without such a rail system not only would the western provinces not have become an integral part of Canada, but also the maritimes and even Ontario and Quebec might not have survived as separate political entities (Berton, 1972). In summary, therefore, although there may not be anything inherent in the legislative process that either facilitates or impedes national integration, it would appear that Canada's first two parliaments did facilitate that process. Moreover, there is good reason to believe that the very concept of a Canadian national entity never would have been operationalized had it not been for internal procedures within the provincial legislature of United Canada.

If these assumptions are realistic, why does Canada suffer from such strong regional cleavages (of which the ethnic and religious are only the most obvious) that her survival in current form periodically has been called into question? Why also, if integration and modernization are empirically overlapping aspects of the larger process of societal development, has Canada achieved a high level of modernization without attaining a correspondingly high level of national integration? Perhaps Canada continues to be plagued by cleavages that threaten her national integrity partly because some of the institutions and processes, other than the legislative, that generally are assumed to facilitate integration (e.g., the party system, a federal structure) in fact may not have made much of a contribution over the years. And, although we have suggested that the first two Canadian parliaments did facilitate both the integration and modernization processes, it may well be that other parliaments in the past hundred years did not make as significant a contribution. Indeed, several parliaments may have done things that actually contributed to the disintegration of Canadian society. Of course, the questions of *whether* and *how* other parliaments, or the party system, or federalism, did or did not facilitate the process of national integration are empirical ones. As such, they could and should be investigated in future research, but their answer obviously is beyond the scope of this chapter.

A second reason for Canada's current integration problem may be that Parliament and other political institutions have provided very few of the unifying symbols that in other countries have served as focal points for the development of national pride, national self-consciousness, and national identification. Mildred Schwartz (1967: vii) makes this point succintly in her important study of Canadian identity:

Until World War II, the term "Canadian" was not even used in Canadian passports. The British flag remained the flag of Canada until the 1960's. Canada's highest court of supreme appeal was the Privy Council of the British House of Lords until recently. Canada's constitution is the British North America Act, passed by the parliament of Great Britain in 1867. Amendments to the Constitution still require *pro forma* ratification by the British parliament. Such symbols of national inferiority which would be outrageous to the citizens of the various new nations of Africa and Asia apparently have bothered few Canadians.

A third reason why Canada has experienced a variety of sharp social and economic cleavages is that her governing elites historically may have preferred such conditions and, in fact, may have encouraged and made use of them to maintain their own privileged positions. This is the thesis of John Porter's remarkably comprehensive study of social stratification and the distribution of power in Canadian society (Porter, 1965). Illustrative of this thesis that Canadian political leaders have combined pious exhortations to unite with themes and practices that divide, because the latter help maintain the socioeconomic status quo and their own positions as elites, is the following passage:

The major themes in Canadian political thought emphasize those characteristics, mainly regional and provincial loyalties, which *divide* the Canadian
population. Consequently, integration and national unity must be constantly
reiterated to counter such divisive sentiments. The dialogue is between unity
and discord rather than progressive and conservative forces. The question
which arises is whether the discord-unity dialogue has any real meaning in the
lives of Canadians, or whether it has become, in the middle of the twentieth
century, a political technique of conservatism. Canada must be one of the few
major industrial societies in which the right and left polarization has become
deflected into disputes over regionalism and national unity. [Porter, 1965:
368–69]

If one wished to cite illustrations that support Porter's thesis, one
could point to the fact that since MacDonald's first ministry, Canadian political leaders have made it clear that Canada is a political
entity in which the two "charter" groups, the British and the French,
have a special status. And, despite the fact that the composition of
the Canadian population has changed dramatically in the past hundred years so that approximately one-third of the current population
is not of either Anglo-Celtic or French descent, the "partnership"
and "bicultural" themes have continued to be promulgated and
encouraged by devices such as appointments to the several federal
cabinets of this century, the establishment of a large and highly
prestigious Royal Commission on Bi-Culturalism and Bi-Lingualism,
the appointment of an official language commissioner, and so forth.
Social scientists might find it interesting (since public policy as to
what information to collect and how to tabulate it very much
reflects official attitudes) that the several Canadian censuses always
have been greatly concerned with such matters as place of birth,
nation of origin, and ethnicity as separate and distinct factors. They
also have avoided the category "Canadian" in tabulating the origins
of the population and even have provided helpful lists of questions
that census enumerators could use for people who fail to provide a
non-Canadian identification (Smith and Kornberg, 1969: 346).[5]

Since public officials over the years seemingly have insisted that
everyone in Canada has a non-Canadian origin, it is not surprising
that scholars and political commentators alike also have ascribed
great importance to matters such as ethnicity and religion as predic-
tors of Canadian political behavior. Nor is it especially surprising that
Canadian political elites should have used ethnic-religious cleavages in
the population to maintain their own privileged positions. In Chapter
7 in this volume Abdo Baaklini, for example, reports that precisely
the same techniques historically have been employed by the elites of
another bicultural society, Lebanon. Assuming Porter and others are

right in their assertions that political elites historically have emphasized factors that divide the Canadian population, it also should be noted that they never have permitted these divisions to "get out of hand." In fact, the federal authorities (and the provincial, for that matter) have not been loath to make use of the available instruments of force and coercion whenever particular individuals or groups posed even a remote threat to current political arrangements. To cite but a few dramatic examples, we may note the use of force by provincial authorities against religious groups such as the Hutterites, Doukhobors, and Jehovah's Witnesses; the federal government's use of the Royal Canadian Mounted Police at Regina to stop a march on Ottawa by the unemployed in 1936; the forced relocation of Japanese-Canadians in 1942; the internment of known Communists and French-Canadian nationalist leaders during World War II; and invocation of the draconian War Measures Act to meet the "October Crisis" of 1970.

With regard to the second question, two reasons have been advanced to help explain how Canada has managed to become a modern industrial state without becoming a fully integrated one in the sense of "creating a territorial nationality . . . which overshadows subordinate parochial loyalties" (Weiner, 1965: 52): (1) the tremendous volume of natural resources with which the country has been blessed, and (2) the ability to continuously attract huge amounts of capital for development purposes, first from Great Britain and then from the United States. These two factors have enabled Canadians to achieve a per-capita income and a standard of living that is among the highest in the world. Regretfully, however, the country's natural resources are unevenly distributed. Further, the investment capital that has been attracted historically has been concentrated largely in extractive and capital-intensive industries. Consequently, only three of the Canadian provinces (Ontario, British Columbia, and Alberta) can be said to be "have" provinces. The other seven continue to be "have-nots"; even the most cursory trip through the Atlantic provinces, rural Quebec, or through Manitoba and Saskatchewan provides a vivid illustration of the uneven quality of modernization-development in Canada. And one can speculate that the very strong regionalism[6] based upon economic particularism that over the years has characterized the social and political attitudes of the population of the maritimes and western Canada is not unrelated to this uneven development. Nor is it unrelated, in all likelihood, to the fact that young French-Canadians still regard Quebec as "underdeveloped" and in a state of "transition" to a modern industrialized society (Hargrove, 1970: 485).

There obviously are many other reasons why national integration has not kept pace with modernization, but it would take a separate volume to develop these reasons. At the beginning of this chapter we observed that national integration rests upon balance and order in society and that integration and modernization are related processes in societal development. Our current thinking is that in Canada both of these processes seem to have rested more upon order than upon balance and that at least some of Canada's problems with nationalist movements and identity crises stem from this fact. This is an assumption we would like to explore in future research.

NOTES

1. For a recent discussion of the problems of Canadian nationalism, see the relevant articles in "Canada 1972," especially pp. 185–93 and 198–202. Other useful collections of materials are in Russell (1966) and Cook (1969).

2. For an account of how an official version of the confederation debates came to be published, see Waite (1963: viii–ix). Note in particular the following comment: "The fact that debates were being reported fully, and officially, encouraged quantities of plain drivel. Moreover members could correct their speeches before they were printed; this meant that speeches were dressed up for public consumption. There are interesting differences between the pungency of a remark on the floor of the House and the pomposity preferred by a member in the 'corrected' version of his speech" (ix).

3. An examination of secondary sources indicated that these issues were extremely relevant at the time.

4. In 1871 MacDonald, then the prime minister, had promised that a railroad connecting British Columbia with the rest of Canada would be completed ten years after British Columbia entered the Confederation (1871).

5. The supportive data in this paper are derived from Origins of the Canadian Population, General Review, Census of Canada, 1961, and the other census volumes of this century. The authors go on to observe that the census provides procedural notes that suggest specific ethnic categories that apparently will satisfy the census-taker. That the entire discussion smacks of a certain petulance on the part of authorities is best reflected in the comment, "Enumerators were instructed to accept the answer 'Canadian' or 'American' if persons insisted on reporting these ethnic origins. The text specifies the exact number of such persons, though these people lose their identities in the printed tables where, we may assume, they fall into such enlightening categories as 'other' or 'not stated'."

6. This regionalism has been manifested in a variety of ways, including the continuous loss of population of less favored areas to Ontario and, until recently, the United States; the generation of protest movements from which the CCF-NDP, the Social Credit-Credi11iste, and the several Quebec nationalist and separatist parties have evolved; and the virtual disappearance of the Liberal party as a major political force west of Ontario.

REFERENCES

ALMOND, G. A. (1966) "Political theory and political science." American Political Science Review 60 (Dec.): 869–79.

BAILEY, A. G. (1967) "The basis and persistence of opposition to confederation in New Brunswick," in Confederation, ed. R. Cook, C. Brown, and S. Berger. Toronto: Univ. of Toronto Press. Pp. 70–93.

BECK, J. M. (1968) Pendulum of Power: Canada's Federal Elections. Scarborough, Ont.: Prentice-Hall of Canada.

BERTON, P. (1972) The Impossible Railway: The Building of the Canadian Pacific. New York: Knopf.

BOURNE, K. (1967) Britain and the Balance of Power in North America, 1815–1908. Berkeley: Univ. of California Press.

BUDD, R. W., R. K. THORP, and L. DONOHEW (1967) Content Analysis Communications. New York: Macmillan.

BURT, A. L. (1971) The United States, Great Britain, and British North America. New York: Russell & Russell.

"Canada 1972" (1972) Current History 62 (Apr.): 177–208.

COOK, R., ed. (1969) French-Canadian Nationalism. Toronto: Macmillan of Canada.

COOK, R., C. BROWN, and C. BERGER, eds. (1967) Confederation. Toronto: Univ. of Toronto Press.

CREIGHTON, D. G. (1958) A History of Canada. Boston: Houghton Mifflin.

––––––. (1967) "Economic nationalism and confederation." In Confederation, ed. R. Cook, C. Brown, and C. Berger. Toronto: Univ. of Toronto Press. Pp. 1–8.

GROSSHOLTZ, J. (1970) "Integrative factors in the Malaysian and Philippine legislatures." Comparative Politics 3 (Oct.): 93–112.

HARGROVE, E. C. (1967) "Political leadership in the Anglo-American democracies." In Political Leadership in Industrialized Societies, ed. L. J. Edinger. New York: Wiley. Pp. 471–91.

–––– (1970) "Nationality, values, and change: young elites in French Canada." Comparative Politics 2 (Apr.): 473–500.

HOLSTI, O. R. (1969) Content Analysis for the Social Sciences and Humanities. Reading, Mass.: Addison-Wesley.

KEENLEYSIDE, H. (1971) Canada and the United States. Port Washington, N.Y.: Kennikat Press.

KORNBERG, A., S. M. HINES, Jr., and J. SMITH (1973) "Legislatures and the modernization of societies." Comparative Political Studies 6 (Jan.): 478–89.

LEVESQUE, R. (1968) An Option for Quebec. Toronto: McClelland & Stewart.

LEVY, M. J. (1972) Modernization: Latecomers and Survivors. New York: Basic Books.

MALLORY, J. R. (1972) "French and English in Canada: uneasy union." Current History 62 (Apr.): 189–93, 210–12.

MEISEL, J. (1963) "The stalled omnibus: Canadian parties in the 1960's." Social Research 30 (Autumn): 367–90.

MERRITT, R. L. (1966) Symbols of American Community, 1735–1775. New Haven, Conn.: Yale Univ. Press.

NISH, E., ed. (n.d.) Debates of the Legislative Assembly of United Canada, 1841–1867. Vol. 1: 1841. Montreal: Les Presses de l'Ecole des Hautes Etudes Commerciales.

"Parliamentary debates on the subject of the confederation of the British North American provinces" (PD) (1865).

PORTER, J. (1965) The Vertical Mosaic: An Analysis of Social Class and Power in Canada. Toronto: Univ. of Toronto Press.

RUSSELL, P., ed. (1966) Nationalism in Canada. Toronto: McGraw-Hill of Canada.

SCHWARTZ, M. A. (1967) Public Opinion and Canadian Identity. Berkeley: Univ. of California Press.

SIEGFRIED, A. (1947) Canada: An International Power, trans. Doris Hemming. New York: Duell, Sloan, Pearce.

SMITH, J., and A. KORNBERG (1969) "Some considerations bearing upon comparative research in Canada and the United States." Sociology 3 (Sept.): 341–57.

STACEY, C. P. (1967) "Britain's withdrawal from North America, 1864–1871." In Confederation, ed. R. Cook, C. Brown, and C. Berger. Toronto: Univ. of Toronto Press. Pp. 9–23.
VAN LOON, R., and M. S. WHITTINGTON (1971) The Canadian Political System. Toronto: McGraw-Hill of Canada.
WAITE, P. B. (1963) Confederation Debates. Toronto: McClelland & Stewart.
WEINER, M. (1965) "Political integration and political development." Annals of the American Academy of Political Science 358 (Mar.): 52–64.
WISE, S. F. (1970) "Conservatism and political development: the Canadian case." South Atlantic Quarterly 69 (Spring): 226–43.
WITTKE, C. F. (1942) A History of Canada. Toronto: Univ. of Toronto Press.

Chapter 7

LEGISLATURES AND POLITICAL INTEGRATION IN LEBANON: 1840–1972

ABDO I. BAAKLINI

INTRODUCTION: THEORIES OF POLITICAL INTEGRATION

In theories of political development, particularly in the context of developing countries, legislatures have been portrayed as inimical to political integration. When institutions favorable to political integration are mentioned, the mobilizing political party, the army, the bureaucracy, or even an authoritarian regime are emphasized rather than the legislature. This chapter will attempt to show that the experience of Lebanon contradicts these theories. Throughout its modern history, the legislature in Lebanon has been the pivotal force in political integration, serving in different ways at different times.

Theories of integration have typically stressed assimilation as the crucial factor. The literature, which is by now quite voluminous (see especially Deutsch, 1953, 1961, and 1964), has generally included theories derived from an idealized and ahistorical version of the Western political experience. But even in the American case, which is normally hailed as the most successful experiment of this kind in the world, integration has been found to be chimerical (Gordon, 1964).

Thus, for example, theories which equate integration with assimilation, having failed to explain the Western experience on which they were purportedly based, are even less applicable to developing countries—and can be misleading guides for political action. In many cases, the coercive and economic capabilities to achieve political integration through cultural and structural assimilation simply do not exist. The experience of Pakistan, Sudan, Iraq, and Nigeria serve as striking reminders that integration through assimilation is not a viable option for many developing nations.

The political actors in Lebanon, by contrast, did not equate integration with assimilation, modernization, or nationalism, as most theorists tend to do.[1] Integration as it was conceived by the Lebanese political elite is not a unidirectional, unidimensional process, but is a conscious choice from among alternative modes of existence that involve many directions and many dimensions. As a process it was not conceived as inevitable. With adequate engineering and manipulation, it was made likely. Integration in Lebanon was not a blind process relying on certain inevitable conditions endemic to modern societies (such as communication, social mobilization, and functions of specialization and structural differentiation), but a process whose conceptualization relied heavily on the "perceptions of interests and values by the actors participating in the process" (Haas, 1968: 11). The contribution of the political elite was to provide the philosophy and the structure of political action for the realization of the perceived interests and values. Both their philosophy and structuring of political actions depended on a system of priorities of actions that were permissible and possible and on a specific sequence in undertaking those actions.

How, then, can developing countries achieve political integration— without disintegrating in the process? The Lebanese experience and the role played by the legislature in achieving political integration can give us one answer. Contrary to the assumptions of Claude Ake (1967), who saw an authoritarian, paternalistic, "identific," and consensual model as the best political system for achieving integration, the Lebanese model works within the context of scarce social, economic, military, and political resources under the command of the political elite, a condition shared by most developing countries. In this model integration is seen as a process taking place within an international context (in which the process of integration can be accelerated or halted if desired)[2] and a local internal context in which the process also can be halted or accelerated. Assimilation as a goal was rejected from the beginning, first because of the inability of the dominant group to impose its culture, values, and structures, and later as an undesired objective which violates the political imperatives of Lebanon and the cultural and civilizational mission in which it came to believe. The uniqueness of the Lebanese approach toward integration is that the achievements needed were not assumed but were worked toward within the constraints of the social, political, economic, and military realities in Lebanon and the outside world.

In a model of this type, which resembles the so-called functionalist model advocated by Haas (1968), differences are assumed and tolerated within the area of indifference or in areas around which there is a consensus. While it calls for the establishment of a central institution to act as a force for allegiance and for the exercise of authoritative decision, the existence of other foci is not negated. Conflict is not eliminated; rather it is seen as controllable and manageable. Both cultural and structural pluralisms are not only tolerated, but are essential for the success of the integrative process. Such a model is obviously more in harmony with the realities of many developing countries. Using Ake's conceptualization in reverse, it is antiauthoritarian, antipaternalistic, antiidentific, and anticonsensual.

THE LEBANESE INTEGRATIVE EXPERIENCE: THE PROMINENCE OF THE LEGISLATURE

Modern Lebanon as an independent political entity owes its existence to a number of historical accidents as well as to internal and external forces that consciously tried to shape the future of the country. Our concern in this study is with one of those variables, namely, the contribution of the legislative institution first to initiating the metamorphosis of Lebanon as a sociopolitical entity and later to consolidating that entity as an autonomous independent state. In no sense is the present analysis intended to underrate the importance of other factors in the political integration of Lebanon, whether these factors be internal or external. Only to the extent that these variables were manipulated by the political elite to achieve their desired goals and objectives shall we touch upon them.

THE KAYMAKAMATE PERIOD, 1842–57

Lebanon's experience in representative forms of government dates back to 1842, when the *imarah* feudal system which had provided political order and legitimacy since the sixteenth century collapsed, setting the tiny Lebanese mountainous province on its search for a new political order and legitimacy.[3] The Lebanese mountains were inhabited by two main communities, the Maronite Christians and the Druze, a religious sect identified with Islam. Since the Maronite Church, and the ideological and economic changes that it created, were at the base of the collapse of the imarah system, the new political order was consciously shaped to take sectarian factors into consideration. Lebanon was thus divided into two provinces called *kaymakamate,* one to be headed by a Christian governor, the other by a Druze. The governor of each district was assisted by a council of representatives from the various sects in the district. Thus, each council was composed of a deputy kaymakam, a judge, and an advisor for each sect; of the Sunni (a dominant Moslem sect), Maronite, Druze, Greek Orthodox, and Greek Catholic sects, and one advisor only from the Shi'a sect (another Moslem sect), since the Ottomans did not recognize the Shi'a as having a separate magistry. The functions of the council included tax assessment, adjudication, and administration of the activities of local government bodies.

The kaymakamate experiment failed for two main reasons. In the first place, the country could not accept sectarian legitimacy as a basis of government. Both the previous three centuries of the imarah rule, as well as the new ideology preached by the Maronite Church, were based on secular legitimacy. In the second place, the new arrangement failed to represent the political power balance in the country. Thus, both the Maronite Church and the newly awakened peasantry failed to identify with the new order. Between 1857 and 1860, Lebanon was immersed in a series of violent internal disorders, culminating in 1860 in a full-fledged civil war taking the form of intersectarian fighting.

THE CENTRAL ADMINISTRATIVE COUNCIL

The Central Administrative Council, a quasi-legislative body sharing with the Mutassarif (the governor of Mount Lebanon) the authority to run the affairs of Mount Lebanon, was to be composed of 12 members distributed among the various religious groups in the order shown in Table 7.1.[4] Members of the CAC were elected through a system of indirect election by all of those, regardless of religion, who resided in a particular region. The people elected the village leaders (or *shaiks*), who in turn elected the members of the CAC. A member of the CAC was supposed to represent all the people in his district rather than just his sect. Every two years one-third of the members of the CAC were to run for election while the remaining two-thirds continued in power. Members whose terms expired were eligible for reelection. The CAC's powers encompassed the sensitive areas of taxes, land tenure, local governments, and public works—all sources of peasant discontent and revolts. In this regard, perhaps, the CAC's main contribution was the creation of a complete *cadastre* (survey) of all the land in Lebanon. After the downfall of the feudal system the most crucial issue was property rights. If the aristocracy and the peasantry were to be brought together under one political system after the 1858–60 civil war, when the peasantry had confiscated much of the aristocracy's land, a complete land survey determining land titles and ownerships was needed. The work of the CAC in this area and its contribution to political stability and integration were outstanding. The land survey, completed by the CAC in the latter part of the nineteenth century, was to remain the basis of land titles until the mid-twentieth century, when another land survey was conducted.

While the constitutional powers of the CAC were limited mainly to the financial sphere (in itself a very important sphere and the source of most revolts and uprisings), it was able to acquire additional powers and to perform other essential functions. Its main long-range contributions were integration, elite recruitment, and institutionalization of political functions. While all of the three functions are related to political integration, we shall concentrate here on integration per se.

Through the work of the CAC the aristocracy of Lebanon was

TABLE 7.1

DISTRIBUTION OF THE MEMBERS OF THE CENTRAL ADMINISTRATIVE COUNCIL BY SECT AND BY REGION

	Christian Sect			Muslim Sect			
Region	Maronite	Greek Orthodox	Greek Catholic	Sunni	Shi'a	Druze	Total
Kisrwan	1						1
Batroun	1						1
Jazzin	1			1		1	3
Matn	1	1			1	1	4
Shuf						1	1
Kura		1					1
Zahle			1				1
Total	4	2	1	1	1	3	12

protected from being completely liquidated by having its property confiscated. While the aristocracy lost its inherited privileges, it continued to play an active political role through the political structure of the Mutasarrifiya, especially the CAC, which provided it with a new legitimacy based on achievement. Gradually this aristocracy turned its attention to commerce, trade, the silk industry, education, and other endeavors as means of preserving its economic lead and consequently its political power. Thus, rather than freezing out the feudal aristocracy or destroying it completely, the CAC opened new dimensions for it and provided it with a new legitimacy to change and readjust to new economic and political realities. Perhaps this very continuation of political leadership under a new political formula is what distinguishes Lebanon from the rest of the Arab and developing countries. Through its role in the central administration, the Lebanese aristocracy has continued to provide Lebanon with a large part of its leadership (Khalaf, 1968).

The CAC not only provided the aristocracy with an outlet for its predicament, but acted in a similar manner with regard to the newly enfranchised segment of the population (especially the Christians). With the establishment of the CAC and the institutionalization of an electoral process for filling vacancies in the CAC, the emerging middle classes found an avenue for assuming political power. Thus the new class of intellectuals, traders, and silk producers was brought into a working relationship with the old feudal aristocracy through the institutions of the CAC. Reviewing the names of those who occupied the presidency of the CAC, we find more who can claim a nonfeudal background than those with a feudal background, as Table 7.2 shows.

After over half a century of working together within the context of the CAC, Lebanon was provided with a leadership that shared a common political and economic vision, as the constitutional debate of 1926 showed (see al-Khateeb, 1970). The CAC became an institution around which various groups (economic and sectarian) could rally. By regulating political conflict over half a century, it was able to put an end to the Maronite Church's attempt to dominate and assimilate the various sectors of Lebanese society. Furthermore, the possibility given to the feudal aristocracy to share in the new system also provided Lebanon with class tolerance between the aristocracy and the emerging middle class. The gap between the rulers and the ruled was not given a chance to deepen, since the demand for change came from below, and the CAC provided the outlet for new leadership. Pluralism in its various shapes—cultural, religious, and eco-

TABLE 7.2
THE PRESIDENTS OF THE CAC*
(YEARS OF SERVICE AND FAMILY BACKGROUND)

1.	Emir Fandi Shihab	1862–64	feudal aristocracy
2.	Eid Abu Hatem	1864–65	nonfeudal
3.	Naom Kikano	1865–67	nonfeudal
4.	Ammoun Yusuf Ammoun	1867–68	nonfeudal
5.	Eid Abu Hatem	1868–74	nonfeudal
6.	Ammoun Y. Ammoun	1874–	nonfeudal
7.	Antoine Ammoun	1874–77	nonfeudal
8.	Eid Abu Hatem	1877–	nonfeudal
9.	Emir Amin Mansour	1877–79	fuedal aristocracy
10.	Emir Sa'd Shihab	1879–87	feudal aristocracy
11.	Emir Fandi Shihab	1888–99	feudal aristocracy
12.	Emir Kablan Abu-al-Lam'	1899–1901	feudal aristocracy
13.	Habib Pasha Assa'd	1902–05	nonfeudal
14.	Salim Bey Ammoun	1908–09	nonfeudal
15.	Emir Kablan Abu-al-Lam'	1910–12	feudal aristocracy
16.	Sa'dallah al Howeik	1912–13	nonfeudal
17.	Habib Pasha Assa'd	1913–15	nonfeudal

*Adapted from Rabbat (1970).

nomic—was accepted as a permanent feature of Lebanese life. The drive for nationalism in Lebanon was modified by a political reality and a political culture that refused to sacrifice cultural, religious, and economic pluralism for the sake of national integration. Since the Mutasarrifiya period, the foundation of an open political, cultural, religious, and economic system has been laid down and has emerged as the main characteristic of present-day Lebanon. Lebanon avoided the experience of a dominant culture trying to integrate or assimilate all other cultures. It also avoided the experience of a mobilizing national party, a main feature of political integration in many newly independent countries. The infusion of the army with aristocratic blood and a professional orientation has shielded the military from playing a national liberation role, the role of "savior" from the "corruption" of the politicians. Instead, as early as 1861, Lebanon had a popularly elected political leadership, thanks to the institution of the CAC.

POLITICAL INTEGRATION UNDER THE MANDATE, 1920–43

The Central Administrative Council was able to mold the feudal aristocracy and the new middle classes of traditional Mount Lebanon proper. The Druzes and the Maronites had been living together for hundreds of years, and therefore the CAC had behind it a whole tradition of unifying imarah institutions to build on. That could not be said of the Lebanon created after 1920. The inhabitants of the four districts added to Mount Lebanon in 1920 (especially Tripoli in the north) were still agitating for unity with Syria. Inhabited predominantly by Sunni, Shi'a, and Greek Orthodox, they identified more with an Arab-Syrian state than with a Lebanese mountain that was dominated by pro-French Maronites under French protection. Furthermore, as the economies of the added districts were predominantly agrarian, they were closely tied with the agrarian Syrian economy. The inhabitants were apprehensive of the traditional ties between France and the Lebanese Maronites. They feared that such ties might lead to French domination, with the Maronites as pawns. It was, therefore, necessary for the proponents of an independent Lebanon to achieve two conflicting objectives if Lebanon were to maintain an independent status. They had to, on the one hand, secure French and international protection for the newly created state, and, on the other hand, secure the cooperation of internal elements who were apprehensive of such foreign protection. In both cases a constitution seemed to be the appropriate answer. A constitution would secure international recognition (since France was required to report to the League of Nations on its actions in Lebanon), transfer part of the authority to the nationals, and assure the many groups that their rights and interests would be safeguarded.

Discussions of the actual process of drawing up the constitution and the unity displayed by the Lebanese political elite in their negotiations with the French are beyond the scope of this study. However, as the incidents that followed the promulgation of the constitution showed, France was outmaneuvered at the debate, and the Constitutional Assembly was able to draft and ratify a constitution concentrating power in the Chamber of Deputies. France's hope that the constitution would serve simply as a facade was soon frustrated. The Chamber of Deputies was determined to exercise its power, a fact that did not meet with the approval of the French, who time and again tried to amend the constitution through the constitutional method. When the French failed to achieve their goal constitutionally because of resistance from the Chamber of Deputies, they often resorted to arbitrary suspension of the Chamber or to unconstitutional amendment.[5] Whatever the French did, it only led to the emergence of the legislature in Lebanon as the center for political life and the structure that was to stir Lebanon into complete independence. Although handpicked by the French in the early 1920s, the

Lebanese parliament in 1943, in a unanimous vote, unilaterally abolished those articles in the constitution which had any reference to the rights and privileges of France as mandatory power and declared Lebanon independent and sovereign. The history of the legislature during the French mandate is the story of an institution that acted as a symbol around which all segments of the Lebanese population could meet in their fight against the colonialists. The resistances to the French left the Lebanese—Christians as well as Moslems—convinced that the way to combat French domination was to present a solid front within the Chamber of Deputies. Religious leaders in this country were satisfied by allowing them to administer the personal and family laws of their various religious sects. The Arab and Syrian nationalists were temporarily placated by the Chamber's act of abrogating the articles of the mandate in defiance of the French Authorities. It was an ardent Arab nationalist and the first prime minister of independent Lebanon, Riadh al-Solh, who delcared in his first ministerial statements to his fellow Arab nationalists: "Our brothers in the Arab countries do not wish for Lebanon except what the proud nationalist sons of Lebanon wish for it. We do not want Lebanon to be used by the colonialists as a pathway to the rest of the Arab countries. So both the Lebanese and the rest of the Arabs want Lebanon to be a proud fatherland and completely independent" (Malhameh, 1965: 23–24).

In the same vein Deputy Abdul Hamid Karami, a Sunni from Tripoli and a vehement antagonist of Lebanese independence, changed his mind as a result of Lebanon's struggle for independence:

> I want to assert in all frankness that our opposition to Lebanon in the past was based on the fact that Lebanon failed to assert its intention toward achieving complete independence. When Lebanon did assert its independence, we have become positive towards Lebanon, especially after the government has declared that Lebanon is Arab in its blood, tongue, and heart. I do not discriminate any longer among Beirut, Damascus, Baghdad, and Cairo. [al-Khateeb, 1970: 306]

However, for Deputy Karami or Premier al-Solh to express belief in the integrity and independence of Lebanon and pledge their allegiance to it as to any other Arab country, the political elites of Lebanon had to decide about the future of the country and the status of the various groups who happened to live there. Their decisions, which came to be known as the National Pact, represented Lebanon's understanding of the kind of political integration it was going to seek.

POLITICAL INTEGRATION IN LEBANON:
ITS MEANING AND SCOPE

Lebanese ideology toward political integration has been shaped by both politics and culture (see Appendix A, page 265). The pluralistic nature of Islamic culture and the way various religious communities had been treated under Islam were not conducive to the emergence of a dominant culture, such as the Anglo-Saxon core culture in the United States. The status accorded Christians and Jews, as holders of a holy book, secured for them the right to lead their communal and religious life in accordance with their time-honored traditions. As long as they paid their taxes, they were free to exercise the precepts of their religions with minimal state interference. The Maronites in Lebanon were the grand beneficiaries of such an open and tolerant policy. Not only were they free to organize and to build a church hierarchy unparalleled by the church hierarchies of that time in that area, they were even allowed to retain their Syriac language, which survives even today in their monasteries and churches. It was therefore unlikely that the Maronite Church, when it became the dominant group in Lebanon, would upset this tradition of religious pluralism even if it could have.

Politically the Maronite Church was in no position to act as a dominant core culture. In the first place, it realized that its survival as a community in an Islamic world was only possible if it assumed a low profile; otherwise it would invite the anger of both the political authorities and the populace. In the second place, the socioeconomic background of the Maronites did not endow them with any aristocratic or special prestige to act as a model for other groups. Coming from the lowest of social and economic classes, the Maronites were derided and perhaps tolerated and accepted simply because of their insignificance and low status. The Druze aristocracy, for example, felt at ease with the Maronite peasants because they considered them as posing no challenge to their status and easily controllable. Even when the Maronite Church became powerful, and some Druze and Muslim aristocrats gained economic and political benefits by converting to Christianity, they did so in secret lest their social status be compromised. Furthermore, under the Mutasarrifiya system and later under the mandate system, the Maronite church came to be associated in the minds of Christian, Druze, and Muslim nationalist leaders with the French colonialists.

Given these cultural and political limitations, it would be difficult to turn these inherent weaknesses into a source of strength. Lebanon's claim for independent statehood and its cultural mission in the area were to stem from the heterogeneous nature of its society and its hybrid Western Arab culture. An autonomous state was needed to preserve this heterogeneity and to enable the Lebanese to continue acting as a cultural and commercial bridge between the West and the rest of the Arab hinterland. No one has captured in a nutshell this paradox better than Michel Cheha, a Catholic, a banker and journalist, a member of the constitutional assembly, and one of the architects of the constitution of present-day Lebanon. Cheha recognized the precariousness of the Lebanese state and felt that its survival required international protection and recognition, at least until it got on its feet. He stated (Cheha, 1966: 40–41):

> What is needed in Lebanon today is adequate knowledge and understanding of its geographical position and of what one might call the natural disabilities under which it labours; and then of the nature of the various groups which together go to make up the Lebanese people. No laws which ignore these profound truths, whether they be organic or ordinary, will ever survive long in Lebanon.

To Cheha, Lebanon was composed of associated religious minorities, a fact that dictated the kind of political and democratic institutions that Lebanon should have. Cheha thought that there was only one way to achieve unity and resist outside pressures:

> Since it is a country comprising associated minorities of different religious communities, Lebanon cannot last long, politically speaking, without an assembly to be the meeting place and centre of unity for those communities with a view to exercising joint control over the nation's political life. Once you abolish the assembly, you unavoidably transpose debate to the sanctuary or to its shadow, and by so much you slow down the formation of a civic sense: (again, when you have no assembly you have nothing to put in the way of too great pressures coming from outside). [Cheha 1966: 4]

The goals and objectives enunciated by Cheha were put into operation in 1943 by Bishara al-Khouri (1961), a Maronite leader of the opposition during the French mandate period and the first president of the republic (1943–52), and Riadh al-Solh, a Sunni Moslem and the first prime minister of independent Lebanon. The various unwritten understandings known collectively as the National Pact provided a formula for political participation by the various religious groups in Lebanon. To avoid recurrent conflicts, the presidency of the republic went to the Maronites, a premiership to the

Sunni, and the presidency of the legislature to the Shi'a. Representation in the legislature was distributed in accordance with the ratio of six Christians to five Moslems.

While it is impossible to predict what Lebanon's destiny would have been without an assembly, Lebanon's history lends evidence to Cheha's assertion of its importance. Whenever the legislative institution was crippled and rendered weak or unrepresentative of the major political forces in the country, Lebanon witnessed traumatic internal troubles like those of 1952, 1958, and 1961.

THE INTEGRATIVE FUNCTIONS OF THE LEGISLATURE AFTER INDEPENDENCE, 1943–70

It may be argued that Lebanon's division into religious minorities is no more than an artificial division, orchestrated and played by the political elites, simply to justify an independent existence of a Lebanese state and to insure the maintenance of their power within that system. As one shrewd Lebanese observer commented, the ruling elite in Lebanon is manipulating both national unity and sectarianism for its own benefit. The logic of the elite is "to divide the country on a sectarian basis and to unite it on everything else; it divides the country for the interests of the regime and it unites the country also for the interest of the regime" (Deeb, 1971: 27). In other words, according to this view, the ruling political elite has so far successfully manipulated sectarianism to its advantage. It has created an independent Lebanon where its political power as well as its economic interests are properly safeguarded. It has also succeeded in delaying the emergence of classes along socioeconomic lines and, more importantly, it has been able to contain the divisive elements and conflict that would have resulted from carrying the sectarian conflict to the logical end, civil war or partition.

Analyzing the achievement of Lebanese system after independence, Dr. Rabbat could not fail to notice the consensus on the need for an independent Lebanon. A minimum of agreement grew to near-unanimity which neither the tensions of 1958 nor those of 1969 were able to upset. Dr. Rabbat stated: "In 1920, when the French declared Greater Lebanon, the Moslems on the whole were asking that they be united with Syria and used to consider the regions they used to inhabit as part of natural Syria" (Rabbat, 1970: 471). In contrast with that attitude, Rabbat cites the message which the

Sunni mufti (the head of the Sunni Church in Lebanon) issued to his coreligionists on the occasion of Fitr (a Moslem holy day). The message came at a time when the government was facing a severe crisis with the Palestinian commandos.

> Each one of us should feel that he is for Lebanon, and that Lebanon is his, and that his duty is to protect Lebanon from all possible harm, by exerting all that we possess from energy, understanding, thinking, faith and knowledge. We should guard it to remain strong and respected, we should guard it as a shield for our Arab nation strong and powerful.[6] [Rabbat, 1970: 472]

To analyze the full contribution of the Lebanese Chamber of Deputies to political integration since independence is tantamount to a full discussion of its contribution to political development, since the two concepts as used in the literature are closely intermingled if not coterminous. That would require a volume by itself. I shall therefore limit this discussion to three areas of integration: (1) between the leaders and the constituencies (i.e., how the gap between the elite and nonelite was bridged) through the electoral process; (2) between the executive and the legislative branches of government through the actual working of the legislature; and finally (3) integration of political parties into the arena of parliamentary politics.

THE ELECTORAL PROCESS

The electoral process has been the subject of a long and continuing controversy in Lebanese political life. It has been criticized and blamed for many evils of the Lebanese political system, such as perpetuating the power of the political elite, establishing and strengthening political sectarianism, preventing the emergence of strong political parties, and weakening the democratic institutions of the country. The electoral process has generally been characterized by government intimidation of the electorates in favor of its supported candidates, by the strong role played by campaign money, and sometimes by falsification of the results of the polls.

Through a detailed statistical analysis, Hudson (1968) and Baaklini (1976) found that the electoral process is characterized by an impressive increase in voting participation, by a steady increase in its competitiveness, by a stabilizing effect, and by promotion of organizational differentiation among the political groups and individuals seeking parliamentary seats. While the rate of new entrants to the

Lebanese chamber has fluctuated widely and unpredictably, the system has remained fluid and flexible (Hudson, 1968: 239; Baaklini, 1976: 141–97).

The electoral laws in Lebanon have two main characteristics: the sectarian distribution of the parliamentary seats and the list system.[7] The main intention behind the sectarian distribution of Chamber seats was to prevent intersectarian competition. Thus a seat assigned to a particular sect is open to competition from candidates belonging to that sect only. However, all the residents of that electoral district are eligible to choose among the candidates regardless of their sectarian affiliation. Since candidates have to compete for the votes of the whole district and not simply for their coreligionists, they normally appeal to the moderate elements of the population. Furthermore, by discouraging intersectarian competition, the electoral system has encouraged intrasectarian and, in many cases, intrafamily competition. More and more, candidates find themselves depending on the support of other sects for their success. Thus, while the electoral law established the sect as a prerequisite for candidacy, the actual working of the system has been constantly militating against the solidarity of the sect as an important factor.

The number of representatives, their distribution, and the number of seats in each district have varied greatly in the modern history of independent Lebanon. The number of deputies thus fluctuated between 44 in 1953 to 99 in 1960, which is the level at which it has continued since then (see Table 7.3). Whenever there was a change in the number of parliamentary seats, a proportional change in the distribution of seats among the sects followed. However, the same ratio of six Christians to five Muslims continued. Dissatisfaction with the electoral laws in recent years has increased. Critics claim that the fixed ratio used does not reflect the actual distribution of the various sects among the population. Calls for a new census have been heard, but the issue has been ignored.

Over the years another variation has been in the size of the electoral district as well as in the number of seats in each district. Earlier electoral districts were coterminous with the *muhafazah* (administrative district).[8] Thus some districts included as many as 17 seats while others had only 7 seats. The 1953 electoral law reduced the number of deputies to 44 and increased the number of electoral districts to 33. Twenty-two of the 33 districts were single-member constituencies and the remaining 11 were double-member constituencies. Table 7.4 shows the fluctuation of electoral districts during the

TABLE 7.3
DISTRIBUTION OF CHAMBER SEATS BY RELIGION

	1943–47	1947–51	1951–53	1953–57	1957–60	1960–64	1964–68	1968–72	1972–
Maronite	18	18	23	13	20	30	30	30	30
Sunni	11	11	16	9	14	20	20	20	20
Shi'a	10	10	14	8	12	19	19	19	19
Greek Orthodox	6	6	8	5	7	11	11	11	11
Greek Catholic	3	3	5	3	4	6	6	6	6
Druze	4	4	5	3	4	6	6	6	6
Armenian Orthodox	2	2	3	1	3	4	4	4	4
Armenian Catholic	—	—	1	1	1	1	1	1	1
Minorities	1	1	1	1	1	1	1	1	1
Protestant	—	—	1	—	—	1	1	1	1
Total	55	55	77	44	66	99	99	99	99

TABLE 7.4
ELECTORAL DISTRICTS, NUMBER OF SEATS BETWEEN 1943 AND 1972

Parliament Elections	Total Number of Seats	Number of Districts	Average Number of Seats Per District	Size of Electoral District 1943–72 and Number of Seats per District																
				1	2	3	4	5	6	7	8	9	10	11	12	13	14	15	16	17
1943	55	5	11							1			1		1					1
1947	55	5	11							1		1	1		1					1
1951	57	9	8.5						2			2	1					1		
1953	44	33	1.3	22			1	1								1				
1957	66	27	2.5	10	11	5	5	1	1											
1960	99	26	3.8	1	6	7	3	6		1	2									
1964	99	26	3.8	1	6	7	3	6		1	2									
1968	99	26	3.8	1	6	7	3	6		1	2									
1972	99	26	3.8	1	6	7	3	6		1	2									

Source: Adapted from Crow (1962: 503).

various elections since 1943. The changes in the number of deputies and the number and sizes of electoral districts were not arbitrary, but were the result of electoral gerrymandering. Through such devices various regimes attempted to control the rate of new admissions to the parliament, to bring about the dismantling of the power of the previous regime in the Chamber, and to reward new supporters and eliminate potential rivals.

President Bishara al-Khouri, in the face of increasing popular dissatisfaction and opposition to his internal policies, found that the best way to deal with the opposition was to increase the number of deputies in the hope of absorbing the popular dissatisfaction. Opposition leaders, he reckoned, would be silenced if they were coopted into the parliament. Apparently his tactics failed, and the opposition leaders, appealing to extraparliamentary support, were able to unseat him in September 1952.

President Chamoun perfected the art of manipulating the results of elections through his control of the number of parliamentary seats and the size of the electoral districts. In 1953, in an attempt to reduce the power base of the pro-Khouri parliamentary group, he promulgated a new electoral law using delegated legislative power which the parliament had temporarily granted him. He enfranchised women, reduced the number of deputies from 77 to 44, and increased the electoral districts from 9 to 33. By so doing, he created 22 single-member constituencies and 11 two-member constituencies, thus preventing any strong alliance of the pro-Khouri forces against his supported candidates. While under the large multimember electoral districts it would have been possible for his opponents to combine forces under one coordinated list, under a single-member constituency each had to fend for himself and compete against the other. Again in 1957 Chamoun resorted to electoral gerrymandering that cut the power bases of his parliamentary opponents. The 1957 parliament, devoid of some of the powerful political forces in the country, was at the root of the 1958 civil war which ushered in the downfall of the Chamoun regime. In 1960 the Shihab regime, in an attempt to weaken the power of the traditional politicians and to strengthen the power of the political forces that emerged as a result of the 1958 civil war, opted for a different method. Rather than decreasing the number of deputies and leaving his political opponents outside the Chamber, Shihab decided to increase the number of parliamentary seats. By so doing he hoped to keep the traditional politicians as well as the newly recruited political elements within the confines of the Chamber. In other words, he tried to follow Cheha's dictum of transferring the political debate from the streets back to the confines of the parliament, and he was successful in doing so.

Essentially, the list system works by making it desirable for several political forces to present a joint list during the electoral campaign for the purpose of winning the election. Each candidate instructs his supporters to vote for the remaining members of the list. While the voters are not required to abide by the list, they generally stick to the bargain of exchanging votes and thus avoid any ticket splitting, which would prove ruinous to all members running on the same list.[9]

Since the list system calls for the cooperation of several political groups, it tends to favor candidates who lack any specific platforms and whose power depends on their financial assets, family background, or personal service in the region. Candidates who belong to political parties with definite platforms find themselves at a disadvantage since it is more difficult for them to compromise, and they are usually avoided by the noncommitted candidates. The successful candidate remains the one who has maintained close relationships with his constituency and has delivered enough personal services to the influential members of the various villages. In other words, the electoral process favors the constituency-oriented, service-oriented member of parliament. Such members, when elected, are not normally bound by any specific platform or overall national commitment. This is the "trustee"[10] type of member who acts not according to the mandate given to him by the electors, but in accordance with his own judgment. This type of member has been the backbone of the Lebanese parliamentary system, since he is free to maneuver and is flexible enough to be able to avoid deadlocks.

The electoral process has thus far given Lebanon a cohesive parliamentary elite[11] which has been able to undertake significant adjustments to meet the changing needs of the newly politicized segments of the Lebanese population. The openness of the electoral process has also made it possible for the system to incorporate new elements into the parliamentary elite (a point that I shall explore when I discuss the political parties in the Chamber).

A significant variable in the Lebanese parliamentary election is the size of the country and the electoral district. In contrast to a large electoral district where the candidate has to rely on an elaborate machine to conduct his campaign, the smallness of the Lebanese electoral district has given rise to what might be called personal politics. Throughout the year Lebanese deputies are in constant contact with members of their constituencies. This contact takes place in a variety of contexts. The member of parliament, in his daily work as the mediator between the government bureaucracy and the public, is continually brought into touch with his constituency. [12] Through the ease of communication and the help of his relatives, the member of parliament attends most of the social functions that occur in his district (funerals, marriages, baptisms, and so on). This personal style of politics has mitigated the importance of interest groups for interest articulation or for political parties for interest aggregation.[13] The deputy has remained the focal contact point between the citizen and the government.[14]

During the last two decades, thousands of individuals have left their villages to work in the capital. However, rather than changing their residence and voting in the capital, they have kept their residence in the village from which they come. During election time they return to their place of birth where they are required by law to cast their vote. Coming back to their villages during election time, they bring with them attitudes and values to which they have been exposed while living and working in the city. The effect of this exchange between the city and the rural areas has not been studied yet; however, it is assumed that it acts as a safety valve in bringing about peaceful and incremental change in Lebanon. Being in close touch with their places of birth, these citizens help to bridge the gap between the city and the rural areas. Voting in their villages helps them to keep in touch with local issues and thus avoid ideological politics. Expert observers of the Lebanese situation will agree that if everyone were required to vote where he lived and worked, the result would be a cleavage between city politics and village politics. City politics would be radicalized, while village politics would remain static. Under the present arrangement, however, incremental social radicalization is taking place even at the village level.[15]

EXECUTIVE-LEGISLATIVE RELATIONSHIPS

Perhaps in no other area in the analysis of Lebanese politics can one find as much contradiction and confusion as in the area of executive-legislative relationships. On the one hand, we are told that the Lebanese political system rests on a precarious balance of power among the various religious sects. Not only must the president of the republic be a Maronite Christian, the prime minister a Sunni Moslem, and the Speaker of the House a Shi'a Moslem, but they are treated as "representing" these sects, with each placing limitations on the activities of the other two (see Binder, 1966). On the other hand, we are told (Salem, 1967) that the powers of the president of the republic are virtually unlimited, not only unchecked by his prime minister, other members of the cabinet, and the president of the Chamber, but even that the whole Chamber is impotent in this regard.

At the formal constitutional level, the president of the republic is simply supposed to be a figurehead, since he cannot act except through his cabinet, which is in turn controlled by the legislature. He cannot undertake a referendum since he himself is elected by the parliament. The constitutional supremacy of the legislature was so overwhelming that it resulted in the crippling of government operations, so that the amendments to the 1926 constitution undertaken in 1927 and 1929 had one main intention, namely to provide the executive with additional leverage over the legislature. The report of the parliamentary committee entrusted with constitutional amendments in 1929 was prefaced with the following statement as part of the rationale for its recommendations: "After three years of experience, it appears that the perfect balance in the power of the government is lacking due to the inequalities between the legislative and the executive powers" (al-Khateeb, 1970: 254).

The same committee went on to list four reasons for that imbalance. In the first place, the Chamber has the ability to force the resignation of the cabinet, simply by withdrawing confidence, while the president has practically no recourse against the Chamber in the form of calling for a national referendum. His ability to dissolve the Chamber was constitutionally limited to cases that rarely obtain. [16] In the second place, the president was limited in the choice of his cabinet, since he had to observe sectarian distribution and to balance the interests of the various parliamentary blocs. In the third place, the president was limited in his relationship with the legislature by the term of his office. According to the 1926 constitution, the president's term of office was limited to three years (now six), while the term of office of the Chamber was four years. Thus a president whose election and reelection to office depended on the good will of the members of the Chamber had less power under his command. Finally, the absence of organized political parties with clear majorities in the chamber imposed limitations on the power of the president, since he had to create majorities to support his policies on each issue.

Constitutional provisions aside, proponents of the supremacy of the executive in Lebanon argued that the political realities and practices in Lebanon had given the president unmatched power. They argued that the domination of the legislature by the executive might be a legacy of the mandatory psychology—where the French high commissioner was all-powerful—carried into the independent period (Khateeb, 1970: 2, 489). Others argued that the dominance of the president of the republic was related to (1) the strength of his personality as compared to the personalities of the ministers who serve with him; (2) the lack of strong political parties in the Chamber, thus leaving individual members free to follow their personal interests; (3) the absence of strong political parties outside the Chamber to mobilize public opinion; (4) the electoral laws and the electoral process; and finally (5) the temporary nature of political alliances within the Chamber that disappear as soon as the issues around which they were formed are solved.

The confusion in the preceding logic stems from two fallacies: a conception of the executive as a monolith overpowering the whole, and a failure to distinguish between normal politics and extraordinary politics. The Lebanese executive is usually portrayed as a monolithic whole, a single actor with one will. The internal dynamics of the decision-making process at the cabinet level or in the various government departments and agencies are normally left unaccounted for. The intrabureaucratic and interbureaucratic rivalries are dismissed as insignificant. The president, under that logic, comes to control a smoothly running bureaucracy whose allegiance and dedication are assumptions not corroborated in reality.

The possibility that the conceptual analysis of the Lebanese society, which used the age-old executive-legislative dichotomy or the Moslem-Christian dichotomy, might be inadequate and distorting was never seriously questioned. If the social phenomenon did not lend itself to the conceptual tools of social science, then the phenomenon was discredited to keep the tool untarnished. In this particular instance the irony is intensified when the same factors that are considered intrinsic to the president's strength by one political analyst are affirmed by another as the source of his weakness. For instance, Muhammad Yakan (1971: 143–57) in his analysis of the factors that contributed to a weak president in Lebanon listed the following: fractured leadership in the executive branch, sectarianism, the National Pact, the contradiction between the constitution and the National Pact, lack of organized public support due to the absence of organized political parties in the chamber, lack of a public opinion, lack of planning and programing, inability to legislate and to undertake direct referenda regarding important issues, and, finally, failure to use his constitutional right to dissolve the parliament or to veto its legislation. The same factors, then, that were used by Crow and Hudson to explain the weakness of the legislature have been turned around by Kerr and Yakan to explain the weakness of the executive. Thus the executive-legislative dichotomy and the Moslem-Christian divisions are simply tools for analysis that should be discarded whenever they fail to illuminate the subject being discussed.

The analysis of Lebanese politics can better be understood within the context of the unity and homogeneity of the political elite in both branches of the government. Not only do the elite share similar socioeconomic backgrounds, family relations, and memberships in social groupings, as discussed earlier, but they also have been shaped and socialized by the same parliamentary institution.

POLITICAL PARTIES AND THE CHAMBER

Compared to parliaments organized around political parties, the Lebanese Chamber does not rank high on percentage of members with party affiliations. Perhaps the small size of the country, ease of communication, face-to-face interaction, strong family and other primary-group ties, sectarian distribution of parliamentary seats, and the electoral process itself—electoral districts, lists system, simple majority—all mitigate against the establishment of strong central party organizations as vehicles for gaining parliamentary seats. Personal politics predominate and are likely to continue to do so. In the summer of 1971 the Arabic newspaper *an Nahar* sent a questionnaire to all members of the current Chamber and to their defeated election opponents and published the results. Ninety-eight % of the 77 members who responded failed to list the political party as the crucial factor in their election. Most of the members and the candidates indicated that the most crucial variable was personal service to their constituents.

Nonetheless, the Lebanese political system has been tolerant of the proliferation of political parties and of their right to organize, mobilize support, and publish literature and their own newspapers. The number of political parties in Lebanon has been on the rise, both inside and outside the Chamber. Since independence, however, political parties in the Chamber have been organized around a strong parliamentary figure (usually an aspirant to the presidency) or—as in recent years—around issues, regional problems, and, increasingly, general and ambiguous programs. However, these parliamentary blocs and caucuses are ephemeral. In Lebanon, parliamentary politics have been more conveniently carried out on the personal level. This is understandable in a small country whose parliamentary elite has been described as a cohesive personally related group. As to its parliamentary elite, Hudson (1968: 146—47) says:

> The cohesion of Lebanon's parliamentary elite is apparent at a glance. Interlocking relationships based on marriage, education, sect, and occupational interests make it very difficult to single out distinct types within the elite.
> The establishment is also remarkably homogeneous and well integrated, compared with the general population. One need only follow the social columns, the marriage announcements and the inexhaustible stream of society photographs that appear weekly in the *Revue du Leban* to see that the contacts among the elite are numerous and usually harmonious.

Given the small size of the elite, the homogeneity, and the frequent contacts of its members with one another, it is no wonder that they do not feel the need to handle their affairs through the impersonal machinery of political parties. Communication, negotiation, and compromises are still manageable and can be handled through personal contacts. Table 7.5 shows the distribution of parliamentary seats in accordance with political parties.

In interpreting this table, we need to consider first that party power in the population or in influencing legislation does not have a one-to-one relationship with party representation, and in some cases the correlation is negligible. For example, the Syrian Social Nationalist party has influenced Lebanese political life at various levels through abortive attempted coups in 1949 and 1961; yet it has been represented in only one parliament by a single member. The Communist party, Ba'ath party, and others not represented in the chamber at all also have influenced legislation and other important political decisions (see Appendix B, page 266).

Second, although the majority of the members in the chamber are independent or have no party affiliation, in the actual operation of the chamber they tend to associate with one parliamentary group, particularly at the time of electing the president of the chamber or at the time of forming a new cabinet. In other words, the chamber tends to divide into two groups with regard to key issues, and the tendency for these two groups to maintain some sort of association has been gradually increasing in recent years.

Third, and a corollary of the second point, despite the low ratio of party or bloc-affiliated members in the parliament, major political debates and issues seem to organize around those few members who

TABLE 7.5

PARLIAMENTARY MEMBERSHIP OF PARTIES IN LEBANON
1951–1972

Party	1951	1953	1957	1960	1964	1968	1972
Lebanese Communist party							
Syrian Social Nationalist party			1				
Ba'ath (Arab Renaissance Socialist party)							
Arab Nationalist Movement							1[a]
Muslim Brethren							1[a]
Ibad-ar-Rahman (The Worshipper of God)							
Muslim Group							
Tahreer							
Dashnak (Armenian party)	2	2	3	4	4	3	3
Hunchak (Armenian party)							
Ramgavar Azadagow (Armenian party)							
Najjada				1		1	
Progressive Socialist party	3	2–4	3	6	6	5	4
National Action Movement					1	1	1
National Appeal			membership flexible and indeterminate				
National Organization				1			
Katáeb (Phalange)	3	1	1	6	4	9	7
Constitutional Union		flexible and indeterminate		5–8	5	4	4[b]
National Bloc	2	3	4	6	2	5	3
National Liberals		party nonexistent		4–5	6	8	6
Democratic Socialist party							2[a]
Democratic party							1[a]
Total	10	8–10	12	32–37	28	36	33[a]
Total members in Chamber	77	44	66	99	99	99	99
Percent of members in political parties	13%	24%	18%	35%	28%	36%	33%

Sources: Crow (1962: "Parliament in the Lebanese Political System," Table 2, p. 284) and Suleiman (1967: 265). Table adapted from Suleiman.

a. The election of 1972 brought to the parliament representatives of three parties that were never represented before, and the creation of a new party, the Democratic Socialist party, headed by Mr. Kamel al-Ass'ad.

b. Membership in the Constitutional Union has been fluctuating; 4 is an approximation.

associate with parties or blocs. Both dynamism and inertia in the chamber, as well as the theatrical parliamentary performances, are apt to be their doing. Of course the blocs they create and the issues they debate are neither permanent nor ideological in nature, thus preserving the fluidity, flexibility, and atmosphere of compromise that has enabled the parliamentary institutions, as well as the elites who man them, to survive, grow, and prosper in an area hostile to the whole parliamentary democratic game. During the mandate period, parliamentary political life was largely engineered by the supporters of Emile Edde, president of the republic between 1936 and 1939 who later organized the National Bloc, and the supporters of Bishara al-Khouri, president of the republic between 1943 and 1952 and organizer of the Constitutional Union party. The main issues of conflict between the two blocs, in addition to rivalry for the presidency, were their attitude toward the French, the continuation of the mandate, and Lebanon's independence.

The National Bloc cooperated with the French, believed Lebanon was not ready for independence, and sought the continuation of the French mandate as a means of self-protection. Its attitude toward the frequent French suspension of the constitution was passive if not implicitly approving.

The Constitutional Union opposed the French suspension of the constitution, agitated for Lebanese independence, and asked for the early termination of the French mandate. Its policy duplicated that of the National Pact as outlined above. Parliamentary politics in the 1940s and early 1950s was dominated by the Constitutional Union. President Chamoun's election in 1952 eclipsed their fortunes. Chamoun's ascension to power resulted from the opposition organized by the National Socialist Front. It was founded in 1951, through the cooperation of two main parties, the Progressive Socialist party of Kamal Jumblat and the National Bloc of Raymond Edde, and headed by Chamoun himself and several other parliamentary personalities, including Ghassan Tweini (who is sometimes counted as a member of the Syrian Social Nationalist party). The Front had a reformist platform and aimed to work for resignation of the president, who was accused of rigging the elections, amending the constitution, and succeeding himself for another term in office. In 1952 the immediate aim was realized when Bishara al-Khouri submitted his resignation to the Chamber. With Chamoun in power, the program of the Front was to emerge as legislation; but the Front itself soon ceased its cohesive activities due to disagreement between Chamoun and Jumblat.

In the 1960s the division in the parliament centered around Shihabism and its opponents. The Shihabist forces were to organize under the leadership of Rashid Karami (several times a prime minister) in what came to be known as the Democratic Parliamentary Front, while the other forces were to organize under the Tripartite Alliance of the Kataeb National Bloc and Chamoun's National Liberal party. Several other parliamentary blocs and fronts have played significant roles regarding particular issues, including the National Struggle Front of Kamal Jumblat, the Popular Social Front, the Parliamentary Reform Front, the Congress of Parties, other organizations, and various national personalities.

Parliamentary bloc politics reached a zenith in 1970 during the election of Suleiman Franjieh to the presidency. Rather than the usual behind-the-scenes maneuvering, the Chamber divided into equal halves around two main parliamentary fronts, that of the Democratic Parliamentary Front of the pro-Shihabi forces and that of the Tripartite League of the anti-Shihabi forces. With a one-vote majority (50–49), the anti-Shihabi forces elected Suleiman Franjieh as the president for the next six-year term. The same division of forces brought Kamel al-As-ad to the presidency of the Chamber in October 1970.

The fourth point that needs to be emphasized in interpreting Table 7.5 is the growing trend toward more party representation in the Chamber, and, more significantly, more party involvement in the electoral process. As the table shows, Lebanon's parliamentary life in the independent era at first involved almost no party representation, but it has grown continuously since then. However, the table does not show the increased party involvement in the electoral process. This involvement is taking two forms: the running of party candidates and the administering of electoral campaigns for nonparty independent candidates. Even what Hudson (1968) calls the "radical outsiders" have been fully involved in this process. The Syrian Social Nationalist party, in the 1960 election, ran more than eight candidates as party representatives and administered the electoral campaign for several other nonparty candidates. This trend is significant for at least two reasons. In the first place, it shows that there is an acceptance, even by the radical outsiders, of the democratic process and a recognition that the road to power in Lebanon is through elections, not coups. Secondly, there is a growing recognition by journalists and political observers of the importance of parties such as the Katab in administering and running an electoral campaign.

Whether the absence of strong parliamentary political parties has been a source for what some call parliamentary weakness is very difficult to demonstrate. Clearly, however, the ability of the parliamentary elites to reach a consensus regarding essential issues in times of crisis has not been impeded by the lack of parties. On the other hand, their flexibility and their ability to adjust and cope with changing situations has definitely been strengthened by the absence of organized, strongly doctrinaire political parties in the Chamber, especially in a system where the social composition of the country tends to favor a multiparty structure. However, considering Lebanon's political space as well as its demographic constitution and distribution, the style of personal politics is likely to continue.

CONCLUSIONS

Political integration in the Western experience presupposes the existence of a strong unified elite having the ability to mobilize economic, social, political, and military sanctions and the willingness and freedom to apply these sanctions. The argument was made earlier in the discussion that what the theories of political integration presuppose as a prerequisite is what the developing countries actually lack. As the experience of Lebanon demonstrates, many developing countries do not have a dominant culture, since two or more cultures have coexisted throughout the ages and one is not likely to abandon its style and form of life or accept the claim of the other as legitimate and superior. Even if a dominant culture exists, the elite is usually fractured, its ability to mobilize sanctions is limited, and, more important, its freedom to use whatever sanctions it can mobilize is extremely limited. Developing countries face the challenge of achieving some sort of political integration in the context of superior and hostile forces, both internal and external. The role of outside forces (economic, political, and military) renders the ability and freedom of the national elite in the application of sanctions very negligible.

The Lebanese model works within the context of pluralistic, competing elites and does not call for the mobilization of strong sanctions or the use of such sanctions. The basic socioeconomic and cultural characteristics of the groups that compose the society as given are accepted. Areas of conflict are depoliticized, contained, and managed within the group, so that their spillover will be limited. Significantly, the Lebanese model not only does not need an authoritarian system, it could hardly make use of such a system. It favors a pluralistic, democratic system with a weak government. Conflict is not considered inimical to political integration, but rather a prerequisite to integration. Political integration is not equated with assimilation, nationalism, or modernization—which, in theories on integration, are frequently depicted as coterminous with integration. It is simply an organizational, structural integration in the realm of politics where each of the component parts can retain its identity and still be relevant and functional to the whole. This incremental model of political integration, with time, can broaden the areas of consensus and commonality among the various groups and thus can expand the political sector in the system. The historical survey of Lebanese political integration can be constructed as a progressive movement toward more and more areas of consensus and the enlargement of the scope of the political sector. The main structure in this process, as I have argued, is the Lebanese legislature.

POSTSCRIPT

This chapter was supposed to cover political integration in Lebanon until 1972 and the role the legislature played in this regard. However, the bloody war in 1975–76 that engulfed Lebanon demands some explanation. While it is too early to formulate a definite judgment as to the causes of the war, its nature and its impact on the political system and the process of integration in that country, a number of observations are nevertheless in order.

First: There is a general consensus among observers that the basis of the conflict is essentially political and not sectarian as often depicted by the press. While sectarian allegiances may have been mobilized one way or another by the various combatants, the fact remained that both Christians and Moslems were internally divided as to the side they supported.

Second: Although there is an internal Lebanese dimension to the conflict, international and Arab components played a crucial part— whether in the Palestinian armed presence in Lebanon, or in the initial Syrian support to the Palestinians and their subsequent massive military intervention, or in the financial and military support of Arab and non-Arab countries to the various combatants.

Third: There is no doubt that the Lebanese institutions failed to head off the conflict or to halt the armed clashes once they began. It should be remembered, however, that the Lebanese institutions were developed to handle normal internal conflict as most state institutions usually are. It is painfully apparent that Lebanon's latest war transcends the boundaries of a normal internal conflict. Though fought internally, it was generated, precipitated, and prolonged by intra-Arab and international conflicts. In this case one is entitled to question the ability of any modern political institution to handle a conflict of this magnitude. There is, moreover, the unique nature of the Lebanese military. The Lebanese political elites refused to develop a strong military institution not because of their lack of consensus, but rather because they agreed that a strong army might be potentially oppressive, inevitably interested in dragging Lebanon into the Arab-Israeli conflict, and economically costly to maintain. As a result, the army was envisioned to resolve purely internal conflicts and maintain a modicum of law and order. It was not intended to act as a strong defensive force against superior external forces.

Even the Palestinian presence in Lebanon was controllable as long as it was an unassuming presence. However, after the six-day war of 1967 and the successive defeats of the Palestinian military presence in Jordan in 1970 and 1971, Lebanon became the only Arab country where the Palestinians could maintain a major military power outside the control of the government. Thus, while Lebanon's decision not to build a strong army served it well between 1943 and 1967, the situation changed radically in recent years, especially since the October war of 1973 and the emergence of the Arab bloc as a strong economic, if not military, power. Lebanon could no longer maintain a neutral posture in the Arab-Israeli conflict. It needed a strong army to defend its territorial integrity in the face of recurrent Israeli strikes against the Palestinian presence within its borders.

Fourth: During the 1975–76 conflict most of Lebanon's political institutions, including the presidency, political parties, and the army showed signs of partisanship and were thus discredited. The legislature was the only institution that maintained the legitimacy of the state by providing a common forum where important decisions were made such as the amendment of the constitution, the election of a new president, and the granting of confidence to the newly composed cabinet. Whatever the outcome of the war in Lebanon might be, one basic feature of the new political order will be a strengthened legislative institution.

Fifth: In spite of the ferocity and barbarity of the fighting, none of the combatants renounced the Lebanese independent state. Even the Moslem population traditionally against an independent Lebanon showed as much concern with the independence and territorial integrity of the country as did the Christians. Furthermore, none of the combatants proposed a new viable economic or political order for a new Lebanon. The competitive capitalist system, the pluralistic nature of political parties, and even the sectarian distribution of political power have continued and are likely to persist. The Syrian-Arab military presence will undoubtedly allow the Lebanese government to play a more active role in regulating the economy, in limiting political competition and freedom of the press and, perhaps, in arriving at a modified formula to distribute power among the various sects and political groups in the country. The Syrian-Arab military presence may also lead to the establishment of a strong Lebanese army. Despite these possible transformations, however, it is unlikely that Lebanon's multireligious and multiethnic population will change; it is also unlikely that Lebanon's pluralistic multinational political system will be radically altered in favor of an assimilationist one. On the contrary, the recent war in Lebanon reaffirmed the right of all groups to exist with a certain degree of cultural and religious autonomy. It shattered the illusion of some political parties which thought that Lebanon's political institutions could be destroyed by a few armed bands. It may have discouraged for sometime to come those who thought that change in Lebanon could come through violence rather than through the polls. What Lebanon now needs, as most of the combatants seem to have lately recognized, are mediating institutions such as the legislature. Even the army's leadership is presently being reorganized to reflect the same sectarian balance which exists in the parliament.

NOTES

1. With the possible exception of Haas (1968) and Sewell (1966).

2. If communication is assumed to be a mechanism conducive to integration, forces working against integration can use it for their purposes as well. The coercive, economic, and political resources of the international community, particularly the colonial West, and more recently the Communist West, are forces not to be minimized by any theory on integration. Integration in developing countries has to take place within the context of the international system, with all its stresses and strains. The resources of the developing countries are no match for those of the international system.

3. For a full discussion of the political development of Lebanon in this period, see Harik (1968).

4. In 1912 the city of Deir al Kamar, which was previously under the direct rule of the

Mutasarrif, was allowed representation in the CAC. One Maronite and one Druze representative were added, raising the number of the CAC from 12 to 14.

5. French High Commissioner General Catroux amended the constitution unconstitutionally by a decree, No. 129 F.C., March 18, 1943.

6. From a speech by Mufti Hassan Khalid, Sunni mufti of the Lebanese Republic, December 10, 1969. Whether the creation and maintenance of an independent Lebanon is a positive value as far as all segments of society are concerned is beyond the scope of this study.

7. Since 1943 Lebanon has had six electoral laws—in 1943, 1950, 1952, 1953, 1957, and 1960.

8. Lebanon is divided into five such administrative districts, each headed by a *muhafiz* (governor) appointed by the council of ministers on the recommendation of the minister of interior.

9. The list system in Lebanon needs to be distinguished from the party-dominated list system prevalent in some European countries. In Lebanon the parliamentary seats in each electoral district are distributed among the various sects to reflect the sectarian composition of the inhabitants of that district. Usually each list is a coalition, composed of candidates who belong to the various sects in each district with the purpose of exchanging votes. For a full discussion of the list system, see Ziadeh (1960).

10. Heinz Eulau found three orientations among United States legislators with regard to their representational role: the trustee, the delegate, and the politico. See Wahlke, Eulau, Buchanan, and Ferguson (1962: 272–80).

11. For the socioeconomic background of the parliamentary elites, see Hudson (1968).

12. During an hour-long interview in the summer of 1971 with a member of parliament, more than seven persons from his district dropped by his office to ask him to intercede on their behalf with the government bureaucracy.

13. Interest groups in Lebanon are organized in big cities, the most influential being the Chamber of Commerce, the Association of Bankers, the Association of Hotel Owners, and the Association of Industrialists.

14. The purpose of President's Shihab's administrative reform movement in 1959 was to strengthen the bureaucracy, fortify it against political pressure, and bring it in direct contact with the people. This attempt was opposed by the professional politicians, who saw in it an attempt to undercut their political power.

15. This is no longer a hypothetical statement. In recent years the effect of the vote of city dwellers who go back to their districts to vote was felt strongly in the rural, Shi'a-dominated districts, since a large proportion of the working classes living around Beirut are Shi'a. Thus, Hudson (1968: 244) found a decrease in the non-Christian landlords represented in the parliament. Comparing the 1964 and 1968 chambers, I found that the number of Shi'a deputies who could be classified as landlords had dropped from 13 to 10.

16. In accordance with the 1927 amendments the president of the republic could dissolve the Chamber under the following conditions: (1) if the Chamber refused to meet during the regular sessions or during an extraordinary session even though it has been requested twice to do so by the president of the republic; (2) if the Chamber refused flatly to appropriate funds for the regular operation of the government with the intention of sabotaging the activities of the government; (3) if the Chamber undertook resolutions aimed at abrogating the status of the mandatory power. See al-Khateeb (1970: 198).

REFERENCES

AKE, C. (1967) A Theory of Political Integration. Homewood, Ill.: Dorsey Press.

BAAKLINI, A. (1976) Legislative and Political Development: Lebanon, 1842–1972. Durham, N.C.: Duke University Press.

BINDER, L., ed. (1966) Politics in Lebanon. New York: Wiley.

CHEHA, M. (1966) "Lebanon today." Les Conferences du Cenacle, Beirut 20th year, 9 and 10.

CROW, R. (1962) "Religious sectarianism in the Lebanese political system." Journal of Politics 24 (Aug.): 82.

DEEB, G. (1971) "An nizam assiyasi wa al muwatin fi Lubnan" (The political system and the citizen in Lebanon). In An nizam assiyasi al-afdal lil-inma (The Preferred Political System for Development), ed. Lebanese Development Studies Association. Beirut: Oweidat Publishing House. Pp. 19–32.

DEUTSCH, K. (1953) "The growth of nations: some recurrent patterns of political and social integration." World Politics 5 (Jan.): 44–74.

––––– (1961) "Social mobilization and political development." American Political Science Review 55 (Sept.): 493–514.

––––– (1964) "Communication theory and political integration." In The Integration of Political Communities, ed. P. Jacob and J. Toscane. Philadelphia: Lippincott. Pp. 143–78.

––––– (1964) "The price of integration." In Integration of Political Communities, ed. P. Jacob and J. Toscane. Philadelphia: Lippincott.

GORDON, M. M. (1964) Assimilation in American Life. New York: Oxford Univ. Press.

HAAS, E. B. (1968) The uniting of Europe, 2nd ed. Stanford, Calif.: Stanford Univ. Press.

HARIK, I. (1968) Politics and Change in a Traditional Society. Princeton, N.J.: Princeton Univ. Press.

HUDSON, M. (1968) The Precarious Republic. New York: Random House.

KHALAF, S. (1968) "Primordial ties and politics in Lebanon." Middle East Studies 4 (Apr.): 243–69.

al-KHATEEB, A. (1970) Dasteur Lubnan: al-munakashat al-barlamaniyah wa alwathaiq (The Constitution of Lebanon: Parliamentary Debates and Documents) 1 and 2. Beirut: n.p.

al-KHOURI, B. (1961) Haqa'iq Lubananiyyah (Lebanese Truths) 1 and 2. Beirut: Awraq lubaniyyah.

MALHAMEH, J. (1965) Majmouat al Bayanat al-Wizaiya (Collection of Cabinet Statements). Beirut: Maktabet Khayyat.

an NAHAR (1971) Series of interviews with members of parliament and defeated candidates. Published every Tuesday, Thursday, and Saturday (June 3–July 27).

RABBAT, E. (1970) al-Wasit fi al-Kanun al-dasteuri al-lubnani (The Umpire in the Lebanese Constitutional Law). Beirut: Dar al-Ilm lil-Malayeen.

SALEM, E. (1967) "Cabinet politics in Lebanon." Middle East Journal 21 (Autumn): 488–502.

SEWELL, J. P. (1966) Functionalism and World Politics. Princeton, N.J.: Princeton Univ. Press.

SULEIMAN, M. (1967) Political Parties in Lebanon. Ithaca, N.Y.: Cornell Univ. Press.

WAHLKE, J. C., H. EULAU, W. BUCHANAN, and L. C. FERGUSON (1962) The Legislative System. New York: Wiley.

YAKAN, M. (1971) "Riasat ad dawla bayna takaleed al madi wa tahadiyat al-mustakbal" (The presidency between the tradition of the past and the challenges of the future). In An-nizam assiyasi al-afdal lil-inma (The Preferred Political System for Development), ed. Lebanese Development Studies Association. Beirut: Oweidat Publishing House. Pp. 143–57.

ZIADEH, N. (1960) "The Lebanese election of 1960." Middle East Journal 14 (Autumn): 367–81.

APPENDIX A
LEBANESE POPULATION BY SECTS AND DISTRICTS (1956)

Sects	Beirut	Mount Leb.	North Leb.	South Leb.	Beka'a	Total
Sunnis	76,116	24,423	118,203	29,889	27,067	286,238
Shiites	17,062	22,716	1,337	148,446	61,044	250,655
Druze	2,457	71,569	19	6,893	7,193	88,131
Maronites	18,101	224,921	111,917	39,509	29,260	423,708
Greek Catholics	3,617	21,520	3,864	23,147	35,630	90,788
Greek Orthodox	25,276	32,239	62,767	10,784	17,861	148,927
Protestants	5,482	3,945	1,357	2,493	1,088	14,365
Latin	2,771	963	330	265	117	4,446
Armenian Catholics	8,809	3,722	345	298	1,448	14,631
Armenian Orthodox	42,762	15,600	1,579	1,833	1,905	63,679
Chaldeans	1,178	62	29	8	189	1,466
Syrian Catholics	4,757	40	194	3	705	5,699
Syrian Orthodox	2,745	257	150	5	1,641	4,798
Jews	5,382	95	40	1,108	67	6,692
Others	215	447	6,064	206	261	7,193
Total	220,849	422,193	307,695	264,716	101,063	1,411,416

Source: an-Nahar (Beirut Arabic daily), April 26, 1956.

LEBANESE POLITICAL PARTIES REPRESENTED IN PARLIAMENT: THEIR SECT AND CONSTITUENCY

Party	1964 Religious Affiliation	1964 Electoral District	1968 Religious Affiliation	1968 Electoral District	1972 Religious Affiliation	1972 Electoral District
Ba'ath					1 S 1 GO 2 AO	1 N. Leb 1 Beirut 2 Beirut
Arab Nasserite Coalition			3 AO	3 Beirut		
Dashnaks	4 AO	3 Beirut 1 Mt. Leb.				
Najjada						
Progressive Socialist party	2 D 1 S 1 GO 1 SH 1 SH	3 Mt. Leb 2 Beka'a 1 Beirut	1 S 1 MI 1 GO 1 M 1 D 1 SH	1 Beká 2 Beirut 3 Mt. Leb.	1 M 1 MI 1 D 1 S	3 M.Leb. 1 Beirut
National Action Movement	1 S	1 Beirut	1 S	1 Beirut	1 S	1 Beirut
Kataeb	2 M 1 AC 1 GC	2 Beirut 1 Mt. Leb. 1 S. Leb.	7 M 1 AC 1 MI	3 Beirut 3 Mt.Leb. 1 Beka'a 1 N. Leb. 1 S. Leb.	5 M 1 AC 1 GC	2 Beirut 2 Mt. Leb. 1 N. Leb. 2 S. Leb.
Constitutional Union	4 M 1 Sh	4 Mt. Leb. 1 Beka'a	2 M 1 D 1 Sh	3 Mt. Leb. 1 Beka'a		
National Bloc	2 M	2 Mt.Leb.	4 M 1 Sh	4 M. Leb. 1 N. Leb.	2 M 1 Sh	3 Mt. Leb.
National Liberals	4 M 1 GO 1 Sh	4 Mt. Leb. 2 N. Leb.	5 M 1 GC 1 S 1 Sh	7 Mt. Leb. 1 N. Leb.	4 M 1 S, 1 SH 1 D	5 Mt. Leb. 1 N. Leb. 1 S. Leb.
Democratic Socialist party	Established only in 1972				3 SH	3 S. Leb.
Democratic party					1 M	1 Mt. Leb.

Key: M = Maronite; Mi = Minorities; GO = Greek Orthodox; GC = Greek Catholic; AC = Armenian Catholic; AO = Armenian Orthodox; D = Druze; S = Sunni; Sh = Shi'a.

CONCLUSION: THE LEGISLATURE AS A VEHICLE
OF NATIONAL INTEGRATION

MALCOLM E. JEWELL
ALBERT F. ELDRIDGE

The chapters in this volume have focused on a single question: under what conditions does the legislature facilitate integration in a plural society, and under what conditions does it have disintegrative consequences? The question might be posed slightly differently: do legislative institutions have characteristics that make them more effective than other political institutions as vehicles of national integration? A comprehensive answer to these questions would require a much more extensive survey of legislatures than is contained in this volume. Case studies in a few countries cannot provide us with the factual base for definitive answers, but they do provide some clues and suggestions. The purpose of this chapter is to suggest what implications these studies, in addition to other selected data, have for these broad questions concerning the impact of legislatures on national integration.

These studies suggest that there are two fundamental conditions that must be met in order for a legislative system to contribute to national integration. First, the system must assure that the demands of the various groups found in the society are represented effectively and articulated in the legislature. Second, there must exist institutions or mechanisms that have the potential to facilitate compromise, so that the legislature is not reduced to an arena in which legislators merely shout the demands of their constituents. There may appear to be a contradiction between the two requisites of legislative integration, but the evidence suggests that the legislature will be ineffective if major groups are unrepresented or if the institution is unable to develop devices for mediating conflicts among contending groups. A number of examples, drawn primarily from these chapters, may be used to illustrate how the presence or absence of these attributes affects the integrative capacities of legislative systems.

EQUITABLE REPRESENTATION

There are both symbolic and tangible reasons why equitable legislative representation of groups in the population is important. If the members of a group are satisfied that they have a fair share of seats in the legislature, their loyalty to the national regime and their willingness to accord legitimacy to the legislature are likely to be enhanced. Without equitable representation, however, the group is likely to question the legitimacy of the values and symbols which affirm a national political community and sustain public authority. Integration requires that groups within a society share certain norms. Among these are agreement on the manner in which public disputes will be resolved and on the general rules and spirit by which the community is to be governed. The degree to which such a consensus can be found within a society is a function of representation. In addition, legislators perform important communication and brokerage functions in the political process. The representative of a group participates in the exercise of power over important sectors of public life through his access to resources and administrative agencies. Any features of the legislative system that reduce the share of seats that can be won by a group have the effect of reducing the group's power in the system.

Chapter 1 by Jewell, "Legislative Representation and National Integration," describes in some detail a variety of electoral devices that either increase or decrease the ability of groups to transform votes into legislative seats. It is obvious that devices such as single-member districts, schemes for proportional representation, separate electorates, and reserved seats affect the share of seats that can be won by a group having a given number of popular votes. Political majorities have sometimes used these devices to reduce the legislative strength of minorities as well as, on other occasions, to assure minority representation. Moreover, electoral devices may force a minority group to form alliances with other groups in order to gain representation or give an advantage to political parties that are based on votes from more than a single group.

Chapter 5, on Northern Ireland, provides the clearest illustration of the disintegrative impact of an electoral system. Budge and O'Leary argue that the single-member district plurality system had the effect of polarizing conflict along religious lines because it virtually guaranteed that only sectarian parties would win legislative seats and that each member would represent exclusively either Catholic or Protestant interests, depending on which group had a majority in the district. Integration has been accomplished in Lebanon, however, in large part because of the careful efforts to protect the rights of the various religious sects that make up the country. One major aspect of that policy has been the allocation of reserved seats in the legislature to each of the sects. At the same time the fact that candidates must win votes in each district from members of other sects forces the legislators to represent a broad range of interests and therefore minimizes the likelihood of serious legislative conflicts along sectarian lines.

For the representation of minority groups to be effective the legislators must have enough skill and experience to make the needs of their constituents known. This may require skill in debate, bargaining, and political maneuvering. The studies of minority representation in the legislatures of plural societies have shed very little light on such matters. Obviously the decision of minority legislators to boycott a legislature, as in Northern Ireland, makes it impossible for the legislators to be effective. Chapter 3, on Afghanistan, suggests that many of the legislators are effective in representing local interests in part because they have sufficient social status and political experience to play the role of middleman or mediator at the national level. If legislators representing a minority are less well educated or belong to lower occupational or social strata (as do members representing the lower castes in India), they are likely to be less effective in debate and negotiation than are those in higher socioeconomic strata. If members of a minority lack legislative experience (as is the case of most Chinese MPs in Malaysia), they may be less effective.

Chapter 2, on Rajasthan, suggests another dimension of effectiveness dealing with the social links between the legislator and the general society. The legislators in many developing countries are transitional or "new men" socialized in a modern culture. Unlike the masses, they are socially, occupationally, and geographically mobile. The resulting gap between the governing elite and the masses might cause the legislator to lose touch with the more traditional perspective of the masses. On the other hand, should the legislator have a traditional perspective in a legislature composed primarily of "new men" he might be quite effective. Sisson and Shrader point out that the MLAs in Rajasthan represent men who have been socialized in both a traditional and modern culture. Their ability to link a relatively traditional general society and the more modern political system effectively derives in part from their personal transitional experiences that incorporate both styles.

The effectiveness of legislators also may depend on the institutions within the legislature. Extensive opportunities for debate on the budget or other legislation and a fully developed question period in legislatures with a British heritage are parliamentary devices that give minority legislators the maximum opportunity to publicize the needs and demands of their constituents. Equally important, though harder to measure, may be a bureaucratic tradition of responding to requests from legislators for special attention to the needs of their constituents. In Afghanistan, for example, the success of legislators as middlemen clearly depends on the willingness and even eagerness of the bureaucrats to respond to their requests. In countries with a highly developed, professional bureaucracy such as India we might expect to find more bureaucratic resistance to pressures from legislators.

The success of the legislature in performing integrative functions depends on the quality as well as the quantity of representation for the minority interests in a society. Measuring the quality of representation requires more detailed study than has yet been conducted on the activities of legislators, particularly in nonwestern countries. We need to know more about their goals and roles, but more important is precise information about how they spend their time and where they spend it (in the district or the capital), what they accomplish, and what factors make some legislators more successful than others. Some of the relationships between the legislator and his constituency are discussed in the chapter on Rajasthan. The authors point out a pattern of affinity between the MLA and his constituency: his mother tongue is the dialect spoken in his constituency; he spends a great deal of his time there and much of his time spent in the capital is taken up with constituency service, the highest priority task for a large proportion of Rajasthani MLAs. We need additional information about how constituents evaluate these activities, and how they are perceived by the bureaucracy, party leaders, and others who compete for power in the political system.

THE LEGISLATIVE SYSTEM AS AN INTEGRATIVE MECHANISM

There is nothing inherent in legislative institutions that makes them necessarily vehicles for integration. We may think of the legislative chamber as an arena equipped with loudspeakers, where the conflicting demands of various groups can be amplified, where the members struggle for a place at the microphones to make sure that the demands of their groups can be heard, but where no one listens or seeks ways of compromising and accommodating the various viewpoints. The question is what can be done to transform such an area into an institution with the capacity for integration. What features of the legislative system might have the greatest effect on integration?

Perhaps the most important stimulus to integration is the existence of political parties with a base of support that cuts across ethnic, racial, religious, or other lines.

As a number of the authors in this volume point out, one of the basic assumptions of democratic pluralism is the existence of an interlocking system of crosscutting associations that meet group conflict and serve as regulators of the quantity and quality of demand placed upon the government. The political party can contribute to the process of compromise, and the need for party unity and loyalty provides legislators with an incentive for compromise. If political parties represent narrow, sectarian interests, they may exacerbate conflict; but if parties represent crosscutting factions, clusters of interests, or if party lines cut across other alignments, the party system may facilitate integration.

The mechanics of the electoral system have some effect on the types of parties that win seats in the legislature, although the effects of any such system will depend on the size and geographical distribution of groups. A system of separate electorates almost guarantees that parties will represent particular interests separately elected and that a multiinterest party will be severely handicapped. A system of reserved seats for particular minorities, as in India or Lebanon, leads to the formation of political parties representing multiple interests or the establishment of factions or alliances that cross sectarian lines. The single-member district system in Northern Ireland seems to have contributed to the establishment of a Catholic and a Protestant party and undermined efforts to build parties on nonreligious bases. In more diverse countries, such as the United States, however, the single-member district system has facilitated, or at least permitted, the development of two major parties each of which represents a diverse group of interests.

In Northern Ireland the distribution of Catholics and Protestants guarantees that most districts will be dominated by one religious group. The MPs are frequently elected without opposition, and they need to be responsive only to the dominant religious group in their districts. Consequently they have nothing to gain by attempting to play a compromising role on religious issues; they would only antagonize their constituents and their party leaders. By contrast, in Lebanon, the larger number of religious sects are scattered somewhat more evenly, and the multimember districts include voters from several sects. The successful legislative candidate is one who forms alliances with a large enough number of the political leaders in the district so that he can win votes from members of the strongest sects in the district. The Lebanese legislator has every reason to support compromises on sectarian questions and if possible to minimize the importance of sectarian issues. Lebanese political parties do represent more than a single religious sect, but they have been slow to develop. Political integration in Lebanon rests more on the efforts of individual power brokers at the district and local level than it does on the efforts of national political parties.

The integrative role of a strong majority party is illustrated by the Congress party in India. The party's willingness to slate Muslims made it possible for some Muslim legislators to be elected, despite the fact that Muslim voters were too scattered to control any significant number of the single-member districts. Obviously the demands of Muslims could be moderated within the Congress party. That this has happened is attested to by the fact that in recent years some Muslim leaders have sought to win elections through separate Muslim parties. In Malaysia the minority Chinese won a share of political power through participation in the multiracial Alliance party, which has held a commanding majority. In recent years, however, the Chinese members of the Alliance have grown less effective in the legislature, and the Alliance party has carried out policies that appear increasingly to serve the interests of the Malay majority. In African countries, where tribal divisions are usually the most important, there has been a tendency for partisan alignments to follow tribal lines, with the result that parties have been less than completely effective as instruments of integration. In some countries the dominant party has represented the interests of the largest tribe. In Nigeria the tribal bases of the parties contributed to disintegration and civil war.

Although the role of parties is not the primary focus of Chapter 6, on Canada, it is clear that early in the history of the Confederation there were differences in their commitments to national integration and unity. The authors also make it clear that the problem of integration has been a persistent one in Canadian history, contributing to the splintering of parties along both ethnic-religious and regional-economic lines. National political parties representing diverse interests have been integrative forces in Canada, but they have had to struggle against substantial odds to win parliamentary majorities.

In Yugoslavia, of course, a major goal of the Communist party has been the integration of the diverse nationalities that make up the Yugoslav state. It is a measure of the party's success that national integrity has been maintained, particularly in the face of the severe pressures from the Soviet bloc in the 1950s. It may be a measure of the party's shortcomings that the Yugoslav leaders tried to use the legislative body as an instrument of integration, as described by Cohen in Chapter 4.

Obviously there is no opportunity for political parties to play an integrative role in Afghanistan, because such parties have not been legalized. Although it is perfectly possible that political parties could develop along tribal and ethnic lines and consequently have a disintegrative effect, what does seem to be clear from Weinbaum's comments is that, in the absence of parties, the national legislature serves virtually no integrative purpose. Its members owe no allegiance to national institutions and devote their time and energies to scrambling for benefits for their constituencies.

In Rajasthan the role of intraparty factions and coalitions in organizing ties among legislators is important. These factions cut across primordial social linkages and aid in the maintenance of secular party institutions. Recruitment into these factions is secularized, which has further broadened the social base of the party system. The authors of the chapter on Rajasthan point out the extent to which pluralized institutions can replace primordial ones as effective linkages within the society. In Rajasthan "factional" competition has contributed to the integration of the Congress party.

Crosscutting factions, like parties, constitute a form of intersocial linkage and may serve as an effective mechanism for political integration.

Whatever the contribution parties may make to national integration, we should consider the possibility that the legislature itself may facilitate integration. How might this occur? What characteristics would be necessary? We suggest that the legislature must have reached an advanced stage of institutionalization. It should be a durable, autonomous institution, with its own norms that affect the behavior of members. Legislative membership should be somewhat stable, so that some of the membership is experienced and members will anticipate continuing careers in the institution. Under these conditions, the legislators can be expected to develop a degree of allegiance to the institution and to the national regime of which it is a part. They will have an incentive to make the legislative system work. The legislature can develop institutional devices, such as party caucuses and committee meetings, in which there are strong norms to compromise. The experienced legislator develops working relationships with other members that facilitate compromise. The legislator needs to develop the political strength and the electoral security that make it possible for him to compromise without running a serious risk of being defeated for reelection as a result of his compromises. The stronger the legislative institution and its component parts, such as legislative parties and committees, the more the legislators will be influenced by participation in their activities and the greater its potential for their integration. Working within the legislative system, the legislators also must be able to provide tangible benefits for their constituencies. As the Canadian case shows, legislation can often serve to strengthen group support for a regime. In fact, as Kornberg and Hines point out, substantive measures such as the enabling legislation for the Canadian transcontinental railroad can contribute directly to integration. Such measures help to dampen particularistic regional cleavages and at the same time facilitate the development of an identification with a new and larger entity called Canada. This does not mean that the legislator becomes inarticulate as a champion of constituency needs but that he learns how to bargain and compromise and succeeds in persuading his constituents to approve the results of his negotiations.

If these are the requisites of an integrative legislature, it should be clear why neither the legislatures in Yugoslavia nor in Afghanistan are capable of contributing to integration. As described by Cohen, the Federal Assembly in Yugoslavia does not appear to be a strong institution, although it has been gradually enlarging the scope of its activities. Until 1967 the representation of nationalities in the Assembly was largely symbolic. It is not clear from the study whether there had been an opportunity for legislative norms to develop or for experienced, career legislators to emerge. It is clear that the system of representation put the members of the Chamber of Nationalities under considerable pressure from their regional constituencies to advance regional interests, and that members lacked the freedom to negotiate and compromise necessary for the Chamber to be an arena for mediating disputes. The Chamber of Nationalities became an arena for accurately measuring and articulating differences but not for resolving them. The legislative institution in Yugoslavia appears to have been too fragile to carry the heavy burden of resolving regional differences.

The legislature in Afghanistan appears to be an even more primitive institution. It meets for relatively brief periods, and then it has difficulty getting a quorum because the members attach higher importance to their activities in the constituencies. It appears that members owe their political strength to their social and economic statuses in their districts rather than to their experience or the positions they hold in the legislature. According to Weinbaum, the legislators use their political strength to protect their constituencies and the parochial demands of their regions, while curbing the powers of the national government. They do not appear to be spokesmen for the national government in their districts, nor do they appear to have a strong allegiance to the national government.

The portrait of the Lebanese Chamber of Deputies drawn by Baaklini in Chapter 7 is very different. In Lebanon the Chamber became the focal point in the struggle for national independence. Since independence was achieved, it appears to have become more fully institutionalized, with a durable internal structure, norms, and substantial continuity of membership. The careful balance of membership among sects has eliminated one potential source of disintegration, and the Chamber has developed into an arena in which compromises are possible.

There may be conditions in some countries under which it is impossible for the legislature to perform integrative functions. If the divisions between groups in a society have become too rigid, it may be impossible for the representatives of those groups to make compromises within the legislature, and the legislative majority may be unwilling to accord rights and privileges to the legislative minority. Budge and O'Leary conclude their study of Northern Ireland with a description of the British plan to create a new assembly and government for that country in which minority (Catholic) interests would be better represented. Given the depth of the divisions that have developed within Northern Ireland, however, the chances for success of the new institutions are obviously small.

One of the weaknesses or disadvantages faced by legislative bodies as integrators is that the groups in control of the government often perceive the legislature primarily as a vehicle for advancing the interests of minorities. Because the dominant group equates national integration and unity with its own ability to maintain control, it sees the legislature as a source of disintegration. This appears to be a major reason why many of the African governments have either reduced the authority of the legislature by a variety of techniques or have abolished it entirely. In Kenya, for example, the original constitution under which the nation gained independence provided for a bicameral legislature, including a Senate that was intended to protect regional and tribal interests. The Senate also proved to be a base of support for the minority party. The majority party, during the first few years of independence, succeeded first in eroding the power of the Kenyan Senate and then abolishing it, in order to bring about greater national unity and minimize the influence of those forces favoring decentralization and regional autonomy.

In a number of African countries the party system has been ineffective as an integrative mechanism because parties have established one-party systems in an effort to make the party system more integrative. Despite the obvious risk that a single party will serve the dominant region or tribe, it is possible that greater diversity will be tolerated within one party and that such a party can serve integrative purposes.

Legislatures are not intrinsically or inevitably integrative in character. The legislature may be a vehicle for total domination of the political system by a majority group, as in Northern Ireland. More commonly, the majority may restrict the authority of the legislature in an effort to prevent minorities from using it to advance their interests. Perhaps the legislature is able to serve integrative goals only when both majority and minority interests recognize that it has this potential and agree to utilize it for that purpose. Under these conditions, the legislature does have several characteristics that are particularly valuable. It is large enough to accommodate a wide variety of interests. The symbolic aspects of representation are important in satisfying the demands of minorities for recognition. The public character of debate and questions in the legislature also serves the needs of minorities. The individual legislators provide an important link between the localities and the national government, a two-way channel of communications that can facilitate integration. The legislature's potential for promoting compromise among competing interests depends on its level of institutionalization, the development of norms and organizational structures that will facilitate bargaining and the management of conflict, and the emergence of a legislative party system that can serve integrative goals because it transcends ethnic, religious, tribal, or other divisions. In fact the party system and the electoral system are so central to the operation of the legislature that they must be analyzed together if we are to understand whether and how the legislature contributes to national integration.

INDEX

Abdul Hamid Karami, 241n
Afghan Assembly. *See* Afghan Parliament
Afghanistan: as ethnic mosaic, 98; political
   history of, 119n; population of, 119n;
   religious animosity in, 100; society of,
   97–101. *See also* Representation, of
   minorities
Afghan legislators, 97; and constituent
   relations, 111; as elites, 111; financial
   interests of, 112; literacy of, 103; as
   mediators, 110, 269; roles of, 118; term
   of office and elections of, 102–3; and
   three classes of mediation, 112
Afghan Parliament: and absence of political
   parties, 104; compared with Middle
   Eastern legislatures, 96–97; composition
   of 102, 106–8; constitution and
   inauguration of, 101–2; vs. executive,
   103–4; and integration, 118; network of
   responsibility in, 113; as primitive
   institution, 275
Afghan politics: governmental restrictions
   on, 116–17; and obstacles to democracy,
   117; and political parties, 273. *See also*
   Pashto *and* Pashtuns
African states: and political parties, 273.
   See also Nigeria
Alberta, 219
Amanullah, King Mohammed, 117
Andrews, J. M., 175, 185, 191
Anglo-Irish Treaty, 170
Arya, Choudhry Kumbharam, 86

Assimilation: and national integration, 234
At-large elections, 37

"Balance": definition of, 204
Belfast, 168–69; effect of depression on,
   173; and hospital secularization issue,
   189; as industrial town in rural area, 180;
   riots in (Catholic vs. Protestant), 169,
   176–78, 184. *See also* Northern Ireland;
   Nationalists, Irish Catholic; Unionist party
Belfast corporation, 186, 190
Belgium: and language issue, 3, 39
Bishara al-Khouri, 243, 249, 257
Brahmans: and Indian Nationalist
   movement, 70; as members of Indian
   Parliament, 67
British Columbia, 219; and transcontinental
   railroad, 220–21, 223
British North America Act of 1867, 203,
   208; method of research on, 206
Brooke, Sir Basil (Lord Brookeborough),
   172, 175, 185
Brookeborough, Lord. *See* Brooke, Sir Basil
Brown, George: joins coalition for change in
   Canadian constitution, 211

Canada, 201; depression of 1873, 222; and
   elites, 227, 228n, ethnic-religious cleavage
   in, 202; expansion of, 219, 222;
   federalism and representation of
   minorities in, 17; influenced by Britain
   and United States, 208; integration of